10,000

WAYS
TO SAY
I LOVE YOU

10TH ANNIVERSARY EDITION

GREGORY J.P. GODEK

10,000
WAYS
TO SAY
I LOVE YOU

10TH ANNIVERSARY EDITION

GREGORY J.P. GODEK

SOURCEBOOKS CASABLANCA™
AN IMPRINT OF SOURCEBOOKS, INC.®
NAPERVILLE, ILLINOIS

Published by Sourcebooks Casablanca, an imprint of Sourcebooks, Inc.
P.O. Box 4410, Naperville, Illinois 60567-4410
(630) 961-3900
Fax: (630) 961-2168
www.sourcebooks.com

Library of Congress Cataloging-in-Publication Data

Godek, Gregory J. P.
  10,000 ways to say I love you : 10th anniversary edition / by Gregory J. P. Godek. — 2nd ed.
      p. cm.
  Includes bibliographical references and index.
  1. Love—Miscellanea. 2. Intimacy (Psychology)—Miscellanea. I. Title.
II. Title: Ten thousand ways to say I love you.
  BF575.L8G63 2009
  306.7—dc22

                    2009030712

Printed and bound in the United States of America.
CHG 10 9 8 7 6 5 4 3 2 1

OTHER BOOKS BY
GREGORY J.P. GODEK

Books by Gregory J.P. Godek from Sourcebooks, Inc.
are available at book and gift stores nationwide

DEDICATION

Thomas Valentine Godek (#904)

ACKNOWLEDGMENTS

Tracey Ellen Godek
Jean Ann Mancuso-Godek
Barbara Jane Godek
Bonnie Whitman
Mara Scribner
Craig Schreiber
Mary Marcell
Celine Dion
Wolfgang Amadeus Mozart

INTRODUCTION

No one in the history of the world has ever attempted to gather a list of 10,000 ways to express love. I've learned that 10,000 is a really, really big number. At one idea per day, this book will last you 27.4 years!

The questions I get asked most often about my books are "How?" "How long?" and "Why?"

"How? How do you gather 10,000 ways to say 'I love you'? I can't even think of ten!" The most important factor is what I call having a "romantic mind-set." It's a way of looking at the world and filtering information—and that filter is *love*. Another important factor is my sophisticated filing system for keeping track of the scraps of paper and napkins that I use to capture ideas as they leap from my brain—plus a high-powered laptop.

"How long? How long does it take you to write your books?" This book took only three months to write. But it's taken forty-three years to research.

"Why? Why would you write *10,000 Ways to Say I Love You*? Do we really *need* 10,000 ways? Aren't you getting a wee bit obsessed?" Of *course* I'm obsessed. Teachers and artists are *always* obsessed by their topics. And yes, we really *do* need 10,000 ways. Every idea doesn't "fit" for every person. And as to "why": Because people (*thousands* of people) continually ask me for ideas, suggestions, and tips. This book is the ultimate practical resource for couples. It contains the basics of romance, the essence of expressing love, creative twists on classic ideas, concepts you probably never thought of, and resources gathered from one thousand sources.

Since the first edition came out, we've been given the iPod, Facebook, Twitter, and countless other tools we can use to express affection. Why not take advantage of all of them? This 10th anniversary edition celebrates all the romance that readers have brought into their lives in the last decade using the ideas here, and gives those fans new ideas and new ways to say, "I love you."

More answers to the question "Why 10,000?" Because it's a big number. Because people are fascinated by numbers. And, by combining the concept of *love* with the concept of *numbers*, you start to get a feeling for how big love is, how big love can be. Actually, love is infinite. And as far as I'm concerned, 10,000 ways to say "I love you" is just the *beginning*.

~Gregory J.P. Godek

1. Honor your partner's individuality
2. Sign your letters: "Forever and a day"
3. Attend a lousy movie, sit in the balcony, and make out in the dark
4. Promise to be her Prince Charming
5. Promise to be his one-and-only
6. Osculate
7. Strive to be an A+ couple
8. Place a heart-shaped sticker on your wristwatch to remind you to call
9. Make your favorite meals and enjoy them in bed
10. Get a bumper sticker that reflects his view of life
11. Romantic resource: www.1800flowers.com
12. Become an artist of your relationship
13. Write custom word balloons on his favorite newspaper comic strip
14. Change one bad habit
15. Give her a gold bracelet made of X's and O's
16. Blindfold him and take him to a new restaurant
17. Take a gondola ride in Venice
18. Keep mistletoe hung in your home *year-round!*
19. Go "above and beyond" for your partner

20. On Monday: Be debonair
21. On Tuesday: Be enchanting
22. On Wednesday: Be sexy
23. On Thursday: Be funny
24. On Friday: Be playful
25. On Saturday: Be romantic
26. On Sunday: Be zany

27.   Send your lover a funny eCard
28.   For harried parents: Hire a babysitter on *retainer*
29.   Hide a pair of earrings in a box of chocolates
30.   Celebrate the anniversary of when you first met
31.   Try to go one week without saying anything negative
32.   Shower together by candlelight
33.   Warm her bath towel in the dryer for her
34.   Upside down stamps mean "I love you"
35.   Kiss her hand—the *proper* way (lower your lips to her hand)
36.   Trust your intuition
37.   Never, never, *never* wallpaper together
38.   Carry a wedding photo in your wallet
39.   Program her computer background to flash a love message from you
40.   Use the little strips of paper from Hershey's Kisses as coupons redeemable for one kiss each
41.   Get a sleeping bag built-for-two
42.   View romance as "Adult Play"

43.   For newlyweds only: Talk about your hopes and dreams for your future together
44.   Write them down and store the document in a safe deposit box
45.   Open it on your twenty-fifth anniversary

46.   "On this earth, though far and near, without love, there's only fear." ~ Pearl S. Buck
47.   Share a Whitman's Sampler
48.   Write to Dear Abby. Share the inspiring story of your relationship

49.   Mail a little box of candy conversation hearts

Songs to Help You Express Your Feelings:
Love & Tenderness

50.   "Always on My Mind," Willie Nelson
51.   "Amazed," Lonestar
52.   "The First Time I Ever Saw Your Face," Roberta Flack
53.   "Breathe," Faith Hill
54.   "I'll Stand By You," The Pretenders
55.   "Longer Than," Dan Fogelberg
56.   "Still," Commodores
57.   "But for the Grace of God," Keith Urban

58.   Get an astrological "Couples Chart" created by master
        astrologer Eric Linter: (617) 524-5275
59.   Plan a "Mystery Date" for sometime next month
60.   Cool travel resource: *Dream Sleeps: Castle & Palace
        Hotels of Europe*, by Pamela Barrus
61.   Plan sexy surprises
62.   Eat in St. Louis' most romantic restaurant: Tony's
63.   Tell your mate that you—love, adore, admire,
        cherish, desire, want, need, prize, esteem, idolize,
        revere, treasure—him/her

Ways to Love a Taurus
(21 April–21 May)

64.   Taurus is an *earth* sign: Cater to his/her grounded,
        practical nature
65.   Gift tip: Quality over quantity
66.   Get the finest chocolates for your Taurus
67.   Elegant items make great gifts

68. Limoges boxes, quality prints
69. Roses, apple blossoms
70. Gourmet and rich foods
71. The rustic and unhurried scenery of Ireland
72. Wrap gifts in pastels for your Taurus

73. Get a vanity license plate with both of your initials
74. "If you judge people, you have no time to love them."
    ~ Mother Teresa
75. Get an ergonomically correct chair if he/she spends
    lots of time at a desk
76. Revive Victorian-era manners
77. Spend a week sightseeing in Katmandu
78. Romantic Play Alert: Shakespeare's *Romeo
    and Juliet*
79. Use your logical *and* creative abilities to express love
80. Cuddle in front of a campfire
81. February 29, "Leap Year Day": Take a private
    romantic holiday every four years
82. Collect photos of the two of you and bind into a
    book on Kodakgallery or Shutterfly
83. Devote yourself to your partner's happiness

Favorite Love Songs from 1931

84. "Dancing in the Dark"
85. "Dream a Little Dream of Me"
86. "Goodnight Sweetheart"

87. "A life lived in love will never be dull." ~ Leo Buscaglia
88. Do something out-of-the-ordinary this weekend
89. Surprise your partner with two tickets to a play

90. Boredom comes from bad attitude, *not* from familiarity

91. Get a charm bracelet with a charm to commemorate each of your children

92. Surprise him/her at the office— wearing an overcoat with nothing on underneath!

93. "I loved him for himself alone." ~ Sheridan

94. If you're an expressive, loud person, try *whispering* your love to your partner

95. Leave written clues that lead her to a restaurant where you're waiting for her

96. Wash windows with you on the outside and your partner on the inside, facing each other

97. "Confidence is the sexiest thing a woman can have." ~ Aimee Mullins

98. Hide a little gift for her so she'll find it during a walk together

99. Save restaurant reviews to use for dates

100. Remember your anniversary

101. Be her groom

102. "I like not only to be loved, but to be told I am loved." ~ George Eliot

103. Romantic Math: Red roses *equal* love

104. Tell your lover something you've never told *anyone* before

105. Hide a love note among a bunch of flowers

106. A note: "I know we're soulmates because…"

107. "In literature as in love, we are astonished at what is chosen by others." ~ Andre Maurois

108. Send postcards

109. Send greeting cards
110. Send an envelope with lingerie
111. Send a love letter via express mail
112. Send a love note in code

113. Say this: "Boy, I'm glad I met you!"
114. Get a charm bracelet with a charm to commemorate each year you've been together
115. A romantic resource: *Bed & Breakfasts and Country Inns*, by Deborah Sakach
116. Be his devoted Lady-In-Waiting
117. Gals: Don't buy him cheap tools
118. Peruse *The Book of Massage*, by Lucinda Lidell
119. "Patience is passion tamed." ~ Lyman Abbott
120. Give phone-kisses
121. For busy couples: Schedule time for romance
122. Clip ads that give you romantic ideas
123. "Imagination is more important than knowledge." ~ Albert Einstein
124. Attend a PAIRS seminar (Practical Application of Intimate Relationship Skills): www.councilforrelationships.org
125. "Live as you would have wished to live when you are dying." ~ Charles F. Gellert
126. Make love your Number One Priority
127. Talk with your mate about how both of you can balance your lives better
128. Live every day with passion
129. Give her your jacket when she's chilly
130. Work overtime, and save up for a romantic vacation
131. "Nothing is impossible to a willing heart." ~ Heywood

132.   Spend a week in New York City
133.   Create an iPod library of romantic music
134.   Visit romantic international cities: London, Paris, and Rome
135.   Touch more
136.   Eat erotic chocolates and pastries
137.   Get a copy of *The Massage Book*, by George Downing; practice one chapter per week on your lover

Questions for Women (That Men Desperately Want to Know the Answers To)

Communication *works* (Once you're a couple, being coy usually backfires)

138.   Have you ever faked an orgasm?
139.   Do you consider yourself a feminist?
140.   What is your most *feminine* trait?
141.   What is your most *masculine* trait?
142.   How do you feel about your masculine traits? Do you *use* or *suppress* them?
143.   What is the *best* thing about being female?
144.   What is the *worst* thing?

145.   Continue to woo your mate
146.   Guys: Hold her dinner chair
147.   "One does not fall 'in' or 'out' of love. One grows in love." ~ Leo Buscaglia
148.   Spend one solid hour shopping for greeting cards
149.   Give lovey-dovey greeting cards
150.   Discuss how you each define "love"
151.   Tease your partner in a subtly sexy way while out in public

152. Freeze a bracelet charm inside an ice cube
153. Send love notes via email every day for a year
154. Practice your cuddling skills while watching TV
155. "Perfection is neither possible nor necessary." ~ Maria Regnier Krimmel
156. Swing together on playground swings
157. Replace the lightbulbs in your bedroom with candles
158. Attend the Tournament of Roses Parade in Pasadena, California
159. Hide a love note in his gym bag
160. Hide a string of pearls in an oyster
161. Create a Gift Closet: Stockpile ahead of time!
162. "Love does not insist on its own way; it is not irritable or resentful." ~ I Corinthians 13:5
163. Go camping together
164. Buy him a new red car; present the key in a velvet jewelry box
165. Attend a Marriage Encounter weekend: www.wwme.org
166. "Loved people are loving people." ~ Katharine Hepburn
167. Read aloud to each other in bed
168. Get season tickets to a local professional theater
169. A note: "Thank you for being the mother of our children."
170. Believe in your partner
171. Blow bubbles on a breezy afternoon
172. Make love to the light of a single candle
173. Get tickets for an event; keep it a secret until the day arrives
174. Cook dinner together
175. Read your partner's mind

176. Spend two weeks sightseeing in Hong Kong
177. Buy your dream home together
178. Go away for a week in Venice
179. "Life is not what you did. It's what you are doing." ~ Jim Burns
180. Romantic Opera Alert: Mozart's *Le Nozze Di Figaro*
181. Spend two weeks in Tahiti
182. Trip the light fantastic

Commitments That Will
Improve Your Relationship

183. Commit yourself to your relationship
184. Commit to spending 10% more time together
185. Commit yourself to being less judgmental
186. Commit to living up to your wedding vows
187. Commit yourselves to having more fun together
188. Commit yourself to practicing your religious beliefs on your partner
189. Commit yourself to seeing your partner's negative behaviors as *calls for love*
190. Commit to communicating your feelings fully
191. Commit yourself to your partner's happiness
192. Commit yourself to *feeling* your feelings of love
193. Commit yourself to *acting* on your feelings of love
194. Commit yourself to listening to the voice of love inside you

195. Enjoy a ski vacation in Switzerland
196. Spend $50 in a Hallmark store
197. A note: "When I think about you in the middle of my day…"

198.   Mark your partner's calendar with your birthday
       and anniversary
199.   Surf www.1001waystoberomantic.com
200.   Guys: Help her put on her coat
201.   Bake homemade muffins together
202.   Use gummy-letter candies to spell out love messages
203.   A note: "I'm uncomfortable saying this out loud, but I
       want you to know how I feel about you…"
204.   Roll up the rug and dance together at home
205.   Place a small bouquet of violets on the table
206.   A Movie Date Coupon: The coupon-holder chooses
       the flick. The coupon-giver treats.
207.   Use a passage from Kahlil Gibran's *The Prophet* to
       inspire your love
208.   "Keep in mind this daily notion: There are no
       ordinary moments." ~ Dan Millman
209.   Explore some used bookstores together
210.   Tattoo his/her name on your left shoulder
211.   Buy her an outfit while she's trying it on
212.   Hide a greeting card under your partner's pillow
213.   Blindfold him and take him away for a romantic
       weekend
214.   Decorate with a Christmas tree ornament that
       symbolizes your partner's hobby or passion
215.   Walk along the Great Wall of China
216.   Do-It-Yourself Romantic Afternoon: 2 bicycles, 5
       hours, 1 bottle of wine
217.   For tea lovers: Keep her tea stash well stocked

218.   Divorce. Divorce yourself from the many distractions
       that keep you from living your love

219. Read *Inner Simplicity*, by Elaine St. James
220. Simplify your life—and you'll find that love is a top priority

221. Give her your house key on a silver chain with a note: "You own the key to my heart."
222. Hang a romantic print by painter Pierre-Auguste Renoir
223. Arrange to have him meet his sports idol
224. "Passionate love is a quenchless thirst." ~ Kahlil Gibran
225. Arrange a *surprise* day off work for your partner
226. Read *The Creative Habit: Learn It and Use It For Life,* by Twyla Tharp
227. Believe in the healing power of love
228. "Intellect strips, affection clothes." ~ Ralph Waldo Emerson
229. Work on your communication skills
230. Learn more about your partner by listening to his/her family
231. You don't have to be your lover's *best* friend—but you must be *a* friend
232. A note: "When I think of you I smile because…"
233. Surprise your partner at work with a red rose
234. Build your self-esteem—you'll be more loving if you love *yourself*
235. Give him a red rose boutonniere to wear during your next date

236. Cultivate humility
237. Practice forgiveness
238. Learn compromise

239.   Foster understanding
240.   Encourage humor

241.   Slip a little love note into his wallet, in between the dollar bills
242.   "Kiss: A contraction of the mouth due to an enlargement of the heart." ~ Anonymous
243.   When attending a wedding, whisper the vows to one another
244.   Save a box of candy conversation hearts—and give them in *July*
245.   Literally *race* to complete your chores—spend time with one another
246.   Splurge on a beach vacation in Jamaica
247.   Slip your photo into his/her wallet
248.   Serve cocktail hour—in bed
249.   Drip chocolate syrup on selected body parts before lovemaking
250.   Keep some greeting cards in a drawer at work—mail one every month
251.   Bum around Europe together
252.   Be waiting for him in the bathtub when he returns from work
253.   On cold days, get up first and turn up the heat
254.   Eat in Toronto's most romantic restaurant: Scaramouche
255.   For tea lovers: Practice the Japanese Tea Ceremony

Yoga Retreats Recommended for Couples

Get away from it all—Get in touch with yourself—Get in touch with your partner

256.   Kripalu Center for Yoga, in Lenox, Massachusetts: www.kripalu.org

257. Expanding Light, in Nevada City, California: www.expandinglight.org

258. Sivananda Ashram Retreat, on Paradise Island, Bahamas: www.sivanandabahamas.org

259. Sivananda Ashram Yoga Camp, in Valmorin, Canada: www.sivananda.org/montreal

260. Satchidananda Ashram, in Yogaville, Virginia: www.yogaville.org

261. Spend a week exploring Cairo

262. Double-date with other fun couples

263. Read the Sunday funnies aloud (use voices)

264. Give him a written bill after dinner: "Salad: One kiss. Entree: Eight kisses. Dessert: Three kisses. (Tipping is *strongly* encouraged.)"

265. Explore some local antique shops together

266. Read Anne Hooper's *Ultimate Sexual Touch—A Lover's Guide to Sensual Massage*

267. Save articles on new sexual techniques

268. Remember: Romance is about the *little things*

269. Little things that bring a smile to her face

270. Little things that remind him of you

271. Little things that bring a tear to his/her eye

272. Little things that have special meaning to just the two of you

273. Little things that are done on a consistent basis

274. Share stories from high school

275. Use body paints!

276. Be his bride

277. Believe in magic

278. Let a poem by Elizabeth Barrett Browning express your feelings
279. The "King for a Day" Coupon: The male coupon-holder is entitled to be treated like royalty for a twenty-four-hour period
280. Stock up on romantic gifts during the Valentine season
281. Wander a local bookstore together
282. Clip newspaper headlines that include your partner's name

Quirky Questions to Help Couples Get Inside Each Other's Heads (and Hearts)

283. What three nouns best describe you?
284. What three adjectives best describe you?
285. If you could save time in a bottle, what would you do with it?
286. What do you want to be remembered for?
287. What are your prized possessions?
288. What did you want to be when you grew up?
289. Would you rather be rich or famous?
290. What's the most fun you've ever had with your clothes on?
291. What's the most fun you've ever had with your clothes off?
292. If you were going to write a self-help book, what would you title it?

293. Leave a blatantly sexual voicemail
294. In your calendar, write a reminder to yourself *one week in advance* of your anniversary
295. Trace your family genealogies together

296. Remove the TV from your bedroom
297. Create a romantic playlist for your next evening out
298. Use the Bible as a guide to living your love
299. Apologize after an argument
300. Be your lover's biggest cheerleader
301. To inspire your romantic creativity, read *A Whack on the Side of the Head: How You Can Be More Creative*, by Roger von Oech
302. Do-It-Yourself Romantic Date: 2 movie tickets, 1 Tub-O'-Popcorn, 2 Cokes
303. "People want riches. They need fulfillment." ~ Bob Conklin
304. Visit a local art gallery together
305. Download songs by his/her favorite singer
306. Shower together (It's sexy—*and* you'll save water!)
307. Love Enhancer: Tenderness
308. Bring home his favorite kind of ice cream
309. Reduce your TV watching to one hour a day
310. Promise that you'll never go on *Jerry Springer* no matter *how bad* things get!
311. Create a Keepsake Album from the memorabilia of your life together
312. Treat her to a facial
313. Read one book per month on improving your relationship
314. Engagement idea: Place the diamond ring in a glass of champagne
315. For *Titanic* movie fans: Recognize April 15 (*they'll* know why)
316. Online resource for sporting events and concerts: Stubhub.com
317. Surprise her with a silhouette portrait

318.   Do-It-Yourself Romantic Picnic: 1 loaf of bread, 1 hunk of cheese, 1 bottle of wine

319.   Encourage your partner's dreams

320.   End each day together with a kiss

321.   Romance Coupon: "Good for a manicure"

322.   "One always loves the person who understands you." ~ Anaïs Nin

323.   Right after Christmas, stock up on wrapping paper and bows—on sale!

324.   Concept: "Date night"

325.   Take a day hike together

326.   Read *Travel & Leisure* magazine: Plan a major vacation

327.   Cherish the present

328.   While you're both out, have a friend deliver a gourmet dinner to your home

329.   Spend this month's golf money on romance

330.   Rent a recreational vehicle for a comfy cross-country vacation

331.   Insert a funny comic in his box of cereal

332.   Inspiration for long-time lovers: "The older the violin, the sweeter the music." ~ Anonymous

333.   Give him a great big bear hug

334.   "People who are sensible about love are incapable of it." ~ Douglas Yates

335.   Give him a hickey

336.   Let a Billy Joel song express your feelings for you

337.   Make your bedroom your romantic hideaway

338.   Control the mood of this intimate environment

339.   Get rid of that desk, TV, and exercise equipment

340.   Surprise her with flowers on the nightstand

341. Add candles and massage oil

342. Gift resource for very quirky stuff: The Neiman Marcus "Christmas Book" catalog: www.neimanmarcus.com

343. After driving his car, return the radio to his favorite station

344. Live your lives as romantic role models

345. Question: Do you want to be *happy*, or do you want to be *right*?

346. Place a rose under the car windshield wiper

347. Live in the moment

348. A note: "Here's something I haven't said to you in a long, long time…"

349. *Life Principles: Feeling Good by Doing Good*, by Bruce Weinstein

350. Create a Facebook group celebrating her

Miscellaneous Skills Lovers Need to Know

351. How to cook your lover's favorite meal

352. How to be affectionate while being sexual

353. How to share your feelings without dumping them on your partner

354. How to do the laundry without destroying your partner's clothing

355. How to be supportive without being controlling

356. How to listen *actively* instead of *passively*

357. How to grow *together* instead of growing *apart*

358. How to be independent without being distant

359. How to be dependent without being co-dependent

360. How to talk about your feelings without using "psycho-babble"

361. How to make love in that "special way" that your partner loves so much
362. How to give a *really skillful* massage
363. How to keep your relationship your number one priority amid life's many demands
364. How to choose gifts that your partner will *love*

365. Get a favorite comic strip blown up to poster size
366. Collect "Love Is…" comics
367. Get familiar with local musicians, and attend their concerts
368. Get a local artist to draw caricatures of you on some eggs; put them in the refrigerator; wait for your partner to notice
369. Proof that "Real Men" *are* romantic: Clint Eastwood in *The Bridges of Madison County*
370. Millionaires need love, too: Diamonds and furs and yachts (Oh, my!)
371. Gently brush her cheek with your lips
372. Sweep her off her feet
373. "All love is sweet, given or returned." ~ Percy Bysshe Shelley
374. Do something *wacky* every full moon

Favorite Love Songs from 1932

375. "You're Getting to Be a Habit with Me"
376. "How Deep Is the Ocean?"

377. When he's away, buy him an *awesome* easy chair
378. Vacation for a month in Australia

379. "Nobody had ever measured, even poets, how much the heart can hold." ~ Zelda Fitzgerald
380. For Married Folks: Seduce your spouse
381. Nibble his ear
382. Send a musical greeting card
383. Gals: Update your concept of Valentine's Day (Many guys don't like all the pink and frills)
384. Believe in miracles

385. Stop expecting your partner to be perfect
386. Stop expecting yourself to be perfect
387. Stop expecting your relationship to be perfect

388. Create a time capsule to be opened on your 50th anniversary
389. Play hooky from work—and spend the day together
390. Watch whales on a cruise in New England
391. Decorate your desk with a heart-shaped crystal paperweight
392. Give him a lottery ticket. Attach a note: "You're one in a million."
393. Spend this month's beer money on romance (which is a better investment?)
394. Keep a file of magazine articles that inspire romantic ideas
395. Spend a week hiking the Alps
396. Do a "time budget" to see where your time *really* goes. Schedule more time for romance
397. Send suggestive notes via email

398. Take a hot air balloon ride; check the Web: www.hotairballooning.com

399. Recite Shakespearean sonnets

400. Check hotels for "Escape Weekend" packages

401. Concept: "Courtship after marriage"

402. While using his car, take it through the car wash

403. Offer to host your in-laws for the holidays

404. Be his "Vargas Girl": Commission an air-brush portrait of yourself for him

405. Write your New Year's resolutions together

406. Create a large and loving family together

407. A date: Dinner and dancing—*at home*

408. Attend an auction together: Buy *something* for each other

409. Be the Best Mother in the World to his children

410. A note: "I first fell in love with you when…"

411. Get matching tattoos

412. Create a DVD of love scenes from his/her favorite movies

413. Subtly flirt with your partner while out at a party

414. "If you would be loved, love and be lovable."
~ Benjamin Franklin

415. Practice "Old World" manners

416. Join a "Show-of-the-Month Club"

417. Bedrooms with fireplaces
(♥ ♥ ♥ ♥ ♥ Household Romance Rating)

418. Spend a month touring Europe

419. On a frosty winter morning, scrape the ice off her car windshield

420. Clip newspaper headlines that are funny or suggestive

421. Enemy of Love: Stress

422. Musical lovenote: "Play the CD *Meet the Beatles*. My message to you is song No. 6"

423. Create your own greeting cards

424. Get your southpaw sweetie *Lefthander Magazine*: Box 8249, Topeka, Kansas 66608

425. Do one of your partner's chores

426. Wear "Sex Appeal" cologne—Show him that you feel he has *plenty already*!

427. Delegate more at work; get home earlier

428. Plan one surprise for next week

429. Become entrepreneurial partners as well as life partners: Go into business together

430. Get him a Mickey Mouse watch

431. Resource for parents: *Trouble-Free Travel with Children*, by Vicki Lansky

432. Put the needs of your relationship ahead of your personal desires

433. Fly to London; have dinner in the West End; fly home

434. Place a love note in the newspaper personal ads

435. Rent a classic car from the year of his/her birth

436. Eat dinner at the best restaurant within one hundred miles

437. Dress in your finest party clothes and dance at home like Fred Astaire and Ginger Rogers

438. Watch a crackling fire together

439. Take your film buff to the Cannes Film Festival

440. Take candles into McDonald's with you: Dine in style!

441. Get season tickets to an amateur theater

442. Save all of your overtime pay for romance

443. Bake homemade cookies together

444. Surprise your partner at the office with his/her favorite candy
445. Learn to read your lover's body language
446. Be creative: Think up two small surprises and one big one
447. A romantic dinner at a restaurant in SoHo
448. Use the song "Shall We Dance" to invite your partner out for a night of dancing
449. Celebrate the first Spring day over 70°
450. Add a "Romance" category to your budget
451. Plan a three-day weekend together
452. Be a gentleman
453. Be a good, old-fashioned Lover Boy
454. While slow dancing at a party, whisper something tender to her

---

455. Watch planes land at the airport
456. Watch the stars appear
457. Watch shooting stars
458. Watch fireflies on a hot summer night
459. Watch the snow fall on a winter day
460. Watch the leaves turn colors in autumn
461. Watch a garden grow on an early spring morning
462. Watch your manners

---

463. When she's away, paint that room she's been bugging you about
464. Create a file of magazine articles on how to improve your relationship
465. Make an appointment for your partner's annual physical exam

466.   Try out together for parts in an amateur theater production
467.   Let a Beatles song speak for you
468.   Use a thesaurus to help you describe how you're— crazy about/mad for/nuts about/smitten with/stuck on/sweet on/wild about—your mate

Kinds of Romantic Surprises

469.   Once-in-a-lifetime surprises
470.   Unfolding surprises
471.   Bait-and-switch surprises
472.   Shocking surprises
473.   Mystery-event surprises
474.   Total surprises
475.   Big surprises
476.   Little surprises
477.   Expected-but-not-right-now surprises
478.   Expensive surprises
479.   Surprise tickets
480.   Group surprises
481.   Surprise vacations
482.   Public surprises
483.   Private surprises
484.   Surprises involving a collaborator
485.   Midnight surprises
486.   Surprises at work
487.   Sexy surprises
488.   Funny surprises
489.   Meaningful surprises
490.   Out-of-character surprises

491.   Romantic Music Library: *Time*, by Lionel Richie

492.   Learn more about her favorite hobby

493.   Whistle at her from across the room

494.   Get backstage passes for your partner to meet her favorite singer

495.   Plan for a romantic retirement: Put extra money into your 401(k) plan

496.   Do something *super* on June 1 (Superman's birthday)

Favorite Love Songs from 1933

497.   "Heartaches"

498.   "Honeymoon Hotel"

499.   "Let's Fall in Love"

500.   "Smoke Gets in Your Eyes"

501.   Clip newspaper articles of romantic ideas

502.   Learn to bake two new gourmet desserts

503.   Celebrate New Year's Eve in Times Square

504.   Romantic Math: Perfume *equals* romance

505.   Share your work bonus with your partner

506.   Share stories from junior high school

507.   Get married on Valentine's Day

508.   Gift & Date Idea: Get the song "I Will Always Love You," by Whitney Houston—

509.   And watch *The Bodyguard*, featuring the song

510.   Carry a photo of your lover in your wallet

511.   When attending a wedding, whisper, "If I had it to do over, I'd marry you again."

512.   Love your partner *unconditionally*

513. Love your partner endlessly
514. Learn to cook three gourmet dishes
515. Get digital downloads to replace all his old albums
516. Add to her collection of horse figurines
517. "In expressing love we belong among the undeveloped countries." ~ Saul Bellow
518. Paint the town red
519. Make up your mind to add more *surprises* to your romantic repertoire
520. Backpack through Europe for a summer
521. Tour the Louvre
522. Go on a trekking vacation in Nepal
523. Make a "Just Married" sign and drive around with it taped to your car
524. Hide a teeny, tiny gift somewhere on your body; make him find it
525. Fill his toolbox with lingerie—make him "work" to get his tools back

---

526. Once-a-week for a year: Jot down two reasons you love your partner
527. Once-a-week for a year: Jot down one great thing he/she did
528. Once-a-week for a year: Jot down one inspirational thought
529. At the end of the year: Print all this out on a big scroll and present it to him/her
530. Repeat next year

---

531. Read the travel section of the Sunday newspaper every week: Dream together

532. Find a local "romantic hideaway"—like a quiet corner at a public garden
533. Take a cruise through the fjords in Scandinavia
534. Visit a local museum together
535. Read *The Enneagram in Love & Work*, by Helen Palmer
536. Classical music lovers celebrate January 27—Mozart's birthday
537. Fold a love note in a fluffy bath towel
538. Toss out letters from previous loves
539. "Kindness is the insignia of a loving heart."
    ~ Anonymous
540. Love Enhancer: Faith
541. Go on an Autumn hayride
542. "Love doesn't make the world go round—but it *does* make the ride worthwhile!" ~ Anonymous
543. Have realistic expectations of love; frankly, love alone *isn't* enough
544. Plan weekend getaways
545. After getting married, have new stationery printed up with both your names on it
546. "Make out" like when you were a teenager
547. Shop at end-of-season sales
548. Volunteer to chaperone a high school dance together—to observe and rediscover what infatuation *really* is!
549. Trekkers celebrate James T. Kirk's birthday: March 21, 2228 A.D.
550. Use one of her pet names for your computer password
551. Surprise your partner with a "trinket gift"

552. Run your hands under warm water before coming to bed

553. Send a love note via FedEx—because your love just can't wait!

554. Replace the Cheerios with candy hearts

555. Put his/her things back where you found them

556. Raise money for a favorite cause together

557. Love Enhancer: Focus of attention

558. Spend *several days* touring the Smithsonian museums: www.si.edu

---

559. Single gals: Accept him as he is—don't try to change him

560. Single guys: Be who you are—don't try to be who you think she wants you to be

---

561. Celebrate Sweetest Day, the third Saturday in October

562. Program your iPod for eight hours of nonstop romantic music

563. Wear matching "friendship rings"

564. Emotions will keep you going when logic tells you to quit

565. Plan one surprise for next month

566. Go to a movie and let him choose the film, snack, drink, and seats

567. Create a personalized "Beer-of-the-Month Club" for him

568. Tear down the walls that separate the two of you

569. Resource: *The Complete Guide to Bed & Breakfasts, Inns and Guesthouses*, by Pamela Lanier

Ways to a Man's Heart

570. Thai Cooking School at the Oriental, in Bangkok, Thailand: orbkk-enquiry@mohg.com

571. L'Ecole des Chefs Relaise Gourmands, at Relais & Chateau Hotels: www.ecoledeschefs.com

572. Jane Butel's Cooking School, in Albuquerque, New Mexico: www.janebutel.com

573. Giuliano Bugialli's Cooking in Florence, Italy: www.bugialli.com

574. A La Bonne Cocotte, in Nyons, France: www.lydiemarshall.com

575. The Apple Farm, in the Napa Valley, California: www.philoapplefarm.com

576. The International Kitchen, for classes in Italy, France, and Spain: www.theinternationalkitchen.com

577. Go on an extravagant date

578. Remember the simple pleasures

579. Work on having more fun

580. Giftwrap even the *smallest* gifts

581. Remember the past together

582. Watch reruns of *The Love Boat*

583. Purchase front row seats to a game of his favorite sports team

584. Be *extra* attentive after your partner has had a tough day

585. Substitute his/her Christmas stocking with a real silk stocking

586. For birthday cards, use design elements from his/her birth year

587. Let a Shakespearean quote speak for you
588. Ask his/her parents for stories about your partner's childhood
589. Become a student of love
590. Gals: Never, never, *never* talk about your past boyfriends in front of him
591. Hire a string quartet to play your wedding music at an anniversary party
592. Take a nap on the couch together
593. While slow dancing at a party, whisper something sexy to him
594. "Say what you feel when you feel it." ~ S. James
595. Make love in slow motion
596. Devote yourself to your partner's growth
597. Sit on his lap
598. Create a time capsule to be opened by your great-great-grandchildren
599. Wink at her from across a crowded room
600. Love Enhancer: Fun-loving attitude
601. Plan anniversary surprises
602. Remind her that you really *do* adore her
603. Attach a gift to the dog's collar, and have him deliver it to her
604. Practice public displays of affection

Ways to Woo Workaholics Away from Work

605. Promise your partner the best sex of his/her life—
606. Follow through on your promise!
607. (If you can't beat 'em, join 'em!): Create a business *together*
608. Test drive cars that are out of your budget!

609. Book a hotel room—within *walking distance* of his office—and invite him over for an afternoon "meeting"

610. Meet him for lunch; dress *very* sexy

611. Have a courier deliver a steamy love letter to her office in the afternoon

---

612. Plan big surprises

613. Sign your letters: "Forever and a day"

614. Write a love letter in the margins of her novel

615. Spend your next commission check on your lover

616. Pick up a gift on a whim

617. Romantic Play Alert: Shakespeare's *A Midsummer Night's Dream*

618. Spend a day at The Art Institute of Chicago

619. Give your partner a kiss, smooch, peck, smack

620. Guys: While out together, stand whenever she enters or leaves the room

621. Eat in Montreal's most romantic restaurant: L'Eau à la Bouche

622. Plan birthday surprises

623. "It takes a smart husband to have the last word and not use it." ~ Anonymous

---

624. "But to see her was to love her, Love but her, and love her for ever." ~ Robert Burns

625. Yes, there *is* such a thing as "Love at first sight." It can be instant, deep, and long-lasting

626. If this is your experience, glory in it!

627. But remember: "Love at first sight" isn't the *only* way to find true love

628. Many people are best friends first, then gradually fall in love

629. If *that's* your path, celebrate your *friendship* as well as your love

---

630. Surprise her with a funny caricature made of the two of you

631. Place a birthday greeting in the personal ads

632. How to arouse an intellectual: *Flesh and the Word: An Anthology of Erotic Writing*, by John D. Preston

633. "Marriage is our last, best chance to grow up."
    ~ Joseph Barth

634. Don't sell his old "junk" at a garage sale before checking with him

635. Learn to play "your song" on the piano or guitar

636. Frame a favorite wedding photo

637. Write a love letter on the chalkboard in your kitchen

638. Remove the ice cream in a single slab; place a love note in a plastic bag in the bottom of the carton; replace the ice cream

639. Celebrate his/her birthday every day for a *month*

640. "Mutual love, the crown of bliss." ~ John Milton

641. Wear green on St. Patrick's Day—even if you're not Irish

642. Acknowledge and validate your partner's feelings

643. A romantic ritual: Kiss at your front door

Favorite Love Songs from 1934

644. "I Get a Kick Out of You"

645. "The Very Thought of You"

---

646. "If you only look at what is, you might never attain what could be." ~ Anonymous
647. Give her a romantic print by painter Claude Monet
648. Weed her garden for her
649. Create a video of favorite scenes from his/her favorite movies
650. Adopt a child, and be the most loving parents in the world
651. Instead of a standard Valentine card, give a copy of "My Funny Valentine" from *Babes in Arms*

Questions for Men (That Women Desperately Want to Know the Answers To)

Very often, the topics that are the most difficult to talk about are those that will bring you much closer

652. Ideally, how often would you like to have sex?
653. Do you feel that you understand women?
654. Do you feel it's *possible* to understand women?
655. What is the *best* thing about being male?
656. What is the *worst* thing about being male?
657. What one thing about women are you most jealous of?
658. Do you feel misunderstood by women?

659. Keep your "pet names" *private*!
660. Give the best chocolate in the world: Varda Chocolate: www.vardachocolatier.com
661. Make a 20-foot HAPPY BIRTHDAY banner
662. Eat dinner at the restaurant with the most romantic atmosphere
663. Be slightly sexy and somewhat sensuous
664. Sign your cards and letters with X's and O's

665. For *proof* that love improves your health, read *Love & Survival: The Scientific Basis for the Healing Power of Intimacy*, by Dr. Dean Ornish

666. Discover cozy little inns

667. Do something so out of the ordinary that you surprise even *yourself*

668. Learn to imitate his favorite actress

669. Send sexy greeting cards

670. Romantic Music Alert: *Oh, What a Night: The Steve Allen Songbook*, by George Bugatti

671. Donate to her favorite charity

672. Play romantic music by Claude Debussy

673. Share a bubble bath

674. Send funny greeting cards

675. Be wild and wacky

676. Fulfill a fantasy: let him fly a real fighter plane: www.fightercombat.com

677. Practice focusing 100% of your attention when listening to him/her

Things to Never, Never, *Never* Do While Making Love

678. Never answer the phone

679. Never call her by a former lover's name

680. Never glance at your watch

681. Never interrupt yourselves for a whining pet

682. Encourage openmindedness, but never push

683. Never leave too little time

684. Never say anything negative about your partner's body

685. Never criticize his/her technique (but do discuss it *later*)

686. Never have sex without discussing birth control first
687. Never criticize your lover in any way
688. Never lose your sense of humor
689. Never videotape without permission
690. Never talk about mundane, un-sexy topics in bed
691. Never fake orgasm
692. Never leave the bedroom door unlocked if kids are in the house

---

693. Romance Coupon: "Good for a pedicure"
694. Spend two weeks in Rio de Janeiro
695. Revisit the site of your first date
696. Wrap your anniversary gifts in *wedding* paper
697. Give him something to carry that will remind him of you…
698. A kerchief or scarf
699. A short verse to carry in his wallet
700. A pair of panties
701. A greeting card *drenched* in your favorite perfume
702. A lock of your hair
703. A current photo
704. A photo of you as a child

---

705. Have sex in the back seat of a car
706. Learn to make origami animals for your nature-loving partner
707. Have big pillows and cozy blankets near the fireplace
708. Find a hobby the two of you can share
709. Visit Los Angeles' most romantic restaurant: Patina
710. Create a "Romantic Idea Jar": 1,001 numbered slips

of paper; choose a number, then refer to the book
1001 Ways To Be Romantic

711. Guys: Dress as her version of Prince Charming...
712. Whether it's in a tuxedo
713. Or a tank-top T-shirt and hardhat
714. Or jeans and a flannel shirt
715. Or silk boxer shorts

---

716. The un-asked-for gesture is most appreciated
717. The surprise gift is most cherished

---

718. Celebrate New Year's Eve in bed together
719. Get a vanity license plate with his/her name on it
720. Watch cartoons together to celebrate Donald Duck's birthday, June 9
721. Gather significant quotes from his/her favorite movie characters
722. Spend time in bed-and-breakfasts
723. Be irrepressible and just a touch irresponsible

---

724. Go through her Victoria's Secret catalog and rate the items 1 through 10
725. Have his/her portrait painted from a photograph
726. Make a list of "Relationship Firsts," and celebrate your *many* anniversaries
727. When your partner has a big deadline, help by doing his/her chores
728. Have popcorn and soda at the movies
729. Live your values

730. Love is timeless—and to prove it, cover up all the clocks in your house for the weekend
731. In your calendar, write a reminder to yourself *one week in advance* of his/her birthday
732. Wrap jewelry in a Big Mac container

---

733. Have your Valentine card postmaked from a romantic city…
734. Valentine, Texas 79854
735. Valentine, Nebraska 69201
736. Loveland, Colorado 80537
737. Loveland, Ohio 45140
738. Loving, New Mexico 88256
739. Bridal Veil, Oregon 97010
740. Kissimmee, Florida 32741

---

741. Take turns taking family photos so you'll *both* be in them!
742. Be more romantic than any other couple
743. Get a vanity license plate with your anniversary date on it
744. Believe in yourself

Favorite Love Songs from 1935

745. "Begin the Beguine"
746. "Cheek to Cheek"
747. "Lovely to Look At"
748. "These Foolish Things Remind Me of You"
749. "You're the Top"

---

750. Treat her to a "make-over" at a spa

751. Create a personalized "Sweet-Treat-of-the-Month Club"
752. "Human beings have the *ability* of logic, but we are not *ruled* by logic; we are ruled by emotion."
      ~ Gregory J.P. Godek
753. Hang mistletoe over your bed
754. Focus on your partner's *wants*, not just on *needs*
755. Review your assumptions
756. Wait on him hand and foot for a day

Bits of Ancient Wisdom for Modern Lovers

757. "One word frees us all of the weight and pain of life. That word is Love." ~ Sophocles
758. "Skill makes love unending." ~ Ovid
759. "Let us not love with words or tongue but with actions and in truth." ~ 1 John 3:18·
760. "Many waters cannot quench love, neither can floods drown it." ~ Song of Solomon 8:7
761. "Take away leisure and Cupid's bow is broken." ~ Ovid
762. "The anger of lovers renews the strength of love." ~ Publilius Syrus
763. "Love is a grave mental disease." ~ Plato
764. "No act of kindness, no matter how small, is ever wasted." ~ Aesop
765. "The madness of love is the greatest of heaven's blessings." ~ Plato
766. "To be able to say how much you love is to love but little." ~ Petrarch
767. "The happiness of your life depends on the quality of your thoughts." ~ Marcus Antonius
768. "To be loved, be lovable." ~ Ovid

769. "The more a man knows, the more he forgives."
     ~ Confucius
770. "To be wronged is nothing unless you continue to
     remember it." ~ Confucius
771. "Union gives strength." ~ Aesop
772. "When male and female combine, all things achieve
     harmony." ~ Tao Te Ching
773. "From their eyelids as they glanced dripped love."
     ~ Hesiod
774. "He is not a lover who does not love forever."
     ~ Euripides
775. "My love for you is mixed throughout my body."
     ~ Ancient Egyptian Love Song

776. Millionaires need love, too: Take her shopping on
     Rodeo Drive
777. Elope (Ladder and all)
778. Take an old bottle of unused medicine capsules;
     empty the medicine; insert *teeny-tiny* love notes;
     write him a "Prescription for Love"
779. Go beyond the expected
780. "Love, and a cough, cannot be hid." ~ George
     Herbert
781. Be strong when your partner is not
782. Write funny messages in the margins of his magazines
783. Love Enhancer: Stay in touch with your feelings
784. Post a love letter video on YouTube
785. Celebrate "Husband Appreciation Day" (a made-up
     holiday; *you* choose when!)
786. Locate a copy of "your song" recorded in French or
     Italian

787. Remember that conversation involves *two-way* communication
788. Be impetuous and impractical
789. Buy two relationship bestsellers per year: Read and discuss them
790. Spend two weeks in Fiji

Relationship Concepts Based on Your Sense of Taste

Just as the variety of tastes are based on just four primary tastes—sweet, sour, salty, bitter—a well-rounded relationship is composed of these four elements:

791. Sweet: The tender, meaningful, deep aspects of life—those we cherish and treasure
792. Sour: The challenging, educational aspects of life—those that help us to grow and learn patience
793. Salty: The zesty, sexy, passionate aspects of life—those high points and memorable times
794. Bitter: The hard, painful, frustrating aspects of life—those that force us to change, mature, and often reach our true potential

---

795. Give a vintage bottle of wine from the year of his/her birth
796. Create a "*perfect* vacation" (your *partner's* definition of perfect)
797. Guys: Don't buy cheap flowers
798. Tell your lover that you're—enchanted by/captivated by/enamored of/fond of—him/her
799. Challenge the cultural stereotypes of men and women
800. Keep a wedding photo on your desk at work

801. Ask your friends to list their favorite romantic restaurants
802. *Practice* kissing
803. Carry a copy of your wedding license
804. Some help for your love letters: "I'm feeling—loving, affectionate, amorous, ardent, erotic, fond, lovesick, hot—for you."
805. Frequent drive-in movies
806. Tell him what you really appreciate about him
807. Give her the window seat when flying together

808. Learn your partner's "hot buttons"—
809. And vow to never hit them
810. Learn your partner's pet peeves—
811. And avoid them
812. Learn your partner's "blind spots"—
813. And help him/her cope
814. Learn your partner's "soft spots"—
815. And indulge them
816. Learn what turns your partner off—
817. And avoid those behaviors
818. Learn what turns your partner *on*—
819. And practice, practice, practice!

820. Write a love letter, and present it to him/her *one sentence at a time*—over two months!
821. Enemy of Love: Overly practical attitudes
822. While out, whisper, "You're the *best*."
823. Provide the popcorn while watching a movie
824. Create monthly files to keep track of romantic things you're going to do

825. Visit the Red Mountain Spa, in Ivins, Utah:
www.redmountainspa.com

826. Ask your friends to share their secrets for keeping
love alive

827. Plan surprise birthday parties

828. Express your love every day, every day, every day

829. Guys: Open the car door for her

830. Love Enhancer: Kindness

831. Buy him penny candy

832. Do one thing to simplify your life

833. Cater to her every whim for a week

834. FYI: Guys really *do* have feelings—it's just that
they're often "on hold"

835. Musical lovenote: "Play *Rock 'N' Roll No.2*, by Elvis
Presley. My message to you is song No. 7"

836. Gals: Please, oh *please*, don't give him boring gifts

837. Remember: A man's ego is fragile

838. (But then again, so is a woman's)

839. Greet her at the door with confetti

840. Love Enhancer: Simplicity

841. "There is no difficulty that enough love will not
conquer." ~ Emmet Fox

842. Hire a harpist to play during brunch at home

843. Put a tiny love note *inside* a balloon

844. Eat dinner at the restaurant with the best view

845. Read *Enchanted Evenings*, by Gregory J. P. Godek

846. Stock up on firewood for cold winter nights

847. Gaze into each other's eyes

848.   English: "I'm in love"
849.   French (to a guy): "Je suis amoureu"
850.   French (to a gal): "Je suis amoureuse"
851.   Italian (to a guy): "Mi sono innamorato"
852.   Italian (to a gal): "Mi sono innamorata"
853.   German: "Ich bin in dich verliebt"
854.   Spanish (to a guy): "Estoy enamorada"
855.   Spanish (to a gal): "Estoy enamorado"
856.   Portugese (to a guy): "Estou apaixonado"
857.   Portugese (to a gal): "Estou apaixonada"

---

858.   Get a fancy brass bed
859.   Wrap a gift in the colorful Sunday comics
860.   Create a "*perfect* date" (your partner's definition of perfect)
861.   Romantic Music Artist: David Sanborn
862.   Visit the store Lover's Lane
863.   Let a poem by Susan Polis Schutz express your feelings of love
864.   A+ Romance Rating: Le Bristol Hotel, in Paris, France
865.   Love Enhancer: Clarity of your life's priorities
866.   Spend $250 on red roses

Romantic Countries to Visit
Gather info on places you'd like to visit on a romantic vacation
867.   Austria: www.austria.info
868.   Belgium: www.visitbelgium.com
869.   England: www.enjoyengland.com
870.   Cyprus: www.visitcyprus.com
871.   Czech Republic: www.czechtourism.com

872. Denmark: www.visitdenmark.com
873. Finland: www.visitfinland.com
874. France: www.franceguide.com
875. Germany: www.germany-tourism.de
876. Greece: gnto.gr
877. Hungary: www.hungarytourism.hu
878. Iceland: www.visiticeland.com
879. Ireland: www.discoverireland.com
880. Italy: www.italiantourism.com
881. Luxembourg: www.visitluxembourg.com
882. Malta: www.visitmalta.com
883. Monaco: www.visitmonaco.com
884. Netherlands: www.holland.com
885. Norway: www.visitnorway.com
886. Poland: www.poland.pl
887. Portugal: www.visitportugal.com
888. Russia: www.russia.com
889. Spain: www.spain.info
890. Sweden: www.visitsweden.com
891. Switzerland: www.myswitzerland.com
892. Turkey: www.tourismturkey.org

893. Go stargazing at a planetarium
894. Decorate the house for the holidays together
895. Announce your wedding anniversary in the newspaper personal ads
896. Learn a dance routine on ice skates
897. A busy mom coupon: "I'll cook the kids' dinner."
898. Create an Easter basket full of chocolate treats
899. Parent's coupon: "It's my turn to stay home with the next sick kid."

900. Text him a romantic message
901. Even one hundred years isn't enough time to express all the love in the human heart.
902. Design a family logo that expresses who you are
903. Turn a wedding photo into a Christmas tree ornament
904. Make a baby!
905. Turn to him/her in public and whisper, "I'm glad I married you."
906. Romantic Math: Champagne *equals* celebration
907. "Thou art to me a delicious torment." ~ Ralph Waldo Emerson

908. Flirt with each other at a party, as if you both were single
909. For beginners: Flirt just a *little*; wink; compliment each other
910. For intermediate students: Act out a complete "pick-up" fantasy
911. For advanced students: Continue the fantasy as you return home
912. For extra credit: At the party, sneak into an empty room and make mad, passionate love!

913. Keep your passports up-to-date for spontaneous foreign travel opportunities
914. Plan a surprise get-away weekend
915. Give a mug with his/her name on it
916. Laugh together
917. Explore your feelings of anger
918. Give one rose for every child

919. Make his/her favorite gourmet dessert
920. Look through your wedding album together

921. "Familiar acts are beautiful through love." ~ Percy Bysshe Shelley
922. Take a familiar act and give it a little, creative, loving twist
923. Tie a ribbon around a cup of bedtime tea
924. Eat dinner by candlelight—*tonight*
925. Say something loving when you wake up
926. Make dinnertime a time for reconnecting
927. Plan some kind of big surprise for next year
928. Buy her a new car; wrap it in a giant red bow
929. Do something so incredible that it would get you into the Romance Hall of Fame
930. Give her a lottery ticket. Attach a note: "Take a chance on me."
931. Serve breakfast tomorrow using your fine china
932. Join the Association for Couples in Marriage Enrichment: www.bettermarriages.org
933. Make a custom romantic button ("I ♥ Tracey")
934. If you're traveling during a holiday, send a romantic I.O.U.
935. Get him a rare baseball card of his favorite player
936. Visit any one of the four Guggenheim Museums

937. Go out dancing
938. Go out of your way for one another
939. Go out on a limb—share your deepest feelings
940. Go out on a limb—build a treehouse for her

941. Go out!

942. "Life is either a daring adventure—or it is nothing."
     ~ Helen Keller

943. Make your daily life a daring adventure

944. Make your next vacation a daring adventure

945. Love Enhancer: Sense of adventure

946. On long car trips, read aloud to each other

947. Plan a wild goose chase that leads to his or her
     favorite restaurant

948. Call to see if you can pick up anything on the way
     home from work

949. Create a library of favorite romantic DVDs

950. Send a dozen roses: 11 red roses and 1 white one.
     The note: "In every bunch there's one who stands
     out—and you are that one."

951. Make a twenty-foot HAPPY ANNIVERSARY banner

952. Design a Web site that features your family histories

953. Create a personalized love song playlist on his/her iPod

954. Take a train ride

955. www.marriagemagazine.org

956. www.sandals.com

957. www.bitsandpieces.com

958. www.travelsmartnewsletter.com

959. www.teaofthemonthclub.com

960. www.kauai-hawaii.com

961. www.supergram.net

962. www.godiva.com

963. http://masteryoga.org

964. Busy parent coupon: "Five 'taxi trips': Hauling the kids to soccer practice."
965. Guys: Don't mess with her junk drawer
966. Leave a small bouquet of daisies on her night stand
967. "The 11th commandment: Thou shalt be happy."
~ Anonymous
968. Serenade her
969. Talk together for ten minutes in bed before rising in the morning
970. Give the Lladro figurine titled "Happy Anniversary"

Questions About Eroticism That Every Couple Should Discuss

A+ Couples understand that no matter how intuitive they are, they still must talk about erotic issues

971. What words do you want to hear during lovemaking?
972. What are the two most sensitive areas on your body?
973. What are your favorite erotic films?
974. How do you define the fine line between "sexy" and "sleazy"?
975. How would you like your partner to *dress* during lovemaking?
976. Which of your five senses is the most sensitive?
977. What's the difference between "sexy" and "erotic"?
978. Do you feel comfortable asking your partner for specific kinds of sexual stimulation?

979. Create a personalized "Wine-of-the-Month Club" for her
980. Classical music lovers celebrate February 23: Handel's birthday

981. Set your ringtone to "your song"
982. Honor your partner's parents
983. Float a love note in a bottle in the bathtub
984. Give subtly suggestive greeting cards
985. Create a shared vision of your future together
986. Greet him at the front door wearing a big red ribbon—and nothing else!
987. Work on being *friends*—as well as *lovers*
988. Bring home dinner from a gourmet take-out café
989. "One forgives to the degree that one loves."
      ~ La Rochefoucauld

Questions to Ask Yourself About Yourself

Understanding *yourself* is required (It wouldn't hurt if your *partner* understood these things about you, too!)

990. How do your balance work and play?
991. Can you make an honest assessment of your weaknesses?
992. Are you using your strengths?
993. How do you rank these priorities in your life? Work, love, family, spirituality, community, money, friends, kids
994. How do you face *change* in your life?
995. In a nutshell, what is your philosophy of life?
996. What motivates you to do your best?
997. What do you feel is your life's central emotional challenge?

998. Sail the South Seas
999. Get a scent ring and a variety of fragrances

1000.   Together, write a letter to your children on every one of their birthdays

1001.   Recreate her bridal bouquet

1002.   Return home with travel brochures and plane tickets sticking out of your pocket. Wait for your partner to notice

1003.   A "Lighthearted Weekend" Coupon: You will be treated to a weekend of silliness and ease

1004.   Read *The Good Marriage: How & Why Love Lasts*, by Judith S. Wallerstein

1005.   Mind-set: Every marriage is a private club for two

1006.   Enemy of Love: Lack of self knowledge

1007.   Carry her up to bed

1008.   Eat dinner at home—*in the nude!*

1009.   Run a bath; leave a note leading her there; leave the house

1010.   Dress her in the morning

1011.   And undress her in the evening

1012.   Remember: Relationships have cycles

1013.   This will help you keep your eye on the future—

1014.   While you act lovingly *today*

1015.   "Love is a little haven of refuge from the world."
        ~ Bertrand Russell

1016.   "Love is the fairest flower that blooms in God's garden." ~ Anonymous

1017.   "Love is, above all, the gift of oneself." ~ Jean Anouilh

1018.   How do you define love? How does your partner?

1019. Revisit this question every year
1020. Keep a journal of your thoughts about love
1021. Collect quotes and verses on love

1022. Anticipate his needs
1023. A+ Rating, Romantic Music Artist: Larry Carlton
1024. During your wedding ceremony, wink at her
1025. Give him a tie that illustrates his favorite sport
1026. Have a picnic at midnight

1027. Argue when you need to
1028. Remember: The *purpose* of arguing with your lover is not to *win*—
1029. (Because even when you *win* you *lose*)
1030. —Its purpose is to blow off steam, then re-connect
1031. "Learn to laugh at your troubles and you'll never run out of things to laugh at." ~ Lyn Karol

1032. Be faithful to your partner
1033. In both word—
1034. And deed

1035. Spend the day at a water park
1036. "You can give without loving, but you cannot love without giving." ~ Amy Charmichael
1037. Love Coupon: The holder is entitled to one candlelight dinner at the most romantic restaurant in town!
1038. Wear matching outfits while on vacation
1039. Use food coloring to create multi-colored popcorn
1040. Meet for coffee after work every Friday

1041. Revisit the place where you proposed
1042. Take along a bottle of champagne
1043. Propose again
1044. Reminisce!

1045. Give each other a "trinket gift" for every day you're apart
1046. Choose to focus on your partner's good points
1047. Resolve to call her more often
1048. Guys: No sexist attitudes
1049. Install dimmer switches on every light in your house
1050. *Get I Love You Coupons* by Gregory J.P. Godek
1051. Slow dance to the light of one candle

1052. Forget "The Golden Rule" ("Do unto others as you would have them do unto you")—
1053. Practice instead "The Platinum Rule," which states: "Do unto others *as they would have you do unto them*"—it promotes more empathy
1054. Get the great book *The Platinum Rule*, by Tony Alessandra

1055. Ride the Napa Valley Wine Train: www.winetrain.com
1056. Explore your feelings of fear—overcoming fear leads to love
1057. Call him at work and say, "Hello, handsome. Are you free tonight?"
1058. Fill your partner's briefcase with flowers

Ways to Love a Gemini
(22 May–21 June)

1059. Gemini is an *air* sign: Cater to his/her light, fun-loving nature

1060. Gift tip: Pairs, sometimes opposites

1061. (Sometimes, one simply isn't enough)

1062. Matching items, like a bracelet and matching necklace

1063. Keep in mind Gemini's dual nature

1064. Lily-of-the-Valley; lavender

1065. Light and subtle foods

1066. The excitement and glamour of New York City

1067. Wrap gifts in yellow for your Gemini

1068. Write a short, romantic and sexy story. Mail it to your mate

1069. Cuddle under a blanket together at a football game

1070. Share your feelings of tenderness

1071. Take your art lover to the Andy Warhol Museum in Pittsburgh

1072. Give your partner his/her favorite movie on DVD

1073. Give your partner more reassurance

1074. Reinforce her good qualities

1075. Compliment his talents and abilities

1076. Be aware that men and women tend to have different styles of communicating

1077. Men tend to view communicating as hierarchical interactions

1078. Women tend to experience communicating as network (connecting) interactions

1079. (But remember that these are *tendencies*—not unassailable truths)

1080. Be *extra* loving after he/she has had a hard week
1081. "The art of love…is largely the art of persistence."
~ Dr. Albert Ellis
1082. Go to a local spa every Friday to unwind together
1083. Get a VW "Love Bug"
1084. Give yourself more *time* for your relationship
1085. Be her bridge partner
1086. Millionaires need love, too: Give one another Rolex watches

---

Sensuality Enhancers

1087. Bring more *sensuality* into your lover's life, and you'll *both* reap many benefits
1088. Run your fingers gently through your lover's hair
1089. Focus on one of the five senses at a time
1090. For one week, create a romantic mood at home through soft lighting
1091. For one week, have great music playing in the background all the time at home
1092. For one week, keep three bouquets of *fragrant* flowers in the house
1093. For one week, focus on touching a different part of your partner's body each day
1094. For one week, prepare an extra-special *taste treat* for your lover
1095. Include more sensuality into your lovemaking
1096. Slow down, make time, relax

1097. Over the next five weeks, get five small gifts that focus on each of the five senses
1098. Focus on the present moment
1099. Buy ten *scented* candles
1100. Give him a great shoulder massage as he watches TV tonight
1101. Buy a basketful of *scented* bath oils and products

1102. Re-enact your first date
1103. Go Christmas caroling together
1104. Change the baby's diaper (when it's not your turn)
1105. Buy a digital picture frame for her and download dozens of photos of the two of you
1106. Lend a hand—without being asked
1107. Three times during the day, stop whatever you're doing, think about your mate, and smile

---

Favorite Spots to Take a Fishing Fanatic

1108. Housatonic River, Cornwall Bridge, Connecticut
1109. Connecticut River, Pittsburgh, New Hampshire
1110. Androscoggin River, Lewiston, Maine
1111. Little Kennebago River, Rangerley, Maine
1112. Falling Springs Creek, Chambersburg, Pennsylvania
1113. Madison River, Ennis, Montana
1114. Rock Creek, Missoula, Montana

1115. Leave a greeting card on his car seat when he's about to run errands
1116. "Love, like death, changes everything." ~ Kahlil Gibran
1117. Create a 10% increase in the amount of fun you have together

1118. The "Flower Power" Coupon: Redeemable for one dozen long-stemmed red roses
1119. Aphrodisiac Alert: *The New InterCourses: An Aphrodisiac Cookbook*, by Martha Hopkins and Randall Lockridge
1120. Write the date on your hidden love notes—they might not be found for a long time!

Favorite Love Songs from 1936

1121. "I've Got You Under My Skin"
1122. "Let Yourself Go"
1123. "The Way You Look Tonight"

1124. Have no hidden agendas
1125. Make love in as many countries as possible
1126. The "Blitz of Balloons" Coupon: Good for: 1) A ride in a big hot air balloon, or 2) One hundred helium-filled balloons!
1127. Love Enhancer: Creative attitude

1128. The gift: A bottle of "Passion" cologne
1129. The activity: A night of passion
1130. The background music: "Passion," by Rod Stewart

1131. Gals: Loosen your inhibitions—and choreograph a *real* striptease for him
1132. The classic music: "The Stripper," by David Rose & His Orchestra
1133. Or "You Can Leave Your Hat On," by Joe Cocker
1134. For inspiration: See Kim Basinger's strip scene in the movie *9 1/2 Weeks*

1135. Text him/her once every hour for a full day
1136. Give *fragrant* flowers: Freesia, Lilies, Lilacs
1137. Make a slideshow featuring pictures and your favorite songs
1138. Take pictures of you poking your heads through cardboard cut-outs of famous people
1139. Celebrate three-day weekends
1140. Mark your partner's birthday in your calendar
1141. Buy her an elegant evening gown
1142. Get a favorite toy from his/her childhood
1143. Offer to go on a long romantic walk

1144. Make some of the notes relate to the title of the album—
1145. *Come Upstairs* by Carly Simon
1146. *This Is Love* by Johnny Mathis
1147. *Lazy Afternoon* by Barbra Streisand
1148. *All The Way* by Frank Sinatra
1149. *Nobody's Perfect* by Deep Purple
1150. *Erotica* by Madonna
1151. *Everybody Loves a Nut* by Johnny Cash
1152. *Help!* by The Beatles
1153. *Goin' Out of My Head* by The Lettermen
1154. *The Language of Love* by Jerry Vale

1155. Record your anniversaries in *Our Marriage Memory Book*
1156. The "Fun-and-Games" Coupon: Your choice of Monopoly, Risk, Yahtzee, chess, or bridge.
1157. Watch reruns of your favorite sitcoms together

1158. When he/she's sick, be the *perfect* caretaker
1159. Stay at the fanciest hotel in Stockholm: Hasselby Slott
1160. Fill his/her entire voicemail box with romantic messages
1161. Write him/her a check for a million kisses
1162. "Love bears all things, believes all things, hopes all things, endures all things." ~ I Corinthians 13:7
1163. Enemy of Love: Impatience
1164. Give tulips. Attach a note: "I've got two-lips waiting for you!"
1165. Prepare for a vacation in the beautiful Bahamas: www.bahamas.com
1166. Give your partner a special good luck charm

1167. Thank him with a hot bath for doing the yard work
1168. (When he's finished, see if you can think of *another* way to thank him)

1169. Find a favorite young artist you both like
1170. Follow and support his/her career
1171. Purchase original pieces of artwork

Romantic Advice from A to Z

1172. **A**lways kiss each other upon departing
1173. **B**e there for each other—always
1174. **C**reate an environment of love
1175. **D**o it—now
1176. **E**scape from the kids
1177. **F**ight fair
1178. **G**ive of your time
1179. **H**andle with care

1180. **I**nspire your partner with your love
1181. **J**udge not
1182. **K**eep your good memories alive
1183. **L**isten to each other
1184. **M**ake love with your partner's needs foremost
1185. **N**ever go to bed mad
1186. **O**ffer to handle an unpleasant chore
1187. **P**raise your partner
1188. **Q**uality time isn't just for kids
1189. **R**espect his/her feelings
1190. **S**ay what you feel when you feel it
1191. **T**ell her you love her every day. Every day
1192. **U**nderstand your differences
1193. **V**alentine's Day is every day
1194. **W**alk together; talk together
1195. **X**-rated stuff is *OK* between consenting, loving couples
1196. **Y**ou can never say "I love you" too often
1197. **Z**ero-in on his little passions

1198. Make a Valentine's Day resolution rededicating yourself to your partner
1199. Install a hot tub in your back yard
1200. Flowers that match her name: Rose, Daisy, Lily
1201. For your anniversary: A lottery ticket and a note: "I hit the jackpot when I married you."
1202. Hire a masseuse to give your partner a professional massage at home
1203. Write a romantic message in sidewalk chalk
1204. Splurge on a $50 shopping spree
1205. Customize his/her horoscope in the paper

1206. Carry love stamps in your wallet at all times
1207. Send your mate silly/cheap souvenirs from your trips

Outrageous Places to Make Love

1208. Make love in a hammock (if you can)
1209. Make love in an elevator (if you dare)
1210. Make love in the bathtub (if you fit)
1211. Make love in the shower (if you can balance)
1212. Make love on a Ferris wheel (if you're not afraid of heights)
1213. Make love in an airplane restroom (if you're both flexible)
1214. Make love in a library (if you're very quiet)
1215. Make love on the hood of your car (if you're fast)
1216. Make love at a party (if you're discreet)
1217. Make love in a pool (if you're good swimmers)

1218. Share your dreams for the future
1219. The "Elegant Sunday Morning Breakfast-In-Bed" Coupon: The coupon-giver will treat you to a gourmet breakfast on any Sunday
1220. Never, never, *never* throw out something that belongs to him/her
1221. Go "above and beyond the call of duty" in expressing your love

Love Songs That Put Women on a Pedestal

1222. "Woman's Worth," Alicia Keys
1223. "Beautiful," Christina Aguilera
1224. "Lady," Kenny Rogers
1225. "Oh, Pretty Woman," Roy Orbison

1226. "When a Man Loves a Woman," Percy Sledge
1227. "Miss Independent," Kelly Clarkson
1228. "I'm Every Woman," Whitney Houston

1229. Switch sides of the bed for a night
1230. Switch housekeeping roles for a day
1231. Switch off the lights: Use candles

1232. Pay attention to your romantic daydreams
1233. Take action the moment a romantic whim hits you!
1234. Buy an acoustic music CD simply because of its romantic cover art
1235. Buy a book with a romantic-sounding title
1236. Eat in the most romantic restaurant in Vienna: Steirereck
1237. Get new wedding bands for your 25th anniversary
1238. On cold mornings warm up her car
1239. Get an alarm clock with radio, CD, or iPod capability—and awaken to romantic selections
1240. Sing "your song" together whenever it comes on
1241. Use a thesaurus to help you describe your—love, beau, beloved, darling, truelove, dearest, flame
1242. The "Favor-On-Demand" Coupon: You want a favor? Just ask the coupon-giver: He or she is obligated to do as you ask
1243. Embark on a safari in Kenya
1244. String a necklace around a stuffed animal's neck— and wait for her to notice

1245. Watch the sun rise
1246. Watch the sun set

1247.   Watch your mouth: Don't say things you'll regret

Best Love Songs by Lionel Richie

1248.   "Endless Love" (with Diana Ross)
1249.   "Truly"
1250.   "You Are"
1251.   "Say You, Say Me"
1252.   "Stuck on You"
1253.   "My Love"
1254.   "Love Will Conquer All"

1255.   Remember: Romance doesn't have to cost a fortune
1256.   It's the size of the *thought*—*not* the size of the price tag—that counts

1257.   Buy matching team jackets
1258.   Make love at midnight on New Year's Eve
1259.   Make your partner your No. 1 priority
1260.   Call your partner when you're running late
1261.   For husbands only: Describe yourself as "uxorious"
1262.   Following a stressful week, consciously spend the weekend *reconnecting*
1263.   Once a month, retire to bed together at 8:00 P.M.
1264.   Slip little love notes in his/her glove compartment
1265.   Plan your vacations around major chocolate-producing locations
1266.   Have a romantic Italian dinner in Boston's North End
1267.   Bring flowers home for no specific reason

Relationship Dos and Don'ts

1268.   Do the *opposite* of everyone *else*

1269. Don't gloat when you're right
1270. Don't sulk when you don't get your way
1271. Don't worry—be happy
1272. Don't try to pack too much into the weekend
1273. Don't over-schedule your vacations
1274. Don't make the same mistake twice
1275. Don't undermine your partner's authority with your kids
1276. Don't reveal the ending of a movie!
1277. Don't spend your "Prime Time" watching *TV*
1278. Don't drink and drive—not ever
1279. Don't stop
1280. Don't be a "cover-stealer" in bed
1281. Don't: Negotiate as if your relationship were a business deal
1282. Don't wait—express your love *right now*
1283. Don't even *try* to leave the house during a blizzard; snuggle together for a romantic day off
1284. Do: Learn the gentle art of loving compromise
1285. Don't interrupt when he/she's talking
1286. Don't hold grudges
1287. Don't take one another for granted
1288. Don't go a single day without saying "I love you"
1289. Don't let your mind wander during conversations!
1290. Don't wait for your partner to read your mind
1291. Don't wait until the last minute to make Valentine's Day dinner reservations!
1292. Do call *in advance* to get a babysitter for Valentine's Day evening!
1293. Don't just sign "Love" on your Valentine's Day card; be *eloquent*

1294. Do reserve a room at a bed-and-breakfast *three months* in advance

1295. Don't be so judgmental

1296. Fill your lover's car with balloons

1297. Go somewhere you've always *dreamed* of visiting

1298. Get pre-decorated boxes for instant giftwrapping

1299. Give sunflowers—along with Stevie Wonder's song "You Are the Sunshine of My Life"

1300. Refurbish an antique table together

1301. Go sledding in the snow

1302. Rent skis for the two of you

1303. A "One Week of Breakfast-In-Bed" Coupon: Seven straight days of luxury!

1304. For your car nut: Make a cake to look like a radial tire

1305. Be romantic on a whim

1306. Give your *partner* a gift on *your* birthday. Surprise!

1307. English: "I'm crazy about you"

1308. French (to a guy): "Je suis fou de toi"

1309. French (to a gal): "Je suis folle de toi"

1310. Italian (to a guy): "Sono pazzo di te"

1311. Italian (to a gal): "Sono pazza di te"

1312. German: "Ich bin verrückt nach dir"

1313. Spanish (to a guy): "Estoy loca por ti"

1314. Spanish (to a gal): "Estoy loco por ti"

1315. Portugese (to a guy): "Eu sou louco por você"

1316. Portugese (to a gal): "Eu sou louca por você"

1317. Create a "photo wall" for displaying your best memories

1318.   Romantic Resource: Scan a bridal magazine for travel and gift ideas

1319.   Newlyweds: Carry her over the threshold

1320.   Place small wagers on various fun events

1321.   Bet on the winner of the Miss America Pageant or the World Series

1322.   Bet odd amounts, like $5.27

1323.   Bet for *services*, like backrubs or making dinner

1324.   Linger over coffee at home together

1325.   Linger over coffee at a local café

1326.   Linger over dinner; enjoy each other's company

1327.   Linger after making love

1328.   Linger in bed together in the morning

1329.   Daily affirmation: "I am a lovable—and loving—person"

1330.   Hide a love note in a book on a bookstore shelf—and give clues to its location

1331.   Visit elegant inns around the country: Check out *Recommended Romantic Inns*

1332.   Add to her collection of tchotchkes

1333.   Enemy of Love: Guilt

1334.   Brush against him "accidentally" in public

1335.   Furniture for lovers: A love seat

1336.   Hire a string quartet to provide musical accompaniment for a picnic

1337.   For every day you've been together give him/her a penny

Time-Saving Tips for Lovers

1338. Every minute you save can be devoted to your relationship

1339. Delegate more responsibilities at work—and get home earlier

1340. Run all your errands *in one place*—don't run all over town

1341. Read *Getting Things Done: The Art of Stress-Free Productivity*, by David Allen

1342. Use paper plates, so you don't have to bother washing dishes

1343. Double your recipes so you can get two days' worth of cooking done at once

1344. Don't leave chores half-done: They prey on your mind

1345. Speed up when you do mindless chores

1346. Slow down; appreciate time *together*

1347. Have designated duffel bags and backpacks for various activities

1348. Buy in bulk!

1349. Get rid of all your extra credit cards

1350. Hold weekly "family meetings" to coordinate schedules

1351. Learn the art of speed cleaning: You can learn to clean the average house in under two hours

1352. Create a travel checklist so you can zip through packing

1353. Assign chores to your children—

1354. And keep *increasing* their responsibilities (and allowances) every year

1355. Shop by catalog whenever possible

1356.   Do your holiday shopping *way* in advance

1357.   Propose in front of the Grand Hotel, Mackinac Island, Michigan

1358.   Write a little love note on your mate's dinner napkin

1359.   Have a dozen red roses delivered to your table

1360.   Musical lovenote: "Play *Songs in the Key of Life, Volume 2*, by Stevie Wonder. Listen to song No. 6"

1361.   Wear matching winter scarves

1362.   Volunteer to walk the dog on a cold winter night

1363.   "Love is always expressed by making a sacrifice." ~ Swami Chinmayaananda

1364.   Tip for writing love letters: Don't worry about being poetic or eloquent. What matters is the thought, the effort, and the emotion

1365.   Get *Love Coupons*, by Gregory J.P. Godek

1366.   Love Coupon: Good for one afternoon of window shopping with the coupon giver. Transportation and lunch included. Wishing and dreaming are encouraged. No purchase necessary

Little Touches That Can Make a *Big* Difference

1367.   Wrap all presents in her favorite color

1368.   A rose on her pillow

1369.   For an anniversary note or certificate, use fonts that were popular that year

1370.   The *perfect* perfume or cologne

1371.   Spray a favorite cologne on a love letter

1372.   Bathe together—*by candlelight*

1373.   TGIF: Unwind together with wine and cheese
1374.   Kiss the nape of her neck
1375.   *Matching* bra and panty sets
1376.   Guys: Hold open doors for her
1377.   Satin sheets on the bed

1378.   Seduce your partner tonight
1379.   Be loving *even when you don't feel like it*
1380.   A good read: *This Is My Beloved*, by Walter Benton
1381.   Get him that car he's been dreaming of his whole life
1382.   Go for a walk in the woods
1383.   Make love with the only goal being to prolong arousal as long as possible
1384.   Be romantic on days that end in the letter "Y"
1385.   The "Romantic I.O.U." Coupon: You are entitled to one evening of romance—on an evening *next month* chosen by you
1386.   The Classic "Bubble-Bath-For-One" Coupon: You'll be pampered with scented bubble bath and refreshments
1387.   Sign your love letters: "Your adoring subject"
1388.   Try out as a couple for a reality show like *The Amazing Race*
1389.   Drop hints about an upcoming mystery date
1390.   Love Enhancer: Patience
1391.   For engaged gals: Make a photocopy of your hand and new engagement ring. Mail it to him with a note: "I've got a piece of the rock"

1392.   Visit theme parks across the country…
1393.   Disneyland in Anaheim, California

1394.   Sea World of California in San Diego
1395.   Six Flags Great Adventure in Jackson, New Jersey
1396.   Knott's Berry Farm in Buena Park, California
1397.   Sea World of Florida in Orlando, Florida
1398.   Paramount's Kings Island in Kings Island, Ohio
1399.   Magic Kingdom at Walt Disney World in Lake Buena Vista, Florida
1400.   Santa Cruz Beach Boardwalk in Santa Cruz, California
1401.   Busch Gardens in Tampa, Florida
1402.   Epcot Center in Lake Buena Vista, Florida
1403.   Cedar Point in Sandusky, Ohio

1404.   Take turns
1405.   Take her out to dinner
1406.   Take him out to the ball game
1407.   (Buy him some peanuts and Cracker Jack)

1408.   Give her some Fireballs candies with a note: "I'm hot for you!"
1409.   Love Coupon: Entitling you to a night of watching shooting stars together
1410.   Make homemade Christmas ornaments

Most Important Relationship Issues Ranked in Order—by Readers of *Marriage Magazine*

1411.   Intimacy
1412.   Communication
1413.   Spirituality
1414.   Sexuality and sensuality
1415.   Dealing with adversity

1416. Leisure/humor/play
1417. Self-empowerment
1418. Family
1419. Romance
1420. Rituals and celebrations

♥ How would *you and your partner* rank these issues?
♥ How would you *grade yourselves* in each area?
♥ Would you add any issues to this list?
♥ How are you going to improve in each area?

1421. Create your own series of custom greeting cards that use lyrics from songs
1422. Throw a party specifically to *honor* your partner
1423. Eat dinner at the best Cajun restaurant around
1424. Emulate those rare couples who have an A+ Relationship
1425. Drink from two champagne flutes with your initials engraved on them
1426. Gather romantic ideas from your friends
1427. Hide a stuffed animal in his gym bag

1428. Does your partner have a "namesake" town?
1429. Plan a surprise trip there
1430. Get postcards and brochures from the town
1431. Have a love letter postmarked from the town

1432–1832
401 "Namesake" Towns Across America

1432. Ada: Kans., Minn., Ohio, Okla.
1433. Adrian: Ga., Mich., Minn., Mo., Ore., Tex., W.Va.

1434.   Albert: Kans.

1435.   Alberta: Va.

1436.   Alexander: Kans., N.Dak., Tex.

1437.   Alexandria: Ind., Ky., La., Minn., Mo., N.H., Neb., Ohio, S.Dak., Tenn., Va.

1438.   Alfred: Maine, N.Y., N.Dak.

1439.   Alice: Tex.

1440.   Alicia: Ark.

1441.   Allen: Kans., Ky., Neb., S.Dak., Tex.

1442.   Allison: Colo., Iowa

1443.   Alvin: Ill., Tex.

1444.   Amanda: Ohio

1445.   Amber: Okla.

1446.   Amelia: La., Neb., Ohio

1447.   Angelica: N.Y.

1448.   Angie: La.

1449.   Anita: Iowa, Pa.

1450.   Anna: Ill., Tex.

1451.   Annabella: Utah

1452.   Anna Maria: Fla.

1453.   Annette: Ala.

1454.   Anson: Maine, Tex.

1455.   Anthony: Fla., Kans., N.Mex., R.I.

1456.   Anton: Colo., Tex.

1457.   Archie: Mo.

1458.   Arden: Calif., Nev.

1459.   Arial: S.C.

1460.   Arnold: Calif., Kans., Md., Mo., Neb., Pa.

1461.   Arthur: Ill., Neb., N.Dak.

1462.   Arvin: Calif.

1463.   Ashley: Ill., Ind., N.Dak., Ohio

1464. Aubrey: Ark., Tex.
1465. Austin: Ky., Minn., Nev., Pa., Tex.
1466. Ava: Ill., Mo., N.Y.
1467. Avery: Calif., Idaho, Tex.
1468. Barry: Ill., Tex.
1469. Beatrice: Ala., Neb.
1470. Benjamin: Tex.
1471. Bennett: Colo., N.C., Wis.
1472. Benson: Ariz., Minn., N.C., Vt.
1473. Bernard: Maine
1474. Bernice: La.
1475. Bernie: Mo.
1476. Bertha: Minn.
1477. Bethany: Ill., Mo., Ohio, Okla.
1478. Beverly: Kans., Mass., N.J., Ohio, Tex., Wash.
1479. Bill: Wyo.
1480. Blaine: Ky., Maine, Minn., Wash.
1481. Blair: Neb., Okla., Wis.
1482. Boyce: La.
1483. Boyd: Minn., Mont., Tex.
1484. Bradford: Ark., Ill., Maine, N.H., Ohio, Pa., R.I., Tenn., Vt.
1485. Bradley: Ark., Calif., Ill., Maine, S.Dak., W.Va.
1486. Brent: Ala.
1487. Bronson: Fla., Kans., Mich., Tex.
1488. Bronte: Tex.
1489. Bruce: Miss., S.Dak., Wis.
1490. Bruno: Mich.
1491. Bryan: Ohio, Tex.
1492. Bryant: Ark., Fla., S.Dak., Wis.
1493. Buford: Colo., Ga., Wyo.

1494. Burke: Idaho, N.Y., S.Dak., Va.
1495. Burton: Mich., Neb., Ohio, Tex., Wash.
1496. Byron: Calif., Ga., Ill., Maine, Minn., Okla., Wyo.
1497. Cameron: Ariz., La., Mo., Mont., N.C., S.C., Tex., W.Va., Wis.
1498. Carlton: Kans., Minn., Ore., Tex., Wash.
1499. Carlyle: Ill., Mont.
1500. Carmen: Ind., Okla.
1501. Carroll: Iowa, Maine, Neb.
1502. Carter: Ky., Mont., Okla., S.Dak., Wis., Wyo.
1503. Cary: Maine, Miss., N.C.
1504. Casey: Ill., Iowa
1505. Catharine: Ala.
1506. Cecil: Ga., Ore., Pa., Wis.
1507. Cecilia: Ky.
1508. Celeste: Tex.
1509. Celina: Ohio, Tenn., Tex.
1510. Chandler: Ariz., Ind., Minn., Okla., Tex.
1511. Charlotte: Mich., N.C., Tenn., Tex., Vt.
1512. Chelsea: Ala., Mass., Mich., Okla., Vt.
1513. Christian: Alaska
1514. Christiana: Tenn.
1515. Christina: Mont.
1516. Christine: N.Dak., Tex.
1517. Christopher: Ill.
1518. Clairemont: Tex.
1519. Clancy: Mont.
1520. Clara: Miss.
1521. Clare: Mich.
1522. Clarence: Iowa, Mo., N.Y.
1523. Clarissa: Minn.

1524. Clark: Colo., S.Dak.
1525. Claude: Tex.
1526. Cliff: N.M.
1527. Clifford: Ky.
1528. Clint: Tex.
1529. Clyde: Calif., Kans., N.Y., N.C., N.Dak., Ohio, Tex.
1530. Cody: Neb., Wyo.
1531. Conrad: Iowa, Mont.
1532. Cornelius: N.C., Ore.
1533. Courtenay: N.Dak.
1534. Craig: Alaska, Colo., Kans., Mo., Mont., Neb.
1535. Crissey: Ohio
1536. Crystal: Maine, Minn., N.Dak.
1537. Curtis: Ark.
1538. Cyril: Okla.
1539. Cyrus: Minn.
1540. Dale: Ill., Ind., Ore., Tex., Wis.
1541. Dana: Ind.
1542. Daniel: Md., Wyo.
1543. Davy: W.Va.
1544. Dawn: Tex.
1545. Dennis: Mass., N.C.
1546. Devon: Ky., Mont., Pa.
1547. Dexter: Ga., Iowa, Kans., Ky., Maine, Mich., Mo., N.M., N.Y.
1548. Diana: Tex.
1549. Dixie: Ala., Ga., Idaho, Wash.
1550. Dolores: Colo.
1551. Domingo: N.M.
1552. Donna: Tex.
1553. Donovan: Ill.

1554. Douglas: Ariz., Ga., Mich., N.Dak, Okla., Wyo.
1555. Drake: N.Dak.
1556. Drew: Miss., Ore.
1557. Dudley: Ga., Mass.
1558. Duke: Ala., Okla.
1559. Duncan: Ariz., Miss., Neb., Okla.
1560. Dustin: Okla.
1561. Dusty: N.M.
1562. Dwight: Ill., Kans., Neb.
1563. Earle: Ark.
1564. Edgar: Mont., Neb., Wis.
1565. Edina: Minn., Mo.
1566. Edith: Ga.
1567. Edmond: Kans., Okla.
1568. Edna: Kans., Tex.
1569. Elbert: Colo., Tex.
1570. Eleanor: W.Va.
1571. Elizabeth: Ill., La., Minn., Miss., N.J., W.Va.
1572. Elliott: S.C.
1573. Elmer: Mo., N.J., Okla.
1574. Elmira: N.Y.
1575. Elsie: Mich., Neb.
1576. Elwood: Ill., Ind., Kans., Neb.
1577. Ely: Minn., Nev.
1578. Emily: Minn.
1579. Enid: Miss., Mont., Okla.
1580. Erick: Okla.
1581. Erin: Tenn.
1582. Ester: Alaska
1583. Ethan: S.Dak.
1584. Ethel: Miss., Wash., W.Va.

1585. Eugene: Ore.
1586. Eunice: La., N.M.
1587. Eva: Tenn.
1588. Everett: Ga., Mass., Pa., Wash.
1589. Faith: S.Dak.
1590. Felicity: Ohio
1591. Ferdinand: Ind.
1592. Floyd: La., N.M., Va.
1593. Francis: Okla., Utah
1594. Frannie: Wyo.
1595. Frederic: Mich., Wis.
1596. Frederick: Colo., Md., Okla., S.Dak.
1597. Gail: Tex.
1598. Garrett: Ind., Ky., Wyo.
1599. Gary: Ind., Minn., S.Dak., Tex.
1600. Gay: W.Va.
1601. Geneva: Ala., Ga., Idaho, Ill., Ind., Minn., Neb., N.Y., Ohio
1602. George: Iowa, Wash.
1603. Georgiana: Ala.
1604. Gerald: Mo.
1605. Gifford: Fla., Pa., Wash.
1606. Gilbert: La., Minn., Ore., W.Va.
1607. Girard: Ga., Ill., Kans., Ohio, Pa., Tex.
1608. Gisela: Ariz.
1609. Gladys: Va.
1610. Gordon: Alaska, Ga., Neb., Tex., Wis.
1611. Grace: Idaho
1612. Grady: Ark., N.M.
1613. Graham: N.C., Tex.
1614. Grant: Mich., Mont., Neb., Okla.

1615. Gregory: S.Dak., Tex.
1616. Griffith: Ind.
1617. Grover: Colo., Pa., Wyo.
1618. Hale: Colo., Mich., Mo.
1619. Hanna: Ark., Ind., Okla., Utah, Wyo.
1620. Hannah: N.Dak.
1621. Harlan: Ind., Iowa, Kans., Ky., Ore.
1622. Harris: Minn., Okla.
1623. Harvey: Ill., La., N.Dak.
1624. Hazel: Ky., S.Dak.
1625. Hector: Ark., Minn.
1626. Henrietta: Neb., N.C., Tex.
1627. Henry: Ill., Neb., S.Dak.
1628. Herman: Mich., Minn., Neb.
1629. Hernando: Miss.
1630. Holly: Colo., Mich., Wash.
1631. Homer: Alaska, Ga., Ill., La., Mich., Neb., N.Y.
1632. Hope: Alaska, Ark., Idaho, Ind., Kans., N.M., N.Dak., R.I.
1633. Horace: Kans., N.Dak
1634. Horatio: Ark.
1635. Howard: Kans., S.Dak.
1636. Hugo: Colo., Minn., Okla.
1637. Ida: La.
1638. Ignacio: Calif., Colo.
1639. Ina: Ill.
1640. Inez: Ky., Tex.
1641. Iona: Idaho, Minn., S.Dak.
1642. Ira: Tex.
1643. Irma: Wis.
1644. Irving: Tex.

1645. Irwin: Tex., Pa.

1646. Isabel: Kans., S.Dak.

1647. Isabela: P.R.

1648. Isabella: Minn.

1649. Ivan: Ark.

1650. Jay: Fla., Maine, N.Y., Okla.

1651. Jean: Nev., Tenn.

1652. Jena: Fla.

1653. Jennie: Ark.

1654. Jerome: Ariz., Ark., Idaho, Pa.

1655. Joanna: S.C.

1656. Joaquin: Tex.

1657. Johnson: Kans., Neb., Vt.

1658. Jordan: Ala., Minn., Mont., N.Y.

1659. Joseph: Alaska, Ore., Utah

1660. Joshua: Tex.

1661. Joy: Ill.

1662. Juanita: Wash.

1663. Judson: N.Dak.

1664. Julian: Calif.

1665. Kathryn: N.Dak.

1666. Katy: Tex.

1667. Kaycee: Wyo.

1668. Kelly: Ky., La., Wyo.

1669. Kendall: Fla., Kans., N.Y., Wis.

1670. Kenney: Ill.

1671. Kent: Conn., Minn., Ohio, Ore., Tex., Wash.

1672. Kevin: Mont.

1673. Kimberly: Idaho, Ore., Wis.

1674. Kirby: Ark., Tex., Wyo.

1675. Kirk: Colo.

1676. Kyle: S.Dak., Tex.
1677. Lacey: Wash.
1678. Lambert: Miss., Mont.
1679. Lane: S.C., S.Dak
1680. Laurel: Del., Ind., Md., Miss., Mont., Neb., Va.
1681. La Verne: Calif.
1682. Laverne: Okla.
1683. Lavonia: Ga.
1684. Lawrence: Ind., Kans., Mass., Mich., Miss., Neb., N.Y., Pa.
1685. Lee: Fla., Maine, Mass., Nev.
1686. Lena: Ill., La., Miss., Wis.
1687. Lenoir: N.C.
1688. Lenora: Kans.
1689. Leo: Ind.
1690. Leon: Iowa, Kans., Okla., W.Va.
1691. Leonard: N.Dak., Tex.
1692. Leroy: Ala.
1693. Leslie: Ark., Ga., Idaho, Mich.
1694. Lester: Wash.
1695. Lewis: Colo., Ind., Iowa, Kans., N.Y.
1696. Libby: Mont.
1697. Lilly: Ga., Ky., S.Dak., Wis.
1698. Linda: Calif.
1699. Lindsay: Calif., Mont., Neb., Okla.
1700. Livonia: Mich., N.Y.
1701. Lloyd: Fla., Mont.
1702. Logan: Iowa, Kans., Mont., N.M., Ohio, Utah, W.Va.
1703. Loleta: Calif.
1704. Lolita: Tex.
1705. Loretta: Wis.

1706. Lorraine: N.Y.
1707. Louann: Ark.
1708. Louisa: Ky., Va.
1709. Louise: Miss., Tex.
1710. Lucas: Iowa, Kans., Mich., Ohio, S.Dak.
1711. Lucerne: Calif., Mo., Wash.
1712. Lucy: Tenn.
1713. Lulu: Fla.
1714. Luther: Mich., Mont., Okla.
1715. Lydia: Minn., S.C.
1716. Lyle: Minn., Wash.
1717. Lyndon: Ill., Kans., Vt.
1718. Lynn: Ala., Ind., Mass.
1719. Mabel: Minn.
1720. Madeline: Calif.
1721. Marcella: Ark.
1722. Marcus: Iowa, S.Dak., Wash.
1723. Margaret: Tex.
1724. Margie: Minn.
1725. Marianna: Ark., Fla.
1726. Marissa: Ill.
1727. Martha: Okla.
1728. Martin: Ky., Mich., N.Dak., S.Dak., Tenn.
1729. Mason: Ill., Mich., Nev., Ohio, Tenn., Tex., Wis.
1730. Mathias: W.Va.
1731. Maud: Ohio, Okla., Tex.
1732. Maurice: La.
1733. Maury: N.C.
1734. Max: Neb., N.C.
1735. Maxwell: Calif., Iowa, Neb., N.M.
1736. May: Idaho, Okla., Tex.

1737. Melba: Ohio
1738. Merlin: Ore.
1739. Merrill: Iowa, Miss., Ore., Wis.
1740. Mildred: Mont., Pa.
1741. Milo: Iowa, Maine
1742. Mitchell: Ga., Ill., Ind., Neb., Ore., S.Dak.
1743. Mona: Utah
1744. Morgan: Ga., Minn., Pa., Tex., Utah
1745. Morley: Mich., Mo.
1746. Morton: Ill., Minn., Miss., Tex., Wyo.
1747. Murphy: Idaho, Mo., N.C., Ore.
1748. Murray: Iowa, Ky., Utah
1749. Myrtle: Miss.
1750. Nancy: Ky.
1751. Neal: Kans.
1752. Nelson: Ariz., Ga., Neb., Nev., Pa.
1753. Neville: Pa.
1754. Nicolaus: Calif.
1755. Noel: Mo.
1756. Nora: Ill., Va.
1757. Norma: S.Dak.
1758. Norman: Ark., Okla.
1759. Olga: N.Dak., Wash.
1760. Olivia: Minn.
1761. Ollie: Ky.
1762. Opal: S.Dak., Wyo.
1763. Pablo: Mont.
1764. Paulina: Ore.
1765. Pearl: Miss., Tex.
1766. Philip: S.Dak.
1767. Pierce: Colo., Idaho, Neb.

1768. Pierre: S.Dak.

1769. Prentice: Wis.

1770. Prentiss: Maine, Miss.

1771. Preston: Ga., Idaho, Iowa, Kans., Minn., Mo., Okla.

1772. Quinn: S.Dak.

1773. Ralph: S.Dak.

1774. Ramona: Calif., Kans., Okla., S.Dak.

1775. Randall: Kans., Minn.

1776. Ray: N.Dak.

1777. Rebecca: Ga.

1778. Rector: Ark.

1779. Rhonda: Ky.

1780. Richey: Mont.

1781. Roberta: Ga.

1782. Roscoe: Mont., N.Y., Neb., S.Dak., Tex.

1783. Rose: Neb.

1784. Rosita: Tex.

1785. Roslynn: N.Y., Pa., S.Dak., Wash.

1786. Ross: Neb.

1787. Ruby: Alaska, S.C.

1788. Rudy: Ark.

1789. Russell: Ark., Iowa, Kans., Ky., Minn., N.Y., Pa.

1790. Ruth: Miss., Nev.

1791. Ryan: Okla.

1792. Sarah: Miss.

1793. Savanna: Ill., Okla.

1794. Savannah: Ga., Mo., Tenn.

1795. Scott: Ga., La., Miss., Pa.

1796. Selma: Ala., Calif., N.C., Ore., Tex.

1797. Shelley: Idaho

1798. Sherman: Maine, Miss., N.Y., Tex.

1799. Shirley: Ark., Ind., Mass., N.Y.
1800. Sidney: Iowa, Mont., Neb., N.Y., Ohio, Tex.
1801. Stella: Neb.
1802. Stephan: N.Dak.
1803. Stephen: Minn.
1804. Stewart: Minn., Miss., Nev., Ohio
1805. Stuart: Fla., Iowa, Neb., Okla., Va.
1806. Sylvester: Ga., Tex.
1807. Sylvia: Kans.
1808. Terry: Miss., Mont.
1809. Theodore: Ala.
1810. Theresa: N.Y.
1811. Thomas: Okla., W.Va.
1812. Tony: Wis.
1813. Tracy: Calif., Minn.
1814. Tyrone: N.M., Okla., Pa.
1815. Ulysses: Kans., Neb., Pa.
1816. Van: Tex.
1817. Vaughn: Mont., N.M., Wash.
1818. Vera: Okla., Tex.
1819. Victor: Colo., Idaho, Iowa, Mont., N.Y.
1820. Victoria: Ill., Kans., Tex., Va.
1821. Vincent: Ala., Tex.
1822. Violet: La.
1823. Virgil: Kans., S.Dak.
1824. Virginia: Ala., Idaho, Ill., Minn.
1825. Vivian: La., S.Dak.
1826. Wesley: Iowa, Maine
1827. Wilbur: Ore., Wash.
1828. Willard: Mont., N.M., Ohio, Utah
1829. Willis: Tex., Va.

1830. Winston: N.M., Ore.
1831. Wynne: Ark.
1832. Wynona: Okla.

1833. If he was in the military, have a 21-gun salute wake him on his next big birthday
1834. Bring home one flower a day for a solid month
1835. To get in the mood for an upcoming vacation, rent movies that take place in that location
1836. *Double* the length of your average lovemaking session
1837. "Love is the most wonderful thing in the world."
      ~ Francoise Sagan
1838. Sing her a song
1839. The "Love Phone" Coupon: On a day of the coupon-holder's choice, the coupon-giver will call you once an hour all day long and give one reason why he or she loves you
1840. Share a steamy hot cocoa on a frosty winter evening

1841. Collect romantic and inspirational quotes
1842. Write them in a journal and give it to your partner as a gift
1843. Frame the quotes that best express your love

1844. Remember: Money can't buy you love—
1845. But it *can* rent you a little romance!

1846. Have a bed custom-designed for the two of you
1847. Create a "Valentine Ad" and post on YouTube
1848. Take turns taking the romantic lead
1849. End the day in a special way: Give each other massages

1850. Leave a love note on an Etch-A-Sketch
1851. The Soothing "Hot Tub for Two" Coupon: The coupon-giver will secure an hour in a Jacuzzi for the two of you. Aaahh!
1852. Share a sauna

1853. Exercise more—so you'll be a healthier lover
1854. Eat better—so you'll be around longer to enjoy one another
1855. Read more—so you'll have more to talk about
1856. Meditate regularly—to center yourself
1857. Take a class—to improve your self-esteem
1858. Slow down—and savor life more

1859. Write a short essay together, titled "What We've Learned About Marriage"
1860. Have it rendered in calligraphy and frame it
1861. Submit it to your local weekly newspaper for publication
1862. Submit it to *Marriage Magazine* (955 Lake Dr., St. Paul, MN 55120)
1863. Include it with every engagement gift and wedding gift you give to others

1864. The "Bicycle-Built-For-Two" Coupon: The coupon-giver will secure the bike, pack a picnic lunch, and plan a romantic afternoon
1865. Stay at the fanciest hotel in Amsterdam: The Pulitzer
1866. Copy the lyrics from a hymn that is especially meaningful to you
1867. Be sensitive

1868. Keep candles in your glove compartment at all times—just in case

1869. Place a giftwrapped item on the mantle, and see how long it takes him/her to notice

1870. Act like newlyweds

1871. Act like you did on your first date

1872. Act like your favorite movie couple

1873. Take an acting class together; it will help you express emotions!

1874. Be charming

1875. Be thoughtful

1876. Be outrageous

1877. Be yourself

1878. Romance is the icing on the cake of your relationship

1879. So spread it on *thick*

1880. Enemy of Love: Too many responsibilities

1881. Compliment him on his cooking

1882. Plan to be spontaneous

1883. Say "I love you"—and really, really, *really* mean it!

1884. Give each other a "trinket gift" every day you're on vacation

1885. Buy $50 of greeting cards—so you'll always be prepared

Ways for Guys to *Stun* Their Gals with Romance

1886. Take her out to dinner during the Superbowl. (Record it and watch it later!)

1887. Get tickets to a *sold-out* show

1888.   Wear a tuxedo home from work and take her out for a night on the town

1889.   Create (what she considers to be) the "Perfect Romantic Date"

1890.   Send her on a $500 shopping spree at the Mall of America!

1891.   Arrange a surprise second honeymoon to her dream vacation spot

1892.   Upgrade the quality of the diamond in her engagement ring

1893.   Treat her to a Saturday evening of *sensual* (not *sexual*) delights

1894.   Read *You Just Don't Understand*, by Deborah Tannen, and discuss it with her

1895.   Tell her you want to learn how to help her experience multiple orgasms

1896.   Rent, and watch with her: *Casablanca* on Friday night, *Gone with the Wind* on Saturday night, and *Titanic* on Sunday night

1897.   Make love by catering to *her* desires 100%—and put *your* desires on hold until tomorrow

1898.   Get tickets to be in the audience of her favorite daytime talk show

1899.   Write a love song for your lover

1900.   Sing her the love song you wrote

1901.   Have the song professionally recorded

1902.   Write the lyrics and present them on a scroll—

1903.   Have the lyrics rendered in calligraphy—

1904.   Then have them framed

1905. Read *The Dance of Intimacy*, by Harriet Lerner
1906. Learn to imitate her favorite actor
1907. Wear matching gold rings
1908. Serve homemade lemonade on a hot summer afternoon
1909. Read *The Seven Levels of Intimacy: The Art of Loving and the Joy of Being Loved*, by Matthew Kelly
1910. Give one dozen red roses
1911. Save menus as mementos of your dates together
1912. Attend Shakespeare-in-the-Park in NYC's Central Park
1913. As a secret surprise: Set up a hammock in your back yard

1914. Compile your combined family history together
1915. Interview each other's grandparents and elderly relatives
1916. Write it down and create a keepsake for your children

1917. Reduce your TV watching by 50%…
1918. Spend half of that time improving *yourself*
1919. Spend the other half improving your *relationship*

Ways for Business Executives to Earn Romantic Dividends

1920. Use your *business* skills to improve your relationship
1921. Use time management techniques so you'll have more time together
1922. Use your customer service skills to "keep your 'customer' satisfied"
1923. Use your sales skills—instead of lapsing into nagging or complaining
1924. Be as considerate of your partner as you are of your best customer

1925. Write an "Inter-Office Memo" complimenting him/her for something

1926. How could you "give your partner a raise" to show your appreciation?

1927. If you can keep your *staff* motivated, you can keep your *mate* motivated!

1928. Work some "overtime" on your relationship

1929. Read *The Art of Kissing Book of Questions and Answers: Everything You Ever Wanted to Know About Perfecting Your Kissing Technique*, by William Cane

1930. The Official Valentine's Day Coupon: In addition to providing you with candy and roses, you will be treated like the unique, special, wonderful person you are

1931. Be the Best Father in the World to her children

1932. Say this: "Will you marry me?"

1933. "Loving is not just caring deeply, it's above all, understanding." ~ Francoise Sagan

1934. Go tobogganing together

1935. Make a music mix that makes you feel *young*

1936. Give flowers that match his/her eyes

1937. Make a regular Saturday date: Listen to Garrison Keillor's *Prairie Home Companion* on National Public Radio

1938. The first ever "Second Valentine's Day of the Year" Coupon: Yes, this coupon allows you to celebrate a *second* Valentine's Day on a day of your choosing!

1939. Ride the Tunnel of Love at a carnival

1940. Have a porch swing picnic

1941. Read *Getting the Love You Want: A Guide for Couples*, by Harville Hendrix

1942. A Classic Dinner Date Coupon: At the most romantic restaurant in town. Coupon-giver's treat

1943. *Another* Dinner Date Coupon: At a local restaurant that you've never visited before

1944. And yet *another* Dinner Date Coupon: The coupon-holder chooses the date, the coupon-giver chooses the restaurant

1945. Favorite gifts for women: Jewelry

1946. Favorite gifts for women: Perfume

1947. Favorite gifts for women: Flowers

1948. Run a marathon together

1949. Buy her a kitten

1950. Trace "I love you" on a stick of butter

1951. While flying, call from the airphone just to say "I love you"

1952. Ask your grandparents to share their secrets for keeping love alive

1953. Spend a weekend at a ski lodge, even if you don't like to ski!

1954. A "Carnival Coupon:" Good for a full afternoon of rides on the roller coaster, tilt-a-whirl, Ferris wheel, and merry-go-round

Best Love Songs by Elvis Presley

1955. "I Need Your Love Tonight"

1956. "I Want You, I Need You, I Love You"

1957. "I'm Yours"

1958. "(Let Me Be Your) Teddy Bear"

1959.   "Love Me"
1960.   "My Wish Came True"
1961.   "The Wonder of You"

1962.   "Don't change a mind; change a mood." ~ Aim Ginott
1963.   Use music to change the mood
1964.   You could use soft lighting to change the mood
1965.   Try changing the mood by changing your *attitude*

1966.   How do you get a guy to be more romantic? *Not* by nagging or manipulating!
1967.   How do you get a gal to be more sexual? *Not* by arguing or cajoling
1968.   You can't change another's *mind*—but you *can* change the environment, the context, the mood

---

1969.   When he/she's traveling alone, have an airline attendant deliver a gift to your mate mid-flight
1970.   Take your partner on your next business trip and upgrade to the Honeymoon Suite
1971.   Reserve your weekends for each other
1972.   Learn how to write the story of your steamy romance: Romance Writers of America: www.rwanational.org
1973.   Splurge on a $100 shopping spree at Frederick's of Hollywood
1974.   New parents coupon: "I'll get up in the middle of the night with the baby"

1975.   A "Sweet Stuff" Coupon: Redeemable for *lots* of your favorite candy or chocolate

1976. Mail a wedding photo to your partner with a romantic note attached

1977. Share your religious beliefs

1978. "Make the most of yourself, for that is all there is of you." ~ Ralph Waldo Emerson

1979. Generate 33% more laughter in your life together

1980. Use the song "All of Me" as part of your marriage proposal

1981. Give flowers that begin with the first letter of your lover's name

1982. Write caption balloons for some funny photos

1983. Touch your partner—*with your eyes*

1984. Touch your partner—*with your words*

1985. Touch your partner—*with your actions*

1986. Touch your partner—*with gifts and presents*

1987. This year: Give twenty *small, inexpensive* gifts for Christmas

1988. Next year: Give just one *perfect, elegant, special* gift

1989. The following year: Give gifts that all reflect a *music* theme

1990. And the next year: Give gifts that all reflect a *sports* theme

1991. And the year after that: Give nothing but *books*

1992. And the year after that: Give gifts that all reflect a *travel* theme

1993. And the year after that: Give the "Gift of Time": Twenty-five hours of your time

1994. On your wedding day: Get a friend to buy fifty current magazines and newspapers

1995. Hide them away—then present them to your partner on your 25th anniversary

1996. Do a *Cosmo* quiz together

1997. Hire a housecleaning service to free more time for yourselves

1998. The "Sex-Sex-Sex" Coupon: The coupon giver promises to fulfill one sexual fantasy of the coupon holder's choosing.

1999. Meet for lunch every Wednesday

2000. Reduce your complaining by 50% and your criticizing by 62%

Favorite Love Songs from 1937

2001. "I've Got My Love to Keep Me Warm"

2002. "In the Still of the Night"

2003. "Shall We Dance?"

2004. "Thanks for the Memory"

2005. An "Adventure Date" Coupon: Your partner will take you somewhere neither of you have been.

2006. Enemy of Love: Over-reliance on logic

2007. The "Ultimate Pizza Date" Coupon: The coupon-holder chooses the pizza joint and the toppings. Coupon-giver's treat!

2008. Go for a walk on the beach

2009. Read *Other People's Love Letters: 150 Letters You Were Never Meant to See*, by Bill Shapiro

2010. When staying with relatives, intentionally sleep together in a single bed

2011. Have a pillow fight
2012. Have a pillow embroidered with your names
2013. Get some heart-shaped pillows
2014. Get monogrammed pillow covers
2015. Get a blow-up airplane neck pillow for your traveler
2016. Get a "maternity body pillow" when she's pregnant
2017. Save the ring bearer's satin pillow from your wedding
2018. Learn the subtle art of "pillowtalk"

Film Festivals to Attend with Your Movie Buff

2019. Chicago International Film Festival, October:
www.chicagofilmfestival.org
2020. Hawaii International Film Festival, December:
www.hiff.org
2021. New York Film Festival, June:
www.filmlinc.nyff/nyff.html
2022. Seattle International Film Festival, June:
www.seattlefilm.com
2023. Telluride Film Festival, August:
www.telluridefilmfestival.org
2024. Wine Valley Film Festival, July:
www.winecountryfilmfest.com

2025. Create quirky, custom "tickets" for your lover—
2026. Season tickets for "Friday Night Mattress Testing"
2027. A ticket for "Dinner for Two at Home (Formal attire required)"
2028. A ticket to "A Personal Striptease"

2029. Always have romantic, acoustic music in the car

2030. The "Queen for a Day" Coupon: The female coupon-holder is entitled to be treated like royalty for a twenty-four hour period

2031. Give your partner a small national flag from the country his ancestors came from

2032. Plant a rose garden together

2033. A Cuddle Coupon: Good for two hours of cuddling with the coupon-issuer in front of a roaring fire or on a porch swing

2034. Pick a recipe from *Pizza on the Grill: 100 Feisty Fire-Roasted Recipes for Pizza & More*, by Elizabeth Karmel and Bob Blumer

2035. Rake leaves together

2036. Soma Intimates: www.soma.com

2037. Agent Provocateur: www.agentprovocateur.com

2038. Frederick's of Hollywood Catalog: www.fredricks.com

2039. La Perla: www.laperla.com

2040. Playboy Catalog: www.playboystore.com

2041. Victoria's Secret Catalog: www.victoriassecret.com

2042. Memorize "How Do I Love Thee (Let Me Count the Ways)" by Elizabeth Barrett Browning

2043. Love Enhancer: Empathy

2044. Bake an outrageous French pastry

2045. Stick up for your partner at all times

2046. Take an enlightening vacation at The Esalen Institute, in Big Sur, California: www.esalen.org

2047. Musical lovenote: "Play the CD *Christopher Cross*; my message to you is song No. 1"

2048. A first anniversary card idea: "Happy 50th Anniversary—49 years early!"

Ways to Turn a Simple Bubblebath into a Memorable Romantic Event

2049. Float rose petals in the bathtub
2050. Add scented bath oils
2051. Add floating candles
2052. Add champagne
2053. Add cheese and crackers
2054. Add soft music
2055. Add a book to read
2056. Have romantic music playing in the background
2057. Do all of the above in a *heart-shaped bathtub*—
2058. At a honeymoon resort *in the Poconos*

2059. Pack a dozen of his favorite cookies in his suitcase
2060. For an Elvis fan: Get collector's original singles of all eighteen of his No. 1 hits
2061. A "Kids-Free Day!" Coupon: You two get to play as the coupon-giver finds a caretaker for the kids for twenty-four hours
2062. Romantic Opera Alert: Mozart's *The Magic Flute*
2063. Compliment her on her looks
2064. Buy her cotton candy
2065. Get an autographed photo of his/her favorite athlete
2066. Drape a giant banner in front of your house to celebrate his/her return from a trip
2067. Stay married—through thick and thin
2068. When you're in the car together, tune in to her favorite station

Ways to Drive Your Lover *Crazy*

2069. Write love notes on all six sides of a Rubik's Cube, then scramble it!
2070. Send sexy text messages
2071. Engage in three hours of foreplay
2072. Give him hints about what his birthday gift is
2073. While he/she's out of town, have "phone sex" every day
2074. Wrap a *tiny* gift in a box, inside a larger box, inside a larger box, etc.
2075. Send a series of sexy notes from "A Secret Admirer"
2076. Circle a date in her calendar in red, but don't tell her *why*
2077. Place her wrapped birthday gift on the mantle *a week early*, and drive her crazy with anticipation
2078. Call him at work and describe in *excruciating detail* your sexy lingerie and what you want to do to him

2079. Gals: Don't mess with his work bench
2080. Start a blog as a love letter to your partner
2081. Bake him a pie
2082. Hang a romantic print by Impressionist painter Paul Cézanne
2083. The "Indoor Picnic" Coupon: You pick the date, and your partner provides goodies
2084. Read *The Love Dare*, by Stephen Kendrick and Alex Kendrick
2085. Give one dozen pink roses
2086. Create a personalized "Music-of-the-Month Club"

2087. Take your car nut to the car show
2088. Take your gardener to the flower show
2089. Take your space nut to Cape Canaveral
2090. Take your fashionable mate to a fashion show
2091. Take your boating enthusiast to the boat show
2092. Take your Trekkie to a Star Trek convention
2093. Take your baseball fan to the World Series
2094. Take your architecture buff on a tour of European cathedrals
2095. Take your art lover to an art museum
2096. Take your race fan to some NASCAR races
2097. Take your ski bum to the Swiss Alps
2098. Take your chef to a gourmet cooking class
2099. Take your motorcyclist to a bike rally
2100. Take your history buff on a tour of Civil War battlefields
2101. Take your theater buff to a Broadway show
2102. Take your sun worshiper to Waikiki
2103. Take your sci-fi fan to the Palomar Observatory
2104. Take your "star gazer" to Hollywood's Avenue of the Stars
2105. Take your tennis fan to Wimbledon

2106. The Wine Lover's Coupon: Redeemable for a favorite bottle of wine.
2107. Understand your feelings of jealousy
2108. The "Field of Dreams" Coupon: Redeemable for a relaxing afternoon in a quiet meadow. Picnic and romantic companionship included
2109. Dine in a revolving restaurant
2110. Say "I love you" 300% more often

2111. When window shopping, secretly note what your partner likes, and return later to buy it

2112. Discuss what comes to mind for each of you when you think of a "Romantic Rendezvous"

2113. Find a "personal shopper" to help you run romantic errands

2114. Celebrate Beethoven's birthday: December 16

2115. Visit the country where your partner's family came from

2116. Use flowers to send *specific* messages of love

2117. Ambrosia symbolizes—Love returned

2118. Amethyst symbolizes—Admiration

2119. Azalea symbolizes—Romance

2120. Camellia symbolizes—Steadfast love

2121. Pink carnations mean—"I'll never forget you"

2122. Cherry blossom symbolizes—Spiritual beauty

2123. Daisies symbolize—Innocence

2124. Gardenias mean—"You're lovely"

2125. Geraniums mean—"A secret rendezvous"

2126. Hazel symbolizes—Reconciliation

2127. Iris symbolizes—A flame of passion

2128. Lilac symbolizes—New love & innocence

2129. Lily symbolizes—Sweetness & purity

2130. Orchids mean—"You're beautiful"

2131. Peach means—"You're unique"

2132. Rosemary symbolizes—Remembrance

2133. Tulips (red) mean—"My perfect lover"

2134. Tulips mean—"You mean everything to me"

2135. Violets mean—Faithfulness

2136.   Eat dinner at the most expensive steakhouse in town
2137.   Choose *fresh* flowers—they'll last *much* longer
2138.   If he/she's a fanatical dog/cat lover, get gifts for the pet, too!
2139.   "In love and war don't seek counsel." ~ French proverb
2140.   Read *The Seven Principles for Making Marriage Work*, by John M. Gottman
2141.   Fill the freezer with twelve boxes of his favorite kind of Girl Scout Cookie
2142.   A+ Rating, Romantic Music Artist: Richard Clayderman
2143.   Give him a football signed by his favorite player
2144.   Give her a scarf that pictures her favorite flowers
2145.   Love Coupon: An Evening of Dancing: Kick up your heels for a night on the town!
2146.   Have a gourmet picnic—complete with candelabra and music

2147.   Create a series of gifts and gestures with "crazy in love" as the theme
2148.   Note: There are seven songs and two movies listed in this book with "crazy" in their titles. Can you find them? Can you use them?

2149.   "A love song is just a caress set to music." ~ Sigmund Romberg
2150.   Create a playlist of songs that fits this description
2151.   Some suggestions: "Make It with You," Bread
2152.   "Lost in Love," Air Supply
2153.   Attach a note that is a "caress set to *words*"

2154.   Incorporate more music into your day-to-day life together

2155.   Try a different ethnic cuisine every night for a week

2156.   Mood music: Create a light-hearted mood with the *Picnic Suite* by Jean-Pierre Rampal and Claude Bolling

2157.   Be unconventional

2158.   The "Romantic Rowboat" Coupon: Your host will man the oars for a romantic afternoon on a local lake with you

2159.   Genie Coupon: Good for three wishes. "Your wish is my command!"

2160.   Single guys: Never wrap *anything* in a ring box except an engagement ring

2161.   Save one flower from *every* bouquet he gives you, and create a new bouquet of dried flowers

2162.   Giftwrap all presents in a special way

2163.   "The Half-Day-Off-Work" Coupon: The coupon-giver will arrange with your employer for half a day off work for you

2164.   Give him cologne that turns you on

2165.   Plan a three-day weekend—as a surprise

2166.   For parents: Create more time for yourselves by creating a "Neighborhood Child-Sharing Program"

2167.   For coffee lovers: Buy a gift certificate from Starbucks

Best Love Songs by Chicago (and/or Peter Cetera)

2168.   "Glory of Love" (Peter Cetera)

2169.   "I Don't Wanna Live Without Your Love"

2170.   "Just You 'n Me"

2171. "The Next Time I Fall" (Peter Cetera and Amy Grant)
2172. "Stay the Night"
2173. "Will You Still Love Me?"
2174. "You're the Inspiration"

2175. "Often the difference between a successful marriage and a mediocre one consists of leaving about three or four things a day unsaid." ~ Harlan Miller
2176. Hang a romantic print by Impressionist painter Camille Pissarro
2177. Place a new item of jewelry in her jewelry box—and wait for her to discover it
2178. Toast marshmallows over a campfire
2179. Send a sexy photo via text message
2180. Take a trolley ride
2181. Make a cake from scratch
2182. Always, always, *always* follow your heart

2183. Creatively create more time for your relationship
2184. Prioritize your household chores into *now*, next week, and *next year*!

2185. "Just do it": Be more loving more often
2186. "It's the real thing": Love
2187. "Have it *your* way": Lovemaking
2188. "Fly the friendly skies": Join the Mile High Club!
2189. "Reach out and touch someone": Physically *and* emotionally
2190. "*Try* it—you'll *like* it": If you're out of practice, *try* being more loving—you'll *like* it

2191. The "Couple's Campout" Coupon: Good for a romantic night in the woods. The coupon-giver will supply the tent, sleeping bags, campfire, etc.
2192. Eat dinner at the best Japanese restaurant around
2193. Love Enhancer: Goodwill
2194. When sipping champagne, intertwine your arms
2195. Keep this book handy—so you can refer to it at a moment's notice
2196. Love Enhancer: Attentiveness
2197. Give her diamond earrings by putting them on a teddy bear's ears
2198. Give one pink rose

Favorite Love Songs from 1938

2199. "This Can't Be Love"
2200. "Two Sleepy People," Bob Hope & Shirley Ross
2201. "You Go to My Head," Kay Kyser

2202. Between lovers: Complete honesty is demanded, assumed, and never questioned
2203. Give one yellow rose
2204. A+ Romantic Restaurant Rating: Au Clocher du Village
2205. Send him/her to a spa Fridays after work
2206. Give her socks that picture her favorite flowers
2207. Photograph your children and make an album
2208. For men married more than ten years: Propose to your wife *again*—and give her a BIG diamond ring

Exercises for Tapping into Your Creativity

Relationships require creativity. These exercises will jump-start yours.

2209. Give it a twist: Start with something basic, then give it a creative twist

2210. Change your routine: Shaking up your routine often leads to new ideas

2211. Consider every crazy idea that pops into your head. You won't use them *all*, but the process *expands* your thinking

2212. Give yourself a deadline: Sometimes working under pressure works!

2213. Learn from your mistakes

2214. Go with your strengths: Do what comes *naturally*, go with the flow

2215. Go *counter* to your natural strengths: Try something *different*

2216. Tap into your unconscious mind: There's a lot going on beneath the surface

2217. Challenge the assumptions

2218. Imagine how *someone else* would do it: How would Einstein create new ideas? Mozart?

2219. Use different "models" of thinking: Think *organically*; think like a *cat*; think like a *millionaire*

2220. Re-frame the question: The question might be, "How can I be more loving?" Or it might be, "How can I be more *spontaneous*?"

2221. Listen to your intuition/sixth sense/Inner Voice

2222. Admit that you're *dissatisfied* with the status quo: It will inspire you to find solutions

2223. Don't go it alone! Brainstorm romantic ideas with a group of friends

2224. Use random ideas to stimulate different avenues of thinking

2225. Change your perspective: See the "Big Picture." Look at the *details*

2226. Borrow (then customize) ideas! From movies, books, other couples

2227. Face your fears: What's holding you back from being more creative? More loving?

2228. Draw pictures; doodle; make diagrams

2229. Try on a different persona: Think like a kid; think like a member of the opposite sex; think like your partner

2230. Withhold judgment: Generate *lots* of ideas before you begin evaluating

2231. Have fun; play with ideas; be *wacky*

2232. Bake one cupcake for every year she has lived

2233. Serve a cake with birthday candles that won't blow out (Ha!)

2234. Buy two beach chairs and watch the waves in a secluded spot

2235. Eat dinner at the best English pub around

2236. The Whimsical "Holiday at Home" Coupon: The coupon-giver will treat you to an at-home weekend vacation

2237. Review all the Valentine specials at restaurants the week prior to Valentine's Day

2238. Wish upon a falling star

2239. Give compliments

2240. Go on a photo safari

2241. Visit the Grand Ole Opry
2242. Right after Valentine's Day, stock up on heart-themed wrapping paper and boxes
2243. Send love notes via fax
2244. If you travel a lot: Make a habit of calling every day *no matter what*
2245. Clip headline words to create a love note in the format of a ransom note
2246. Plan a treasure hunt for her birthday that leads to all of her favorite places; be creative!

Relationship "Experiments" to Try

2247. Compliment your partner once a day for thirty days in a row
2248. Stop nagging for one solid month
2249. Listen *without interrupting* for one week
2250. Try being *totally supportive* of your partner for one entire week
2251. For one solid week, *give without taking*; ask *nothing* of your partner
2252. Program your unconscious mind to *act* on your loving thoughts whenever they pop up
2253. Say nothing negative or judgmental for three days
2254. Slow down the pace of your lovemaking: Take *twice* as long as usual
2255. Act as if you feel loving—*even if you don't*—for one week. Act like you did when you first fell in love
2256. Tell the truth—no fibs, for one week
2257. See who can be more *creatively romantic*: Take turns being "it" for one week each, over a period of two months

2258. Guys: Do something *with* her that you hate to do
2259. It only counts as a loving gesture if you do it cheerfully and without complaint
2260. Go shopping with her, see a chick flick

2261. Support and encourage your partner to stop smoking
2262. Make love on a Sunday afternoon
2263. "It is when we earn love least, that we need it most." ~ Anonymous
2264. Give him a cap from his favorite basketball team
2265. The "Sleep In Late" Coupon: You are entitled to sleep 'til noon! Your partner will be responsible for the removal of all disturbances
2266. Enemy of Love: Lack of time
2267. "Who you are shouts so loud, I cannot hear what you're saying." ~ Ralph Waldo Emerson
2268. Eat in the most romantic restaurant in Zurich: Tubli
2269. Go out of your way for your partner
2270. Gather movies with his/her favorite stars
2271. Love Coupon: This coupon entitles the holder to one sensuous backrub, no less than thirty minutes long
2272. As part of foreplay, read aloud to him a sexy passage from an erotic book
2273. Massage her feet

366 Things to Celebrate—
Every Day of the Year Is Special!

2274. January 1: New Year's Day—Make a new year's resolution!
2275. January 2: Isis Celebration—The goddess of love

2276. January 3: Tom Sawyer's Cat's Birthday

2277. January 4: Tom Thumb's Birthday—Honoring all short people

2278. January 5: Twelfth Night—The last of the Twelve Days of Christmas

2279. January 6: Sherlock Holmes' Birthday

2280. January 7: Film fest—Nicolas Cage's Birthday

2281. January 8: Rock 'n Roll Day & Elvis Presley's Birthday

2282. January 9: National Clean-Off-Your-Desk Day

2283. January 10: Rod Stewart's Birthday

2284. January 11: Naomi Judd's Birthday

2285. January 12: Family Communications Day

2286. January 13: Ha! It's Rip Taylor's birthday

2287. January 14: Faye Dunaway's Birthday

2288. January 15: Hot and Spicy Food International Day

2289. January 16: National Nothing Day

2290. January 17: Benjamin Franklin's Birthday

2291. January 18: Winnie the Pooh Day! (A. A. Milne's Birthday)

2292. January 19: Popcorn Day: Snuggle with your loved one and pop some kernels!

2293. January 20: Penguin Awareness Day

2294. January 21: National Hugging Day

2295. January 22: Don't Stop Believin'—Steve Perry's Birthday

2296. January 23: Humphrey Bogart's Birthday—Watch *Casablanca*

2297. January 24: Neil Diamond's Birthday—Sing out!

2298. January 25: Virginia Woolf's Birthday—A Room of One's Own Day

2299. January 26: Spouse's Day
2300. January 27: National Chocolate Cake Day—Plan a chocolate cake party or have a cake contest!
2301. January 28: Sarah McLachlan's birthday
2302. January 29: It's Oprah Winfrey's Birthday
2303. January 30: FDR's Birthday
2304. January 31: Bring Sexy Back—Justin Timberlake's Birthday
2305. February 1: Clark Gable's Birthday—Watch *Gone with the Wind*
2306. February 2: Groundhog Day
2307. February 3: Elmo's Birthday!
2308. February 4: Gumby's Birthday—Plan a Clay Party in honor of the famous green icon
2309. February 5: Henry "Hank" Aaron's Birthday
2310. February 6: Ronald Reagan's Birthday
2311. February 7: Laura Ingalls Wilder's Birthday
2312. February 8: James Dean's Birthday—Be cool
2313. February 9: National Bagels And Lox Day
2314. February 10: Umbrella Day
2315. February 11: *Archie* comic book debuts in 1942
2316. February 12: Abraham Lincoln's Birthday
2317. February 13: Chuck Yeager's Birthday
2318. February 14: Valentine's Day
2319. February 15: National Gumdrop Day
2320. February 16: Sonny Bono's Birthday—I got you, Babe
2321. February 17: Play one-on-one—Michael Jordan's birthday
2322. February 18: John Travolta's Birthday
2323. February 19: National Chocolate Mint Day

2324. February 20: National Cherry Pie Day
2325. February 21: *The New Yorker* magazine first published in 1925
2326. February 22: National Margarita Day
2327. February 23: Anniversary of the Tootsie Roll (1896)
2328. February 24: National Tortilla Chip Day
2329. February 25: George Harrison's Birthday
2330. February 26: Carnival Day
2331. February 27: Polar Bear Day
2332. February 28: Anniversary of the final episode of M*A*S*H
2333. February 29: Leap Day
2334. March 1: Crack open a cold one—Beer Day
2335. March 2: Theodor "Dr. Seuss" Geisel's Birthday
2336. March 3: I Want You to Be Happy Day
2337. March 4: Knute Rockne's Birthday
2338. March 5: Penn Jillette's birthday—go see a magic show
2339. March 6: National White Chocolate Cheesecake Day
2340. March 7: Willard Scott's Birthday
2341. March 8: International Women's Day
2342. March 9: Barbie's Birthday—Debuted in 1959
2343. March 10: Sharon Stone's Birthday
2344. March 11: Johnny Appleseed Day
2345. March 12: Plant A Flower Day
2346. March 13: Good Samaritan Day
2347. March 14: Ha! Billy Crystal's Birthday
2348. March 15: The Ides of March
2349. March 16: Jerry Lewis' Birthday
2350. March 17: St. Patrick's Day
2351. March 18: Oatmeal Cookie Day

2352.   March 19: Bruce Willis' Birthday
2353.   March 20: Big Bird's Birthday!
2354.   March 21: Fragrance Day
2355.   March 22: National Goof-Off Day
2356.   March 23: National Chip and Dip Day: Throw a wild and crazy dip party with your friends! Have everyone bring over a different dip
2357.   March 24: Harry Houdini's Birthday: Throw a magical fiesta!
2358.   March 25: Elton John's Birthday
2359.   March 26: Make Up Your Own Holiday Day
2360.   March 27: Mariah Carey's Birthday
2361.   March 28: Beer Brewers Day (August Anheuser Busch Jr.'s Birthday)
2362.   March 29: Oscar Meyer's Birthday—Hot dog!
2363.   March 30: Take A Walk In The Park Day
2364.   March 31: Anniversary of the Eiffel Tower
2365.   April 1: April Fool's Day
2366.   April 2: Giovanni Jacopo Casanova's Birthday
2367.   April 3: National Find-A-Rainbow Day
2368.   April 4: Arthur Murray's Birthday—Dance!
2369.   April 5: Paula Cole's Birthday
2370.   April 6: Twinkies Day
2371.   April 7: No Housework Day
2372.   April 8: Zoo Lover's Day
2373.   April 9: W.C. Fields' Birthday
2374.   April 10: Encourage a Beginning Writer Day
2375.   April 11: Write Your Memoirs Day
2376.   April 12: National Tap Dance Party Day
2377.   April 13: Thomas Jefferson's Birthday
2378.   April 14: International Moment of Laughter Day

2379. April 15: Watch a "Harry Potter" movie—Emma Watson's Birthday
2380. April 16: National Eggs Benedict Day
2381. April 17: Listen to the Beatles—Paul McCartney debuts first solo album in 1970
2382. April 18: Pet Owner's Day
2383. April 19: Movie night—Ashley Judd's Birthday
2384. April 20: *Love Story*—Ryan O'Neal's Birthday
2385. April 21: Webster's Dictionary Published
2386. April 22: Enlighten your mind: Immanuel Kant's Birthday
2387. April 23: William Shakespeare's Birthday
2388. April 24: Pig In A Blanket Day
2389. April 25: Hoo-ahh! Al Pacino's Birthday
2390. April 26: Hug A Friend Day
2391. April 27: Tell A Story Day
2392. April 28: Kiss Your Mate Day
2393. April 29: Duke Ellington's Birthday—Jazz it up!
2394. April 30: Get a belly full of laughs: Jerry Seinfeld's Birthday
2395. May 1: May Day
2396. May 2: Baby Day
2397. May 3: World Press Freedom Day
2398. May 4: Naked Day
2399. May 5: Cinco de Mayo
2400. May 6: International No Diet Day
2401. May 7: Beethoven's Ninth Symphony premiered in 1824
2402. May 8: World Red Cross Day
2403. May 9: The Piano Man, Billy Joel's Birthday
2404. May 10: Fred Astaire's Birthday—Gotta dance!

2405. May 11: Eat What You Want Day
2406. May 12: Limerick Day (Edward Lear's Birthday)
2407. May 13: Stevie Wonder's Birthday
2408. May 14: May the Force be with you on George Lucas' Birthday
2409. May 15: National Chocolate Chip Day
2410. May 16: Love A Tree Day
2411. May 17: Sugar Ray Leonard's Birthday
2412. May 18: *Dracula* by Bram Stoker is published in 1897
2413. May 19: Circus Day
2414. May 20: Turn back time and listen to some hits— Cher's birthday!
2415. May 21: National Waitresses Day
2416. May 22: Buy A Musical Instrument Day
2417. May 23: Joan Collins' Birthday
2418. May 24: Bob Dylan's Birthday
2419. May 25: *Star Wars* is released in 1978: Host a costume party and watch the movie
2420. May 26: Celebrate the first American woman in space—Sally Ride's Birthday
2421. May 27: Wild Bill Hickok's Birthday
2422. May 28: Whale Day
2423. May 29: Bob Hope's Birthday—Thanks for the memories
2424. May 30: Water A Flower Day
2425. May 31: American Poetry Day (Walt Whitman's Birthday)
2426. June 1: Marilyn Monroe's Birthday
2427. June 2: Jerry Mathers' birthday—Leave it to Beaver!
2428. June 3: Tony Curtis' Birthday

2429. June 4: Celebrate women's right to vote! The 19th amendment passed in 1919
2430. June 5: World Environment Day
2431. June 6: Kenny G's Birthday
2432. June 7: National Chocolate Ice Cream Day
2433. June 8: Best Friends Day
2434. June 9: Donald Duck's Birthday
2435. June 10: Judy Garland's Birthday
2436. June 11: The movie *E.T.: The Extra-Terrestrial* was released (1982)
2437. June 12: Red Rose Day
2438. June 13: Spend time in detention with the "Breakfast Club"—Ally Sheedy's Birthday
2439. June 14: Flag Day
2440. June 15: Magna Carta Day
2441. June 16: Fudge Day
2442. June 17: Barry Manilow's Birthday
2443. June 18: Paul McCartney's Birthday
2444. June 19: Garfield's Birthday (1978)
2445. June 20: Lionel Richie's Birthday
2446. June 21: Summer Solstice— The First Day of Summer
2447. June 22: Doughnuts Day
2448. June 23: Midsummer Eve
2449. June 24: Celebration of the Senses Day
2450. June 25: Carly Simon's Birthday
2451. June 26: Start the party! Gretchen Wilson's Birthday
2452. June 27: Sunglasses Day
2453. June 28: Gilda Radner's Birthday
2454. June 29: Camera Day
2455. June 30: *Gone with the Wind* published in 1936

2456. July 1: International Joke Day
2457. July 2: National Literacy Day—Read a romantic book
2458. July 3: Half-Way Point of the Year
2459. July 4: American Independence Day
2460. July 5: Bikini swimsuit premiered in 1946
2461. July 6: Beatrix Potter's Birthday
2462. July 7: Ringo Starr's Birthday
2463. July 8: Buy stock for her: first issue of the Wall Street Journal is published
2464. July 9: National Sugar Cookie Day
2465. July 10: Bahamas Independence Day—Plan a vacation!
2466. July 11: Read *Charlotte's Web*—E.B. White's Birthday
2467. July 12: Pecan Pie Day
2468. July 13: Harrison Ford's Birthday
2469. July 14: Bastille Day
2470. July 15: Linda Ronstadt's Birthday
2471. July 16: Pop some popcorn—It's Orville Redenbacher's Birthday
2472. July 17: Disneyland founded in 1955
2473. July 18: Nelson Mandela's Birthday
2474. July 19: Anthony Edwards' Birthday
2475. July 20: Anniversary of the first Moon landing, 1969
2476. July 21: National Junk Food Day
2477. July 22: Oscar de la Renta's Birthday—Celebrate *in style*
2478. July 23: National Hot Dog Day
2479. July 24: Amelia Earhart's Birthday
2480. July 25: Merry-Go-Round invented, 1871
2481. July 26: Mick Jagger's Birthday

2482. July 27: Bugs Bunny's Birthday (1940)

2483. July 28: Jacqueline Kennedy Onassis' Birthday

2484. July 29: Martina McBride's Birthday

2485. July 30: National Cheesecake Day

2486. July 31: Perry Como's Birthday

2487. August 1: Friendship Day

2488. August 2: Watch a horror movie together—Wes Craven's Birthday

2489. August 3: Tony Bennett's Birthday

2490. August 4: Champagne invented by Dom Perignon in 1693

2491. August 5: National Mustard Day

2492. August 6: Jamaican Independence Day—Plan a vacation!

2493. August 7: Garrison Keillor's Birthday

2494. August 8: Dustin Hoffman's Birthday

2495. August 9: Book Lover's Day

2496. August 10: S'Mores Day

2497. August 11: Play in the Sand Day

2498. August 12: Go play tennis—Pete Sampras's Birthday

2499. August 13: International Lefthanders Day

2500. August 14: Read a romance novel—Danielle Steel's Birthday

2501. August 15: Julia Child's Birthday

2502. August 16: *Sports Illustrated* first published in 1954

2503. August 17: "Wizard of Oz" premiered in NY in 1939

2504. August 18: Bad Poetry Day

2505. August 19: National Aviation Day (Orville Wright's Birthday)

2506. August 20: Sit Back and Relax Day

2507. August 21: National Senior Citizen's Day

2508.   August 22: Be An Angel Day

2509.   August 23: Hug Your Boyfriend or Girlfriend Day

2510.   August 24: Make a deal with your mate—It's Monty Hall's Birthday

2511.   August 25: Kiss and Make-up Day

2512.   August 26: Women's Equality Day—19th Amendment certified

2513.   August 27: Beauty Is in the Eye of the Beholder Day

2514.   August 28: Dream Day—Anniversary of MLK's "I have a dream" speech

2515.   August 29: Michael Jackson's Birthday

2516.   August 30: Ted Williams' Birthday

2517.   August 31: Gloria Estefan's Birthday

2518.   September 1: Lily Tomlin's Birthday

2519.   September 2: Jimmy Connors' Birthday

2520.   September 3: Charlie Sheen's Birthday

2521.   September 4: The Beatles record their first single, "Love Me Do"

2522.   September 5: National Cheese Pizza Day

2523.   September 6: Read A Book Day

2524.   September 7: Do It! Day

2525.   September 8: International Literacy Day

2526.   September 9: Teddy Bear Day

2527.   September 10: Swap Ideas Day

2528.   September 11: Patriot Day

2529.   September 12: Chocolate Milkshake Day

2530.   September 13: Positive Thinking Day

2531.   September 14: Star Spangled Banner Day

2532.   September 15: First issue of *USA Today* published in 1982

2533.   September 16: B.B. King's Birthday

2534. September 17: Citizenship Day
2535. September 18: National Cheeseburger Day
2536. September 19: Holy Birthday, Batman—It's Adam West's Birthday
2537. September 20: Sophia Loren's Birthday
2538. September 21: Tiffany's founded in 1837
2539. September 22: Hobbit Day
2540. September 23: Autumnal Equinox
2541. September 24: F. Scott Fitzgerald's Birthday
2542. September 25: Christopher Reeve's Birthday
2543. September 26: National Pancake Day
2544. September 27: Ancestor Appreciation Day
2545. September 28: Confucius' Birthday
2546. September 29: National Coffee Day
2547. September 30: Breakfast at Tiffany—it's Truman Capote's Birthday
2548. October 1: World Vegetarian Day
2549. October 2: Snoopy's Birthday
2550. October 3: Mickey Mouse Club Debut in 1955
2551. October 4: National Taco Day
2552. October 5: Kate Winslet's Birthday
2553. October 6: German-American Day
2554. October 7: John Mellencamp's Birthday
2555. October 8: Chevy Chase's Birthday
2556. October 9: John Lennon's Birthday
2557. October 10: Wear a tux—Anniversary of the tuxedo in America, 1886
2558. October 11: Ha! *Saturday Night Live's* premiere, 1975
2559. October 12: Luciano Pavarotti's Birthday—Sing out!
2560. October 13: Modern Mythology Day
2561. October 14: National Dessert Day

2562.　October 15: *I Love Lucy* debuts in 1951

2563.　October 16: Winnie the Pooh's Birthday

2564.　October 17: Black Poetry Day

2565.　October 18: Chocolate Cupcake Day

2566.　October 19: Evaluate Your Life Day

2567.　October 20: Mickey Mantle's Birthday

2568.　October 21: Dizzy Gillespie's Birthday

2569.　October 22: The Supremes become first all-female group to attain #1 selling album in 1966

2570.　October 23: Johnny Carson's Birthday

2571.　October 24: International Forgiveness Day

2572.　October 25: Pablo Picasso's Birthday

2573.　October 26: Walt Disney airs first TV program, *Disneyland* in 1954

2574.　October 27: Enjoy an old favorite—*ET* released on video in 1988

2575.　October 28: National Chocolate Day

2576.　October 29: Halley's Comet Day! Sir Edmond Halley's Birthday

2577.　October 30: Henry "The Fonz" Winkler's Birthday

2578.　October 31: Halloween

2579.　November 1: National Author's Day

2580.　November 2: Burt Lancaster's Birthday

2581.　November 3: Sandwich Day

2582.　November 4: Booklover's Day

2583.　November 5: Roy Roger's Birthday

2584.　November 6: Saxophone Day

2585.　November 7: Punsters Day

2586.　November 8: National Cappuccino Day

2587.　November 9: International Guinness World Records Day

2588. November 10: Debut of *Sesame Street*, 1969
2589. November 11: Veterans Day
2590. November 12: Have a gathering with *Friends*—David Schwimmer's Birthday
2591. November 13: *Fantasia* premiered, 1940
2592. November 14: *Moby Dick* by Herman Melville published in 1851
2593. November 15: American Enterprise Day
2594. November 16: Birth of the Blues (W.C. Handy's Birthday)
2595. November 17: Homemade Bread Day
2596. November 18: Mickey Mouse's Birthday
2597. November 19: Meg Ryan's Birthday
2598. November 20: Buy her a printed dress—Emilio Pucci's Birthday
2599. November 21: World Hello Day
2600. November 22: Anniversary of the National Hockey League, 1917
2601. November 23: Anniversary of *Dr. Who*'s premiere, 1963
2602. November 24: Dale Carnegie's Birthday
2603. November 25: Rudolph, the Red-Nosed Reindeer premiers (1949)
2604. November 26: National Cake Day
2605. November 27: Jeans Day (Levi Strauss's Birthday)
2606. November 28: Radio debut of the *Grand Ole Opry*, 1925
2607. November 29: Electronic Greetings Day—Send your loved one an e-card with love
2608. November 30: Mark Twain/Samuel Clemens's Birthday

2609. December 1: Anniversary of the invention of Bingo, 1929

2610. December 2: Celebrate the pop princess—Britney Spears's Birthday

2611. December 3: Katarina Witt's birthday

2612. December 4: National Candy Day

2613. December 5: Raise a toast—Prohibition repealed on this day in 1933!

2614. December 6: Ira Gershwin's Birthday

2615. December 7: National Cotton Candy Day

2616. December 8: National Brownie Day

2617. December 9: Kirk Douglas' Birthday

2618. December 10: Human Rights Day

2619. December 11: Rock out to the King. Elvis' "Blue Hawaii" hits #1 on the charts

2620. December 12: Poinsettia Day

2621. December 13: Ted Nugent's Birthday

2622. December 14: The screw was patented in 1798—celebrate as you will

2623. December 15: *Gone with the Wind* premiered on this day in 1939

2624. December 16: Boston Tea Party Day—Have a cup of tea

2625. December 17: National Maple Syrup Day—Think sticky and sweet thoughts!

2626. December 18: Listen to the Stones: Keith Richards' Birthday

2627. December 19: Edith Piaf's Birthday

2628. December 20: Position of American Poet Laureate established in 1985

2629. December 21: Anniversary of the first crossword puzzle in 1933

2630. December 22: Winter Solstice
2631. December 23: Susan Lucci's Birthday
2632. December 24: Christmas Eve
2633. December 25: Christmas Day
2634. December 26: National Candy Cane Day
2635. December 27: The Hagia Sofia is finished
2636. December 28: Bairn's Day (Unluckiest Day of the Year)
2637. December 29: Anniversary of the invention of the bowling ball, 1862
2638. December 30: Tiger Woods' Birthday
2639. December 31: New Year's Eve

2640. Attend the Valentine's Day/mid-winter carnival in Quebec City, Canada
2641. Using resources around you, discover three new romantic ideas per week
2642. "To live is to love—all reason is against it, and all healthy instincts for it." ~ Samuel Butler
2643. Surprise him with a vintage bottle of wine from the year you met
2644. Take a walk down the Avenue of the Stars in Hollywood
2645. Gift resource: Figi's Gift Catalog: www.figis.com
2646. Find one romantic thing in today's paper

2647. Don't give *cash* as a gift
2648. (Unless it's a *lot* of money!)
2649. (Or unless you give it creatively)…
2650. Stack one hundred one dollar bills and wrap them with a red ribbon

2651. Create origami animals made of $100 bills
2652. Fill her purse with quarters

Great Beaches of the World

2653. Barbuda, West Indies—A+ for *unspoiled*
2654. Isla de Cozumel, Mexico—A+ for *lazing*
2655. Kea, Greek Islands—A+ for *unspoiled*
2656. Mindoro, Philippines—A+ for *beachcombing*
2657. Molokai, Hawaii—A+ for *lazing*
2658. Mustique, West Indies—A+ for *unspoiled*
2659. Naxos, Greece—A+ for *hedonism*
2660. North Island, New Zealand—A+ for *lazing*
2661. Pamana, Indonesia—A+ for *beachcombing*
2662. Sanibel Island, Florida—A+ for *beachcombing*

2663. Love Enhancer: Generosity
2664. Send a rose to him at work
2665. Wear a ribbon—and nothing else!—and wait under the Christmas tree
2666. Stand in line together at TKTS in Times Square to get discount tickets to Broadway shows
2667. A "Lover's Lane" Coupon: This coupon entitles you to one make-out session at your local Lover's Lane (The coupon-issuer is responsible for providing a car with a roomy back seat)

2668. Guys: Remember—She usually wants you to simply *listen* to her
2669. Gals: Remember—He usually wants you to just *appreciate* him

2670. Choose one day of the week, and be extra, *extra* romantic on that day

2671. Sign your love letters: "Always, forever, eternally, perpetually, unceasingly, evermore"

2672. Fold a love note inside her dinner napkin

2673. Go on a spur-of-the-moment vacation

2674. Buy a "Coupon Book" for local restaurants and services

2675. Create a "word scramble" puzzle using all romantic words

2676. Butterfly kisses: Where you brush your eyelashes against his/her cheek

2677. Plan surprise anniversary parties

2678. Get an autographed photo of his/her favorite actor

2679. Teach your toddlers to read "Do Not Disturb"—and hang a sign on your bedroom door

2680. Integrate his/her lucky number into your life as much as possible…

2681. Get a vanity license plate with that number on it

2682. Get him/her that number of balloons

2683. At hotels, arrange to stay on the "lucky" floor number

2684. At hotels, arrange to get "lucky" room numbers

2685. Get your mate that number of gifts on his/her birthday

2686. Mail him/her that number of roses

2687. Have that number made into a custom piece of jewelry

2688. Use that number in your ATM code

2689. Get a football jersey with that number on it

2690. Play that number in the lottery—You *could* win!

2691. Rent a classic roadster for a day
2692. Create a picture-perfect wedding
2693. Wear "Contradiction" cologne, and show that you're masculine *and* gentle
2694. Always give (and receive) flowers with your *right* hand—it symbolizes positive wishes
2695. "Unconditional love is the most powerful stimulant to the immune system." ~ Bernie Siegal

2696. For grandparents only: Write "The Story of Our Life Together"
2697. Self-publish twenty copies of the book
2698. Give copies of this keepsake to your family

2699. Choose some daily affirmations
2700. Remember: As couples endure, we trade *newness* and *excitement* for *understanding* and *meaning*
2701. Learn what he/she considers *cool*

Favorite Love Songs from 1939

2702. "All the Things You Are"
2703. "I Concentrate on You"
2704. "If I Didn't Care"
2705. "Some Like It Hot"

2706. Use a fountain pen to write elegant love letters
2707. Aphrodisiac Alert: *Fork Me, Spoon Me: The Sensual Cookbook*, by Amy Reilly
2708. Write a love note in a rainbow of colors
2709. For new dads: Give 100% and expect nothing in return for the first three months

2710. "The best way to know God is to love many things."
~ Vincent Van Gogh

Songs to Help You Express Your
Feelings: *Intense Love & Infatuation*

2711. "Can't Take My Eyes Off You," Frankie Valli

2712. "Do the Walls Come Down," Carly Simon

2713. "Every Breath You Take," The Police

2714. "Head Over Heels," Tears for Fears

2715. "I Am Waiting," Yes

2716. "I Fall to Pieces," Patsy Cline

2717. "I Will Always Love You," Whitney Houston

2718. "Nights in White Satin," Moody Blues

2719. "When a Man Loves a Woman," Percy Sledge

2720. "(Your Love Has Lifted Me) Higher and Higher,"
Rita Coolidge

2721. Create a personalized "Sexual-Favor-of-the-Month
Club"

2722. "In thy face I see/The map of honor, truth, and
loyalty" ~ Shakespeare

2723. Greet her at the airport when she flies

2724. Order her personalized M&Ms: www.mymms.com

2725. The "Don't Worry, Be Happy" Coupon: Good for
one truly carefree day. The coupon-giver will arrange
for a fun-filled day of escape

2726. Fill her desk drawers with her favorite candy

2727. FYI: A+ Couples are child*like*, but not child*ish*

2728. Stop taking your partner for granted

2729. Stop suppressing your feelings

2730. "Stop Draggin' My Heart Around," by Stevie Nicks & Tom Petty and the Heartbreakers
2731. Stop arguing over which way the toilet paper should roll
2732. Stop saying, "I told you so"
2733. Set a date to break a bad habit. Do something fun and romantic with your partner to celebrate your accomplishment
2734. "Stop and Think It Over," by Dale & Grace
2735. Stop reading this book and call your partner *right now* to say "I love you"

2736. Visit a butterfly aviary
2737. Enemy of Love: Lack of awareness
2738. Visit an Arboretum
2739. Apologize to your partner for being too busy to pick her up at the airport—then surprise her by showing up there

Ways to Love a Cancer
(22 June–22 July)

2740. Cancer is a *water* sign: Cater to his/her dreamy, romantic nature
2741. Gift tip: Luxurious
2742. Try deluxe soaps and creams, lush music
2743. Often appreciates antiques
2744. As Cancer is ruled by the moon, items with a moon motif
2745. Lilies; trees in general
2746. Smooth and creamy foods
2747. The beauty and romance of Venice
2748. Wrap gifts in silver for your Cancer

2749. Read aloud to her an erotic poem
2750. Enemy of Love: Temper

2751. For everything there is a season, and a time for every matter of the heart:
2752. A time for passion, and a time for patience,
2753. A time for him to lead, and a time for her to lead,
2754. A time to talk, and a time to listen,
2755. A time for sex, and a time for love,
2756. A time to hold on, and a time to let go,
2757. A time to learn, and a time to teach,
2758. A time to stand firm, and a time to compromise,
2759. A time for masculinity, and a time for femininity,
2760. A time to shout for joy, and a time to express your fears,
2761. A time for yourself, and a time for your mate,
2762. A time for tradition, and a time for change,
2763. A time for you as a couple, and a time for you as a family.
2764. (Read Ecclesiastes 3: 1-8)

2765. Send him to a Fantasy Baseball Camp
2766. For your math lover: There's an *awesome* love poem written in the language of mathematics in "Trurl's Electronic Bard" in the book *The Cyberiad*, by Stanislaw Lem
2767. Stay at the fanciest hotel in New Orleans: The Soniat House
2768. Love Coupon: Good for one "choreographed" lovemaking session! Choose your favorite romantic/ erotic music, and then make love to match its mood and rhythms

Unusual-But-Romantic Places
to Have a Memorable Dinner Together

2769. In a greenhouse full of flowers
2770. At the foot of a beautiful waterfall
2771. On a hillside in Venice
2772. Under a giant redwood tree
2773. Aboard a friend's yacht
2774. At midnight in your backyard
2775. At the foot of Mount Everest
2776. At the top of the Empire State Building
2777. In a hot air balloon
2778. In a meadow under the stars
2779. At the brink of a butte in Montana
2780. In the shadow of the Eiffel Tower
2781. In a cable car in the Alps

2782. FYI: Women tend to like: Lingerie in *pastels*
2783. FYI: Men tend to like: Lingerie in *black* or *red*

2784. As a secret surprise: Study a book on massage techniques
2785. Go apple picking together in the fall
2786. Give her socks that picture her favorite animal
2787. Bake her a cake
2788. "Oh love, as long as you can love." ~ Ferdinand Freiligrath
2789. The Decadent "Dinner-In-Bed" Coupon: Forget *breakfast* in bed—you're being treated to an elegant *dinner* in bed sometime this week
2790. Eat dinner at the restaurant with the best food

2791. On Monday: Give one red rose with a lyric from a Beatles song
2792. On Tuesday: Give one red rose with a lyric from a Billy Joel song
2793. On Wednesday: Give one red rose with a lyric from a Barbra Streisand song
2794. On Thursday: Give one red rose with a lyric from a Moody Blues song
2795. On Friday: Give one red rose with a lyric from a Billie Holiday song
2796. On Saturday: Give one red rose with a lyric from a Frank Sinatra song
2797. On Sunday: Give one red rose with a lyric from a song that *you* composed

2798. Guys: Be nice to her during her menstrual periods
2799. Be aware of the dates
2800. Don't joke about it
2801. Honor femininity

2802. Get tickets to see Cirque du Soleil—be enchanted together!
2803. Serve his favorite dessert
2804. Read *Anatomy of Love: A Natural History of Mating, Marriage, and Why We Stray*, by Helen Fisher
2805. "The only way to speak the truth is to speak lovingly." ~ Henry David Thoreau
2806. Serve her tea in her favorite mug
2807. Hire a neighbor kid to cut the lawn; use that time *romantically*
2808. Use sparklers on his/her birthday cake

2809. Attend a Sunday afternoon concert in the park
2810. Have a picnic in the living room in front of the fireplace

2811. Words that *men* love to hear: "I *want* you"
2812. Words that *women* love to hear: "I *need* you"

Characteristics of a True Romantic

2813. Taps into his/her creativity regularly
2814. Is just a *little bit* "naughty"
2815. Takes love seriously—
2816. But has a great sense of humor
2817. Makes his/her intimate love a top priority
2818. Makes romantic gestures without ulterior motives
2819. Is flexible
2820. Celebrates sexuality
2821. Understands the importance of little touches, brushes, caresses
2822. Appreciates his/her partner's uniqueness
2823. Celebrates both the *masculine* and the *feminine*
2824. Is a pretty good mind reader
2825. Sees the world in a slightly offbeat way
2826. Maintains a deep, spiritual connection with his/her partner
2827. Is spontaneous
2828. Defines him/herself as a "lover"—regardless of other roles
2829. Remembers important dates and anniversaries
2830. Continuously learns and grows
2831. Is in touch with his/her feelings
2832. Pursues new and different experiences
2833. Gives of himself/herself without expectations

2834. Does lots of *little* things
2835. Gives without being asked

2836. Steal a kiss
2837. Give it back

2838. As a secret surprise: Sign him/her up for sailing lessons
2839. The "Cinderella" Coupon: Redeemable for one elegant night of dining and dancing
2840. Splurge in Salzburg, Austria: Experience the *Sound of Music* Tour
2841. It's the Great Pumpkin, Charlie Brown! Give a gift on Halloween
2842. Surprise him with the CD from *Phantom of the Opera*, by Andrew Lloyd Weber
2843. Adopt a new pet!

2844. Monday: Arrive home with champagne
2845. Tuesday: Arrive home with one flower
2846. Wednesday: Arrive home with love in your heart
2847. Thursday: Arrive home with tickets to *something*
2848. Friday: Arrive home with dinner
2849. Saturday: Arrive home with a romantic movie
2850. Sunday: Arrive home with fine chocolate

2851. Surprise her with a vintage bottle of wine from the year of your wedding
2852. The Second Honeymoon Coupon! You choose the *type* of vacation, your partner chooses the *location*. You choose the length of vacation, your partner chooses the departure date

2853.   Leave a trail of your clothes, leading from the front door to your bedroom

2854.   Honor your partner's cultural heritage

2855.   Let a Billie Holiday song express your feelings

2856.   Drink coffee at the best café

2857.   Have a picnic on the roof

2858.   Take a Japanese flower arranging course together

2859.   The "Extra Birthday" Coupon: Without having to get older, your partner will supply you with gifts and cake. No candles needed

Hit Songs with "Love" in Their Titles

2860.   "The Way You Love Me," Faith Hill

2861.   "Accidentally In Love," Counting Crows

2862.   "All 4 Love," Color Me Badd

2863.   "All Out of Love," Air Supply

2864.   "Another Sad Love Song," Toni Braxton

2865.   "April Love," Pat Boone

2866.   "Baby I Love Your Way," Big Mountain

2867.   "Baby I Love Your Way/Freebird Medley (Free Baby)," Will to Power

2868.   "Because I Love You (The Postman Song)," Stevie B

2869.   "Because of Love," Janet Jackson

2870.   "Best of My Love," The Emotions

2871.   "Bye Bye Love," Everly Brothers

2872.   "Caribbean Queen (No More Love on the Run)," Billy Ocean

2873.   "Come and Get Your Love," Redbone

2874.   "Cradle of Love," Billy Idol

2875.   "Dedicated to the One I Love," The Shirelles

2876.   "Do You Love Me," The Contours

2877. "Everybody Loves Somebody," Dean Martin
2878. "Friendly Persuasion (Thee I Love)/Chains of Love," Pat Boone
2879. "Greatest Love of All," Whitney Houston
2880. "Have I Told You Lately That I Love You," Ricky Nelson
2881. "I Love a Rainy Night," Eddie Rabbitt
2882. "I Love Your Smile," Shanice
2883. "I Wanna Dance With Somebody (Who Loves Me)," Whitney Houston
2884. "I Want to Know What Love Is," Foreigner
2885. "I'd Do Anything for Love (But I Won't Do That)," Meat Loaf
2886. "I'd Really Love to See You Tonight," England Dan & John Ford Coley
2887. "I'll Never Love This Way Again," Dionne Warwick
2888. "I'm in Love Again," Fats Domino
2889. "If I Ever Fall in Love," Shai
2890. "It Must Have Been Love," Roxette
2891. "Jump (For My Love)," Pointer Sisters
2892. "Love Hangover," Diana Ross
2893. "Love Is a Battlefield," Pat Benatar
2894. "Love Is Alive," Gary Wright
2895. "Love Is," Vanessa Williams & Brian McKnight
2896. "(Love Is) Thicker than Water," Andy Gibb
2897. "Love Letters in the Sand," Pat Boone
2898. "Love Machine (Part 1)," The Miracles
2899. "Love on the Rocks," Neil Diamond
2900. "Love Rollercoaster," Ohio Players
2901. "Love Theme from *Romeo and Juliet*," Henry Mancini
2902. "Love to Love You Baby," Donna Summer
2903. "Love Will Keep Us Together," The Captain & Tennille

2904. "Love Will Never Do (Without You)," Janet Jackson
2905. "Making Love Out of Nothing at All," Air Supply
2906. "Muskrat Love," The Captain & Tennille
2907. "My True Love," Jack Scott
2908. "Real Love," Mary J. Blige
2909. "Send One Your Love," Stevie Wonder
2910. "Sending All My Love," Linear
2911. "Show Me Love," Robin S.
2912. "Bleeding Love," Leona Lewis
2913. "Sometimes Love Just Ain't Enough," Patty Smyth
2914. "That's the Way Love Goes," Janet Jackson
2915. "This Guy's in Love with You," Herb Alpert
2916. "To Know Him Is to Love Him," The Teddy Bears
2917. "To Sir with Love," Lulu
2918. "What Is Love," Haddaway
2919. "What's Love Got to Do With It," Tina Turner
2920. "When a Man Loves a Woman," Michael Bolton
2921. "Why Do Fools Fall in Love," The Teenagers & Frankie Lymon
2922. "Will You Love Me Tomorrow," The Shirelles
2923. "Woman in Love," Barbra Streisand
2924. "You Give Love a Bad Name," Bon Jovi
2925. "Young Love," Sonny James
2926. "Young Love," Tab Hunter
2927. "(Your Love Has Lifted Me) Higher and Higher," Rita Coolidge

2928. Wear a T-shirt from his alma mater
2929. "Love is not the dying moan of a distant violin— it's the triumphant twang of a bedspring." ~ S.J. Perelman

2930. Love with all your soul
2931. Picnic in a secluded spot—and make love afterward
2932. Wear "Opium" perfume, and show him why he should be addicted to *you*
2933. Learn what he/she considers *relaxing*
2934. While at work, imagine your partner in a sexy outfit... then call her
2935. Learn the waltz
2936. Take your music lover to the Buddy Holly Center in Texas: www.buddyhollycenter.org
2937. Get an autographed photo of his/her favorite singer
2938. Make love in the living room
2939. Create a scrapbook for her of your favorite vacation
2940. Take private dance lessons together
2941. Give the gift of Pez
2942. Give her socks in shades of her favorite color

The 12 Birthstones—and Their Meanings

Accompany the jewelry with a poem about the symbolic meaning of his or her birthstone:

2943. January: Garnet—*faith & constancy*
2944. February: Amethyst—*happiness & sincerity*
2945. March: Aquamarine—*courage & hope*
2946. April: Diamond—*innocence & joy*
2947. May: Emerald—*peace & tranquillity*
2948. June: Pearl—*purity & wisdom*
2949. July: Ruby—*nobility & passion*
2950. August: Sardonyx—*joy & power*
2951. September: Sapphire—*truth & hope*
2952. October: Opal—*tender love & confidence*

2953.   November: Topaz—*fidelity & friendship*

2954.   December: Turquoise—*success & understanding*

2955.   A Romantic Movie Coupon: Choose one: *Out of Africa, Somewhere in Time, Splendor in the Grass, Top Hat, Casablanca, Tootsie, Key Largo, Moonstruck*

2956.   Order long-stem chocolate roses!

2957.   The "Convenience Store" Coupon: Your partner will run to the store for you at a moment's notice

2958.   Save placemats from all the restaurants you visit

2959.   Go for a walk someplace where you can see a beautiful skyline

2960.   Give one rose for every month you've been together

2961.   Hide a diamond ring in a box of Cracker Jacks

2962.   Go on vacation without luggage: Buy everything you need *there*—including clothes!

2963.   The "Create-A-Date" Coupon: Where? Wherever you want. When? Whenever you want. The coupon-giver pays all expenses.

2964.   "The applause of a single human being is of great consequence." ~ Samuel Johnson

2965.   Buy her an antique armoire for her lingerie

2966.   Send her one dozen roses at work

2967.   Lie—in bed together on a Saturday morning

2968.   Cheat—on your budget, just a little bit: Go on a big date

2969.   Steal—time from your other responsibilities: Give it to your mate

2970.   Get "namesake gifts"—

2971.   If her name is *Lucy*, get her an *I Love Lucy* T-shirt

2972. If his name is *Tommy*, get the CD *Tommy* by The Who
2973. If her name is *Barbara*, get a Barbie doll
2974. If his name is *Charlie*, get him some *Peanuts* books
2975. If her name is *Patricia*, get her some Peppermint Patties
2976. If his name is *Arnold*, get all of Schwarzenegger's movies
2977. If her name is *Gloria*, get a copy of "Gloria," by Laura Branigan
2978. If his name is *George*, get him *Curious George*

2979. Massage his hands
2980. FYI: Phenylethylamine: A possibly aphrodisiac chemical in chocolate
2981. The "Knight in Shining Armor" Coupon—in which he will rescue you from Saturday errands and whisk you away for a romantic day together
2982. Create a perpetual bouquet: Bring home one flower a day, for a solid month
2983. Enemy of Love: Jealousy
2984. Learn to tango (it takes two)
2985. Give *fragrant* flowers: Camellia, Peonies, Lavender
2986. Love Enhancer: Having a Sense of Humor

2987. The anticipation is often just as much fun as the event or gift itself
2988. Tell her to reserve a specific future date, but don't tell her *why*
2989. Drop hints about an upcoming surprise event
2990. Use the song "Anticipation," by Carly Simon, to help build the suspense

Unusual **Gift Tips for Lovers**

2991. Buy one blue gift, two red gifts, and one green gift

2992. Find two gifts for under $5, three gifts for $20-$25, and one gift for $50-$100

2993. Get two sentimental gifts, one gag gift, and one practical gift

2994. Get one gift in a toy store, one in a hardware store, and one in a grocery store

2995. Get one gift that will appeal to the *mind*, and one gift that will appeal to the *sense of beauty*

2996. Find one gift that will stimulate his/her sexuality, and one that will stimulate good memories

2997. Get one gift for each sense—sight, hearing, touch, smell, and taste

2998. Get one gift that represents the past, the present, and the future

2999. Give one gift to use in the morning, one to use in the afternoon, and one to use at night

3000. Get one gift for the outdoors, and one gift for the indoors

3001. Get one gift that will make him/her laugh, and one gift that will bring tears to his/her eyes

3002. Get one gift for each of the four seasons

3003. Find a restaurant with a spectacular view

3004. Use a thesaurus to help you describe your feelings of love: Infatuated, crazy, frantic, frenetic, mad

3005. Learn to jitterbug

3006. Give her theater tickets taped to the CD of the show

3007. After you've bought a new house, give her a house key wrapped in a jewelry box

3008. Give him a baseball signed by his favorite player
3009. Have candles on hand at all times
3010. Serve him coffee in his favorite mug
3011. Give him a cap from his favorite baseball team

Ways to *Take Care* of the One You Love

3012. Purge your house of all fatty foods if he/she's on a diet
3013. Install a home security system
3014. Sign your partner up for AAA
3015. Install dead bolt locks on her apartment doors
3016. Buy fire extinguishers for your home
3017. Teach him how to sew on a button—
3018. But do it for him when he's home
3019. Install an alarm system in her car
3020. Bring homemade chicken soup when she's sick
3021. Make sure your cars have jumper cables
3022. Have a complete First Aid Kit for your home
3023. Don't let him over-exert with heavy lifting
3024. Send her to a self-defense class
3025. See a chiropractor every once in a while
3026. Have your cars serviced regularly
3027. Sprinkle salt on the icy steps and sidewalk
3028. Wire an extra set of keys under her car for her
3029. Post a variety of emergency numbers by the phone
3030. Check the air in your car tires
3031. Take a CPR class together
3032. Get him "The Club" to protect his car
3033. Hire a kid to shovel the snow from your driveway
       (protect his back and heart!)
3034. Wear safety helmets when riding bicycles
3035. Change the oil in her car

3036.   Install safety reflectors on your bicycles
3037.   Teach your partner how to drive in bad weather
3038.   Take an Outward Bound excursion together
3039.   Take martial arts classes together

3040.   Read each other's favorite book for a new perspective
3041.   Increase the number of compliments you give your partner by 100%

3042.   Toast one another every time you hold a wine glass
3043.   Toast your good fortune for finding each other

3044.   Have an "aphrodisiacs only" picnic
3045.   Take a music appreciation class together
3046.   Play "She loves me, she loves me not," with a daisy
3047.   Give her jade jewelry
3048.   "Only little boys and old men sneer at love." ~ Louis Auchincloss
3049.   Give him a tie that illustrates his hobby
3050.   Go for a stroll in the park

3051.   Express your faith together
3052.   Meet with others of the same faith regularly
3053.   Live your faith day-to-day

3054.   Pamper her
3055.   Paint her toenails
3056.   Brush her hair
3057.   Cook breakfast, lunch, and dinner for her
3058.   Do a load of laundry
3059.   Nuzzle her neck

3060. Give her a basketball signed by her favorite player
3061. Learn more about his favorite sport
3062. Say this and mean it: "I'm sorry"
3063. Visit Fanny Farmer and select gifts for each other
3064. Toast your many happy years together
3065. *The Good Enough to Eat Breakfast Cookbook*, by Carrie Levin and William Perley
3066. Gals: Greet him at the door wearing high heels, a garter belt, and stockings
3067. Provide more memory for her computer
3068. Read *Making Marriage Work*, by Joyce Meyer
3069. Never, never, *never* betray a confidence
3070. "We can judge others or we can love others—but we can't do both." ~ Mother Teresa
3071. String streamers in the family room, just for fun
3072. Order pizza with all the toppings *she* likes best

3073. Give your partner 100% of everything he/she *needs*
3074. Give your partner 50% to 75% of everything he/she *wants*

3075. Flirt
3076. Kiss
3077. Touch
3078. Hug
3079. Caress
3080. Tease
3081. Whisper
3082. Cuddle
3083. Nuzzle

3084.   Take a photography class together

3085.   Take a camera with you wherever you go

3086.   Model for one another

3087.   Take *erotic* photos of each other!

3088.   Photograph *yourself*—and give the photos to your partner

3089.   Kiss every square inch of his body

3090.   Celebrate your anniversary

3091.   Giftwrap with *real flowers* instead of bows

3092.   Take the day off work to celebrate his/her birthday

3093.   A "Putt Putt" Coupon: Good for one round of miniature golf. Coupon-giver pays the golfing fees; the loser of the game pays for snacks

3094.   Have extra sets of car keys and house keys handy

3095.   Listen to your inner voice

3096.   Some help for your love letters: "Without you I'd be—lost, lonely, devastated, annihilated..."

3097.   Create an Easter basket full of romantic I.O.U.s hidden in plastic eggs

3098.   Create a "love" themed gift...

3099.   Read *The History of Love: A Novel*, by Nicole Krauss

3100.   And the song "Love Is a Many Splendored Thing," by The Four Aces

3101.   And the movie *Can't Buy Me Love*

3102.   And the book *Love Is Letting Go of Fear*, by Gerald Jampolsky

3103.   And the song "Love Me Tender," Elvis Presley

3104.   And the movie *For Love or Money*

3105. And the book *The Secret Language of Love,* by Megan Tresidder

3106. And the song "Love Is," by Vanessa Williams & Brian McKnight

---

3107. "A man is rich according to what he gives, not what he has." ~ Henry Ward Beecher

3108. Learn what he considers *adventurous*

3109. "Life is like a ten-speed bike. Most of us have gears we never use." ~ Charles M. Schulz

3110. Millionaires need love, too: Give him/her a $25,000 coupon redeemable at Tiffany's

3111. Visit a local public garden together

3112. Have all of her jewelry professionally cleaned

3113. "Treat your wife like a thoroughbred and she'll never be a nag." ~ Bumper Sticker

3114. Keep this book hidden from your partner: Use it as your romantic "secret weapon"

Fun/Whimsical Love Songs

3115. "Can't You Hear My Heartbeat," Herman's Hermits

3116. "Crazy Little Thing Called Love," Queen

3117. "Groovy Kind of Love," Phil Collins

3118. "Hello Goodbye," The Beatles

3119. "I Think I Love You," The Partridge Family

3120. "If I Had a Million Dollars," Barenaked Ladies

3121. "I'm Gonna Be (500 Miles)," Proclaimers

3122. "Let's Call the Whole Thing Off," Fred Astaire and Ginger Rogers

3123. "Nobody Does It Better," Carly Simon

3124. "Silly Love Songs," Paul McCartney and Wings

3125. "Sugar, Sugar," The Archies
3126. "When I'm Sixty-Four," The Beatles
3127. "You're the One That I Want," John Travolta & Olivia Newton-John

3128. Plan a lunch date
3129. Send an anniversary greeting via telegram
3130. Get every book featuring his/her favorite comic character
3131. Save the last slice of pizza for him
3132. Give a mug with both of your names on it
3133. Keep a leather-bound Bible with your names embossed on the cover
3134. Take turns giving each other a back rub

3135. Collect ticket stubs from every movie you attend
3136. Collect postcards from all your vacations
3137. Add to her collection of stuffed animals
3138. Add to his collection of rare magazines
3139. Add to his stamp collection
3140. Add to her coin collection

Most Romantic Movies of All Time

3141. *An Affair to Remember*
3142. *The Bodyguard*
3143. *Bull Durham*
3144. *Casablanca*
3145. *Dirty Dancing*
3146. *Doctor Zhivago*
3147. *Flashdance*
3148. *From Here to Eternity*

3149. *Ghost*
3150. *Gone with the Wind*
3151. *Intersection*
3152. *The Last of the Mohicans*
3153. *An Officer and a Gentleman*
3154. *Prelude to a Kiss*
3155. *Shadowlands*
3156. *Somewhere in Time*
3157. *Titanic*
3158. *Top Gun*
3159. *Untamed Heart*
3160. *The Way We Were*
3161. *When Harry Met Sally*

3162. Present him with silver jewelry
3163. Give equipment for his/her favorite hobby
3164. Plan little surprises
3165. Eat dinner at the best Vietnamese restaurant
3166. Work on your listening skills
3167. The Music-Lover's Coupon: Good for one CD by your favorite musical artist—courtesy of the coupon-giver
3168. "Love is a flower and you its only seed." ~ Amanda McBroom
3169. Use Twitter! Send romantic tweets @[your partner] for PDA
3170. Or send direct messages for private love notes
3171. Gather several heart-shaped boxes in February and save them for later
3172. For an adventure vacation: Above the Clouds Trekking: www.aboveclouds.com
3173. Take ballroom dancing classes together

3174. Get a "Silly Slammer" toy to help you express your feelings

3175. Frame your wedding vows
3176. Frame her favorite poem
3177. Frame his favorite song lyrics
3178. Frame an autumn leaf
3179. Frame a lock of her hair
3180. Frame your wedding invitation
3181. Frame your marriage license
3182. Frame a greeting card he sent you
3183. Frame a love note from her

3184. Be interested
3185. Be interesting

3186. Give a mug representing his/her hobby
3187. Give a bottle of wine from the state in which your partner was born
3188. Make love dressed in your finest lingerie
3189. Tour Chocolate World in Hershey, Pennsylvania: www.hersheys.com/chocolateworld
3190. Resource: *Real Simple: Celebrations*, by Editors of *Real Simple* magazine
3191. Take a wine-tasting class together
3192. "The word love has by no means the same sense for both sexes, and this is one cause of the serious misunderstandings that divide them." ~ Simone de Beauvoir

3193. The gift: A 14-karat gold key-shaped pendant

3194.   The note: "You hold the key to my heart"

Top Love Song Duets

3195.   "A Whole New World," Peabo Bryson & Regina Belle
3196.   "After All," Cher & Peter Cetera
3197.   "Ain't No Mountain High Enough," Marvin Gaye & Tammi Terrell
3198.   "Ain't Nothing Like the Real Thing," Marvin Gaye & Tammi Terrell
3199.   "All I Ever Need Is You," Sonny & Cher
3200.   "All My Life," Linda Ronstadt & Aaron Neville
3201.   "Baby (You've Got What It Takes)," Dinah Washington & Brook Benton
3202.   "Beauty and the Beast," Celine Dion & Peabo Bryson
3203.   "The Beat Goes On," Sonny & Cher
3204.   "Can't We Try," Dan Hill & Vonda Sheppard
3205.   "Close My Eyes (Forever)," Lita Ford & Ozzy Osbourne
3206.   "Close Your Eyes," Peaches & Herb
3207.   "The Closer I Get to You," Roberta Flack & Donny Hathaway
3208.   "Dancing in the Street," Mick Jagger & David Bowie
3209.   "Deep Purple," Donny & Marie Osmond
3210.   "Deep Purple," Nino Tempo & April Stevens
3211.   "Easy Lover," Philip Bailey & Phil Collins
3212.   "Ebony and Ivory," Paul McCartney & Stevie Wonder
3213.   "Friends and Lovers," Gloria Loring & Carl Anderson
3214.   "The Girl Is Mine," Michael Jackson & Paul McCartney

3215. "Guilty," Barbra Streisand & Barry Gibb
3216. "Her Town Too," James Taylor & J.D. Souther
3217. "Hey Paula," Paul & Paula
3218. "How Do You Do," Mouth & McNeal
3219. "(I Believe) There's Nothing Stronger Than Our Love," Paul Anka & Odia Coates
3220. "I Can't Help It," Andy Gibb & Olivia Newton-John
3221. "I Finally Found Someone," Bryan Adams & Barbra Streisand
3222. "I Got You Babe," Sonny & Cher
3223. "I Just Can't Stop Loving You," Michael Jackson & Siedah Garrett
3224. "I Knew You Were Waiting (For Me)," Aretha Franklin & George Michael
3225. "I Like Your Kind of Love," Andy Williams & Peggy Powers
3226. "I'm Leaving It Up to You," Dale & Grace
3227. "I'm Leaving It (All) Up to You," Donny & Marie Osmond
3228. "If I Could Build My Whole World Around You," Marvin Gaye & Tammi Terrell
3229. "Islands in the Stream," Kenny Rogers & Dolly Parton
3230. "It's Only Love," Bryan Adams & Tina Turner
3231. "Kookie, Kookie (Lend Me Your Comb)," Edward Byrnes & Connie Stevens
3232. "Leather and Lace," Stevie Nicks & Don Henley
3233. "Let It Be Me," Jerry Butler & Betty Everett
3234. "Love Is Strange," Mickey & Sylvia
3235. "Mockingbird," Carly Simon & James Taylor
3236. "Morning Side of the Mountain," Donny & Marie Osmond

3237. "The Next Time I Fall," Peter Cetera & Amy Grant
3238. "No More Tears (Enough Is Enough)," Barbra Streisand & Donna Summer
3239. "On My Own," Patti LaBelle & Michael McDonald
3240. "One Man Woman/One Woman Man," Paul Anka & Odia Coates
3241. "Playboy," Gene & Debbe
3242. "Put a Little Love in Your Heart," Annie Lennox & Al Green
3243. "Set the Night to Music," Roberta Flack & Maxi Priest
3244. "Shake Your Groove Thing," Peaches & Herb
3245. "Should've Never Let You Go," Neil Sedaka & Dara Sedaka
3246. "Solid," Ashford & Simpson
3247. "Somethin' Stupid," Nancy Sinatra & Frank Sinatra
3248. "Somewhere Out There," Linda Ronstadt & James Ingram
3249. "Stumblin' In," Suzi Quatro & Chris Norman
3250. "Suddenly," Olivia Newton-John & Cliff Richard
3251. "Surrender to Me," Ann Wilson & Robin Zander
3252. "Then Came You," Dionne Warwick & the Spinners
3253. "This Old Heart of Mine," Rod Stewart & Ronald Isley
3254. "To All the Girls I've Loved Before," Julio Iglesias & Willie Nelson
3255. "Tonight, I Celebrate My Love," Peabo Bryson & Roberta Flack
3256. "Too Much, Too Little, Too Late," Johnny Mathis & Deniece Williams
3257. "True Love," Elton John & Kiki Dee

3258. "Unforgettable," Natalie Cole & Nat King Cole
3259. "What Have I Done to Deserve This?" Pet Shop Boys & Dusty Springfield
3260. "What Kind of Fool," Barbra Streisand & Barry Gibb
3261. "Where Is the Love," Roberta Flack & Donny Hathaway
3262. "Wild Night," John Mellencamp & Me'shell NdegéOcello
3263. "With You I'm Born Again," Billy Preston & Syreeta
3264. "Yah Mo B There," James Ingram & Michael McDonald
3265. "Yes, I'm Ready," Teri DeSario & KC
3266. "You and I," Eddie Rabbitt & Crystal Gayle
3267. "You're a Special Part of Me," Diana Ross & Marvin Gaye
3268. "You're All I Need to Get By," Marvin Gaye & Tammi Terrell
3269. "Young Lovers," Paul & Paula
3270. "Your Precious Love," Marvin Gaye & Tammi Terrell

3271. Get married *again* (to your current spouse)
3272. Create a fun rededication ceremony
3273. Read *The Wedding Ceremony Planner*, by Reverend Judith Johnson Ph.D.
3274. Read *Altared: Bridezillas, Bewilderment, Big Love, Breakups and What Women Really Think About Contemporary Weddings*, by Colleen Curran
3275. Read *Weddings from the Heart: Contemporary and Traditional Ceremonies for an Unforgettable Wedding*, by Daphne Rose Kingma

3276. Enemy of Love: Arrogance

3277. Remind yourself to be more loving
3278. Use your brain to help your heart: Read *Jump Start Your Brain*, by Doug Hall and David Wecker
3279. Ignore "call waiting" when talking with her on the phone
3280. Once a month: Have dinner brought in by a caterer
3281. Look for the unstated assumptions in your relationship—they often block your creativity and passion
3282. Do her mother a favor
3283. Do "The Twist"
3284. Learn what he/she considers *romantic*
3285. Give a subscription to the magazine that covers his/her hobby
3286. A+ Romance Rating: Hotel Gritti Palace, in Venice, Italy
3287. Have a wine and cheese picnic
3288. Stroll along the city streets

Favorite Love Songs from 1940

3289. "All or Nothing at All"
3290. "Come Down to Earth, My Darling," Fats Waller
3291. "The Nearness of You," Dinah Shore
3292. "Pennsylvania 6-5000," Glenn Miller
3293. "Taking a Chance on Love"
3294. "You Stepped Out of a Dream"
3295. "You Are My Sunshine," Jimmie Davis

3296. Don't assume you know everything there is to know about your partner
3297. Don't assume "your way" is always right
3298. Don't assume you know all the best sexual techniques

3299. Don't assume you know what's on his/her mind

Most Romantic Spots in America

3300. Big Sur, California
3301. Charleston, South Carolina
3302. Grand Canyon, Arizona
3303. La Jolla, California
3304. Maui, Hawaii
3305. Nantucket, Massachusetts
3306. New Orleans, Louisiana
3307. Niagara Falls, New York
3308. San Francisco, California
3309. Sedona, Arizona

3310. Get in touch with your sense of adventure
3311. Get in touch with your sense of humor
3312. Get in touch with your feelings
3313. Get in touch with your dreams
3314. Get in touch with your creativity
3315. Get in touch with your inner child
3316. Get in touch with your mate
3317. Get in touch with your hopes for the future
3318. Get in touch with your wild side
3319. Get in touch with your inner teenager
3320. Get in touch with your inner romantic

3321. "To fear love is to fear life." ~ Bertrand Russell
3322. Kiss every square inch of her body SLOWLY
3323. The Wacky "Half-Birthday" Celebration Coupon:
       You are entitled to celebrate your half-birthday.
       Included: cake and candles, ice cream and presents

3324. Make one new romantic gesture every day for a year
3325. Propose on Valentine's Day
3326. Hide a love note in his/her napkin at a restaurant
3327. Flowers that match nicknames: Buttercup, Poppy, Sweet Pea
3328. Never, never, *never* say "What's for dinner?" before saying "I love you"
3329. "I will act as if I do make a difference." ~ William James
3330. Secretly buy him/her a movie he/she wants, place it in your DVD collection and tell them to choose a movie of their choice
3331. Spend a weekend in New York City
3332. View your life as a story, and strive for a happy ending
3333. Go on a *fourth* honeymoon

3334. List the three best lessons in love you learned from your parents
3335. Write a letter to your parents thanking them for these lessons

3336. Unlearn the worst relationship habit you learned from your parents
3337. Unlearn the dumbest attitude about love you learned from TV
3338. Gals: Unlearn the "Men are from Mars" attitude: He's an *individual*, not a stereotype
3339. Guys: Unlearn the "Women are from Venus" attitude: All women are *not* the same

3340. Skim the Yellow Pages, looking for companies that might help you in your romantic endeavors

3341. Give her a crystal bud vase

3342. "The heart has reasons that reason does not understand." ~ Jacques Bossuet

3343. Practice daily affirmations to improve your attitude and outlook

3344. Enemy of Love: Poor timing

3345. The Ultimate Picnic Coupon: You are entitled to an all-out, elegant, dinner picnic. Included: 3 course meal, fine wine, candles, and music.

3346. Toast your partner while out with friends

3347. Pre-order her favorite meal and drinks when out for dinner

3348. Send loving thoughts to your lover via ESP

3349. Know *all* of your partner's sizes!

3350. Visit Verona, Italy (A+ Romantic City, and setting of *Romeo and Juliet*)

Tips for Married Men

3351. Flirt with your wife

3352. Don't tell mother-in-law jokes

3353. Never, *never* refer to your wife as "My Old Lady"

3354. Refer to your wife as "My Bride"

3355. Don't abandon your role as "lover" after you take on the role of "husband"

3356. Do your fair share of the household chores

3357. Be a loving role model for your children

3358. Don't take your wife for granted

3359. Visit Redenvelope.com for romantic gifts

3360. Plan your future together
3361. "We love the things we love for what they are."
~ Robert Frost

3362. For Halloween, dress as a *famous couple*—
3363. (Pick a new couple every year!)—
3364. Rhett Butler & Scarlett O'Hara
3365. Romeo & Juliet
3366. Fred & Wilma
3367. Adam & Eve
3368. Antony & Cleopatra
3369. Tom Sawyer & Becky
3370. Napoleon & Josephine
3371. Raggedy Ann & Andy
3372. Lil' Abner & Daisy May
3373. Barbie & Ken
3374. Cupid & Psyche

3375. Sing "your song" to him or her
3376. Pick a bouquet of wildflowers
3377. Learn what he/she considers *soothing*
3378. Celebrate Valentine's Day on the 14th of every month
3379. Buy her gold jewelry
3380. Learn to two-step
3381. Surprise her with an elegant jewelry box
3382. "Too much of a good thing is wonderful." ~ Mae West
3383. Give her an umbrella in her favorite color

3384. Dance cheek-to-cheek

3385. Sleep cheek-to-cheek

3386. Buy an antique bed—
3387. Wear Victorian lingerie—
3388. Trade all electric lights for candles—
3389. Play music by Mozart and Debussy—
3390. And create a weekend of old-fashioned romance

3391. Learn to country line dance
3392. Ask a local travel agent to alert you to special vacation deals
3393. Volunteer together for a community organization
3394. "Perhaps that is what love is—the momentary or prolonged refusal to think of another person in terms of power." ~ Phyllis Rose
3395. Share an inspirational passage from a favorite book
3396. Wrap yourself as a Christmas gift and wait under the tree
3397. Love Enhancer: Commitment
3398. Send him an invitation: "Needed: An audience of one for an intimate Lingerie Fashion Show"

3399. English: "I adore you"
3400. French: "Je t'adore"
3401. Italian: "Ti adoro"
3402. German: "Ich mag dich sehr"
3403. Spanish: "Te adoro"
3404. Portugese: "Eu te adoro"

3405. Buy her lingerie that turns you on
3406. Buy him an outfit that turns you on

3407. Watch a movie that turns you on
3408. Talk about what he/she does that turns you on
3409. Suggest a new sexual activity that turns you on

3410. Play "Role Reversal"—do each other's chores
3411. Play "Role Reversal"—when you next make love

3412. Learn more about the emotional and psychological aspects of sex
3413. Love Coupon: An All-Sports Weekend! The coupon-issuer will pay for and accompany you to any pro sporting event taking place in your vicinity within the next month

Favorite Love Songs from 1941
3414. "Green Eyes," Jimmy Dorsey
3415. "The Anniversary Waltz"
3416. "This Love of Mine," Stan Kenton
3417. "You Made Me Love You," Harry James
3418. "You and I," Glenn Miller

3419. Give equipment for his/her favorite sport
3420. Rent a limousine to be at her service for a solid week
3421. "There is no fear in love, but perfect love casts out fear." ~ 1 John 4:18

Rules for Fighting Fair
3422. Stick to the issue
3423. Stay in the present
3424. Say what you feel when you feel it
3425. Don't generalize

3426. Don't accuse
3427. Don't threaten
3428. Get all of your emotions out
3429. But don't use emotion as a weapon
3430. Don't say anything you'll regret
3431. Compromise, but don't negotiate
3432. Work toward resolution

3433. Celebrate your anniversary every *month*
3434. Kiss the back of his neck
3435. Dance—and sing—in the rain
3436. Prepare dinner together wearing matching aprons— and nothing else!
3437. "Love cannot be bought except with love." ～ John Steinbeck
3438. Enjoy a little "Afternoon Delight"

3439. "Happiness and love are just a choice away." ～ Leo Buscaglia
3440. Remember: While love *is* an emotion, it is also a *choice*
3441. Choose—very specifically—to act like newlyweds for one day
3442. Choose—very consciously—to make the most of every waking hour today
3443. Choose—with care—the words you say

3444. Hide a love note in a bottle of vitamins
3445. Invite her to try some "Vitamin L"

3446. Spend an evening stargazing together

3447. Romantic music alert: Michael Bolton CDs: *All That Matters; The One Thing*

3448. Write three paragraphs on "I Remember When We First Met"
3449. Write it in the style of a romance novel
3450. Or write a poem with the same title
3451. Present it to your partner on your anniversary

12 Things Lovers Can Do—If They Try

3452. You can give without losing anything
3453. You can change without losing your uniqueness
3454. You can grow without growing apart
3455. You can compromise without compromising *yourself*
3456. You can open up without being judged
3457. You can disagree without arguing
3458. You can feel without losing control
3459. You can be affectionate without being sexual
3460. You *can* keep the passion alive in a long-term relationship
3461. You can be mature without losing the child inside of you
3462. You can listen without having to solve the problem
3463. You can be part of a couple without losing your individuality

3464. Give her perfume that turns you on
3465. Businessperson's Tip: Your mate is the most important "customer" you'll ever have!
3466. "Who, being loved, is poor?" ~ Oscar Wilde

3467. Guys: Stop judging, correcting, lecturing
3468. Gals: Stop nagging, complaining, whining

3469. Give her a ruby ring…
3470. Along with a CD with "Rubylove," by Cat Stevens
3471. Wrapped in ruby red wrapping paper

3472. Learn sign language together
3473. Communicate intimate messages across crowded rooms
3474. *Talking With Your Hands, Listening With Your Eyes: A Complete Photographic Guide to American Sign Language*, by Gabriel Grayson
3475. *American Sign Language The Easy Way*, by David A. Stewart, Elizabeth Stewart, and Jessalyn Little

3476. Connect love, creativity and spirituality: Read *The Artist's Way: A Spiritual Path to Higher Creativity*, by Julia Cameron
3477. "The most useless day is that in which we have not laughed." ~ Charles Field
3478. Give her Ralph Lauren "Romance" perfume
3479. Begin planning your 50th anniversary—during your honeymoon
3480. Buy gifts during end-of-season sales

Things That Come in "Twos"—Ideas for Couples

3481. Bicycles built-for-two
3482. Double sleeping bags
3483. Two-seater sports cars

3484. A Chinese pu-pu platter for two
3485. Mozart's Sonata in D Major for Two Pianos, K. 448
3486. Two-person kayaks
3487. Two-for-the-price-of-one specials at stores
3488. Two-for-the-price-of-one specials at restaurants
3489. Duets: "Endless Love," Luther Vandross & Mariah Carey
3490. Loveseats
3491. Stravinsky's Concerto for Two Pianos
3492. Singing songs in two-part harmony
3493. Double solitaire
3494. Wedding rings
3495. Double beds
3496. See-saws
3497. Double-scoop ice cream cones
3498. Two-person hot tubs

3499. Celebrate with a bottle of scented massage oil
3500. A "Quickie Picnic" Coupon: The coupon-issuer will provide the wine, cheese, blanket, transportation, and fascinating conversation
3501. Scatter rose petals over your bed
3502. At every event, save the "Anniversary Waltz" for the two of you
3503. Buy her that special something that she's always wanted, but wouldn't buy for herself

Items for a *Lifetime* Romantic Checklist

3504. Improve your relationship in a *specific* way, once-a-month, *forever*

3505. Never forget a *single* anniversary, birthday, or Valentine's Day

3506. Do something *so outrageous* that it becomes a story your family will tell for *generations*

3507. Make love in Paris

3508. Celebrate your 25th anniversary by renewing your wedding vows

3509. Give a gift that is so special it becomes a keepsake/ family heirloom

3510. Make love one thousand times

3511. Kidnap him/her!

3512. Drive around till he/she's disoriented

3513. Then go to that favorite restaurant

3514. Or away for a surprise romantic weekend

3515. Cater to your cat lover

3516. Get a subscription to *Cat Fancy Magazine*: www.catfancymagazine.com

3517. Visit the "Cat Cabinet" museum in Amsterdam, Holland

3518. Take dancing lessons

3519. Create a collage from your favorite photos of the two of you

3520. Buy a claddagh ring

3521. Attend Oktoberfest in Germany: www.oktoberfest.de/en

3522. Order fancy foods from Norm Thompson: www.normthompson.com

Favorite Love Songs from 1942

3523. "String of Pearls," Glenn Miller
3524. "Paper Doll," The Mills Brothers
3525. "That Old Black Magic"
3526. "We'll Meet Again"
3527. "You'd Be So Nice to Come Home To"

3528. A "Fantasy Island" Coupon: The coupon-giver agrees to play along with any sexual fantasy your fertile imagination can invent.
3529. "Love is strongest in pursuit; friendship in possession." ~ Ralph Waldo Emerson
3530. Give one dozen yellow roses
3531. Buy blank greeting cards—Express your love in your own words
3532. Burn incense

3533. Create one *simple* ritual—maybe around dinner
3534. Create one *elaborate* ritual—maybe around your anniversary
3535. Create one *meaningful* ritual—for when one of you leaves on a trip
3536. Create one *silly* ritual—for brightening a bad mood
3537. Create one *intimate* ritual—as part of foreplay
3538. Create one *family* ritual—for including and acknowledging your kids

3539. Guys: Always open her car door for her
3540. Gals: Pack a special lunch for him before he leaves for work

3541. "Everyone on the planet is given the same weekend. Some people just use it better." ~ An ad for the *Wall Street Journal*
3542. Take a weekend drive with no map
3543. Do all your chores during the week: Free up your weekend for love!
3544. Take a weekend vacation at home
3545. Take a three-day weekend every three months

3546. "To love deeply in one direction makes us more loving in all others." ~ Madame Swetchine
3547. Blow her a kiss
3548. Read *Intimacy: A 100-Day Guide to Lasting Relationships*, by Douglas Weiss
3549. Program yourself to be more loving
3550. Massage his aching shoulders

Favorite Love Songs from 1943

3551. "Cross Your Heart," Artie Shaw
3552. "One for My Baby"
3553. "People Will Say We're in Love"
3554. "Taking A Chance on Love," Benny Goodman

3555. Design a family coat-of-arms
3556. Eat dinner at the restaurant with the best service
3557. Find obscure recordings by his/her favorite singer
3558. Create a custom crossword puzzle that has romantic messages in it
3559. Give her *anything* in one of those distinctive turquoise Tiffany's boxes

3560. The "Jewelry, Jewelry, Jewelry!" Coupon: This amazing coupon is redeemable at any jewelry store anywhere in the world. You choose your gift. The coupon-issuer pays the bill. Up to $_____.

3561. Serve a cheap champagne with your next TV dinner

3562. Eat dinner at the best pizza joint in town

3563. "The only abnormality is the incapacity to love." ~ Anaïs Nin

Favorite Love Songs from 1944

3564. "A Lovely Way to Spend an Evening"

3565. "Dream"

3566. "Irresistible You"

3567. "This Heart of Mine," Vaughn Monroe

3568. Learn a foreign language together

3569. "To speak of love is to make love." ~ Honore de Balzac

3570. Play "All-Day Foreplay"

3571. Pack a picnic basket, and have lunch in his office

3572. "To get the full value of joy you must have someone to divide it with." ~ Mark Twain

3573. A+ Romance Rating: The CD *Let's Talk About Love*, by Celine Dion

3574. Teach your grandchildren everything you know about love

3575. Take a hike in the mountains

3576. Wear matching friendship rings to remind you that you're *friends* as well as lovers

3577. On your anniversary bake a cake with the appropriate number of candles

3578. "We can forgive as long as we love." ~ La Rochefoucauld

3579. Eat dinner at the best Italian restaurant around
3580. Take a walk in the rain

3581. Work on your *friendship* as well as your *love*
3582. Read *Love & Friendship*, by Allan Bloom

Most Romantic Country Songs of All Time

3583. "Blue," LeAnn Rimes
3584. "Diamonds and Dirt," Rodney Crowell
3585. "Dream On, Texas Ladies," John Michael Montgomery
3586. "Everything I Love," Alan Jackson
3587. "Flame in Your Eyes," Alabama
3588. "He Stopped Loving Her Today," George Jones
3589. "It Don't Happen Twice," Kenny Chesney
3590. "I'll Always Love You," Dolly Parton
3591. "It's Your Love," Tim McGraw & Faith Hill
3592. "Look at Us," Vince Gill
3593. "Love Me Like You Used To," Tanya Tucker
3594. "Love Will Find Its Way to You," Reba McEntire
3595. "Love Without End, Amen," George Strait
3596. "Stand By Your Man," Tammy Wynette
3597. "Tell Her," Lonestar
3598. "The Dance," Garth Brooks
3599. "This Night Won't Last Forever," Sawyer Brown
3600. "To Be Loved By You," Wynonna Judd
3601. "Unchained Melody," Rodney McDowell
3602. "You Win My Love," Shania Twain

3603. Send him flowers from "a secret admirer"
3604. "When love beckons you, follow him, though his ways are hard and steep." ~ Kahlil Gibran

3605. Give *fragrant* flowers: Casablanca Lilies, Stephanotis
3606. A "Day at the Races" Coupon: Good for a fun day at the racetrack or ballpark.
3607. Enemy of Love: Laziness
3608. Love Coupon: One romantic dinner at home. Prepared by the coupon-issuer.

3609. "A happy marriage is a long conversation which always seems too short." ~ André Maurois
3610. *Many* couples in long-term A+ Relationships express this thought
3611. Experiment: View your relationship as a *conversation*: It involves give-and-take; expressing yourself; listening; responding

3612. Visit a spiritually meaningful place, like Rome
3613. Daydream together
3614. Restore the Connection: www.gettingtheloveyouwant.com
3615. If you share the same literary tastes, organize a book discussion group

Ways to Love a Leo
(23 July –23 August)

3616. Leo is a *fire* sign: Cater to his/her passionate, sexual nature
3617. Gift tip: Small and expensive
3618. Expensive perfumes and colognes
3619. Gold jewelry, and gold-colored items
3620. Leos will love surprise parties
3621. As the sun rules Leo, items with a sun motif
3622. Sunflowers; bay trees

3623. Elegant and sophisticated foods
3624. The charm of medieval Prague
3625. Wrap gifts in golden tones

3626. For one full day, don't use *words*, but *touch*, to express your love
3627. Always have scented candles on hand
3628. Write a special toast to your partner
3629. Flaunt your sexuality

Recommended Anniversary Gifts

1st

3630. Traditional: *Paper* • Modern: *Clocks* • Godek's: *Lingerie*

2nd

3631. Traditional: *Cotton* • Modern: *China* • Godek's: *French lingerie*

3rd

3632. Traditional: *Leather* • Modern: *Crystal* • Godek's: *Roses*

4th

3633. Traditional: *Fruit* • Modern: *Appliances* • Godek's: *Champagne*

5th

3634. Traditional: *Wood* • Modern: *Silver* • Godek's: *Perfume*

6th

3635. Traditional: *Iron* • Modern: *Wood* • Godek's: *Books*

7th

3636. Traditional: *Copper* • Modern: *Desksets* • Godek's: *Wine*

8th

3637. Traditional: *Bronze* • Modern: *Linen* • Godek's: *Time*

9th

3638. Traditional: *Pottery* • Modern: *Leather* • Godek's: *Music CDs*

10th

3639. Traditional: *Aluminum* • Modern: *Diamond jewelry* • Godek's: *Silk*

11th

3640. Traditional: *Steel* • Modern: *Fashion jewelry* • Godek's: *Software*

12th

3641. Traditional: *Linen* • Modern: *Pearls* • Godek's: *Toys*

13th

3642. Traditional: *Lace* • Modern: *Furs* • Godek's: *Umbrellas*

14th

3643. Traditional: *Ivory* • Modern: *Gold jewelry* • Godek's: *Furniture*

15th

3644. Traditional: *Crystal* • Modern: *Watches* • Godek's: *Chocolate*

16th

3645. Godek's: *Lingerie*

17th

3646. Godek's: *Lingerie*

18th

3647. Godek's: *Lingerie*

19th

3648. Godek's: *Lingerie*

20th

3649. Traditional: *China* • Modern: *Platinum* • Godek's: *Gemstones*

21st

3650. Godek's: *Cedar*

22nd

3651. Godek's: *Pine*

23rd

3652. Godek's: *Maple*

24th

3653. Godek's: *Mahogany*

25th

3654. Traditional: *Silver* • Modern: *Silver* • Godek's: *Poetry*

26th

3655. Godek's: *Frivolous*

27th

3656. Godek's: *Serious*

28th

3657. Godek's: *Cheap*

29th

3658. Godek's: *Expensive*

30th

3659. Traditional: *Pearl* • Modern: *Diamond* • Godek's: *Sapphire*

31st

3660. Godek's: *Educational*

32nd

3661. Godek's: *Practical*

33rd

3662. Godek's: *Simple*

34th

3663. Godek's: *Complex*

35th

3664. Traditional: *Coral* • Modern: *Jade* • Godek's: *Pearl*

36th

3665. Godek's: *A round-the-world cruise*

37th

3666. Godek's: *Computers*

38th

3667. Godek's: *Balloons*

39th

3668. Godek's: *Leather*

40th

3669. Traditional: *Ruby* • Modern: *Ruby* • Godek's: *Theater tickets*

41st

3670. Godek's: *Candy*

42nd

3671. Godek's: *Leather*

43rd

3672. Godek's: *Her choice*

44th

3673. Godek's: *His choice*

45th

3674. Traditional: *Sapphire* • Modern: *Sapphire* • Godek's: *Emerald*

46th

3675. Godek's: *Timepieces*

47th

3676. Godek's: *Calligraphy*

48th

3677. Godek's: *Fruit*

49th

3678. Godek's: *Something heavy*

50th

3679. Traditional: *Gold* • Modern: *Gold* • Godek's: *Paris*

51st

3680. Godek's: *Violets*

52nd

3681. Godek's: *Sculpture*

53rd

3682. Godek's: *Something masculine*

54th

3683. Godek's: *Something feminine*

55th

3684. Traditional: *Emerald* • Modern: *Emerald* • Godek's: *Gold*

56th

3685. Godek's: *Red*

57th

3686. Godek's: *Blue*

58th

3687. Godek's: *Yellow*

59th

3688. Godek's: *Green*

60th

3689. Traditional: *Diamond* • Modern: *Diamond* • Godek's: *Sapphire*

61st

3690. Godek's: *Outdoor-oriented*

62nd

3691. Godek's: *Indoor-oriented*

63rd

3692. Godek's: *Sex-oriented*

64th

3693. Godek's: *Sports-oriented*

65th

3694. Godek's: *Pearl*

67th

3695. Godek's: *Traditional*

68th

3696. Godek's: *Modern*

69th

3697. Godek's: *Purple*

70th

3698. Godek's: *Diamond*

71st

3699. Godek's: *Venice*

72nd

3700. Godek's: *Antiques*

73rd

3701. Godek's: *Her choice*

74th

3702. Godek's: *Rolls Royce*

75th

3703. Godek's: *If you make it this far you get to start all over again!*

3704. Surf the Internet for romantic ideas
3705. Give her your car key on a gold chain with a note: "You drive me wild!"
3706. Cover the ceiling with helium balloons
3707. Rent costumes to inspire and enhance a fantasy
3708. Take a limo ride

3709.   Buy lots of *little* diamonds for one another

3710.   Watch cloud formations

3711.   Watch your children grow

3712.   Watch your love grow

3713.   Watch out for each other's best interests

3714.   Watch your partner's favorite TV show

3715.   Watch him or her mature

3716.   Watch your relationship deepen

3717.   Watch your pennies so you can buy that special gift

3718.   Watch your favorite movie together—for the tenth time

3719.   Watch an eclipse of the sun

3720.   Watch an eclipse of the moon

3721.   Watch the clock turn to midnight on New Year's Eve

3722.   Watch time go by

3723.   Watch your weight so you stay healthy

3724.   A "Couch Potato" Coupon: You're entitled to a weekend of sitting in front of the TV, while the coupon-giver caters to all of your junk food needs

3725.   "The little things? The little moments? They aren't little." ~ Jon Kabat-Zinn

3726.   Take an extra five minutes in bed to welcome each other to a new day

3727.   Mood music: Create a comfortable, jazzy mood with the *Chase the Clouds Away* CD by Chuck Mangione

---

3728.   Prescription for romance: Hug!

3729.   Minimum dosage: two per day

3730.   Average dosage: four per day

3731. Recommended dosage: ten per day
3732. Words that *men* love to hear: "I *believe* in you"
3733. Words that *women* love to hear: "I *cherish* you"

3734. Match your love notes to your flowers
3735. "The red rose is my passion for you; the pink rose is my commitment to you; the yellow rose is the sunshine you've given me"
3736. "One flower for each day I'll be away from you (I'm glad it's a *small* bouquet)"
3737. "She loves me—She loves me not—She *loves* me!"

3738. Give him a Mont Blanc pen so he can write love letters to you in style!
3739. Buy snacks at the best café
3740. Drink a bottle of rare French wine together

Favorite Love Songs from 1945
3741. "Autumn Serenade"
3742. "If I Loved You"
3743. "The More I See You," Carmen Cavallaro
3744. "Sentimental Journey," Doris Day
3745. "This Heart of Mine," Judy Garland

3746. A "Chocoholic" Coupon: You are entitled to a massive no-holds-barred celebration of chocolate! Included: an *extraordinary* amount of chocolate
3747. Eat dinner at the best German restaurant around
3748. Tour the great vineyards of France
3749. When traveling, mail a greeting card every day you're gone

3750.   Write a letter together to your grandchildren

3751.   And one to your great, great, great grandchildren

9 Songs to Help You Express Your
Feelings: *Desire & Sexual Attraction*

3752.   "Afternoon Delight," Starland Vocal Band

3753.   "Feel Like Makin' Love," Bad Company

3754.   "I Want Your Sex," George Michael

3755.   "Kiss You All Over," Exile

3756.   "Let's Spend the Night Together," Rolling Stones

3757.   "Natural Woman," Aretha Franklin

3758.   "Sexual Healing," Marvin Gaye

3759.   "Slave to Love," Bryan Ferry

3760.   "The Sweetest Taboo," Sade

3761.   Get *front row center* seats to see her favorite performer

3762.   Tell her about the event, *but not about the seats*

3763.   Sing "your song" to your lover at a Karaoke bar

3764.   A "Saturday Night Fever" Coupon: Dance your cares
        away this Saturday night.

3765.   Enemy of Love: TV

3766.   Learn what he/she considers *sexy*

3767.   Take an extra five minutes to reconnect

3768.   Fill her shoes with penny candy

3769.   Dab perfume on intimate places on your body

3770.   "The ideal day never comes. Today is ideal for him
        who makes it so." ~ Horatio Dresser

3771.   Put notes on household products…

3772. Joy dishwashing liquid: "Every day with you is a *joy*"
3773. Cheerios: "Just knowin' you love me cheers me up"
3774. Old Spice: "You spice up my life"
3775. Ritz Crackers: "Let's 'Put on the Ritz' tonight"
3776. A roll of Lifesavers: "You're a lifesaver"
3777. Caress soap: "Let's do this tonight"
3778. Hershey's Kisses: "I'll trade you *these* for some of *yours*"

3779. Think-up your *own* suggestive notes to attach to Snickers bars...
3780. Godiva basket of goodies
3781. Mounds candy bars
3782. Fire Balls

3783. Enjoy an autumn hayride together
3784. As a secret surprise, learn to cook a gourmet meal
3785. Catch a new act at a local comedy club
3786. Take a horse-drawn carriage ride
3787. Give a balloon bouquet
3788. Locate a nearby meadow where you can pick wildflowers
3789. Give him movie tickets taped to its soundtrack
3790. "The road to the heart is the ear." ~ Voltaire
3791. Give her ice capades tickets inside a pair of ice skates
3792. Make two *incredible* banana splits
3793. Enclose pressed flowers with a love note
3794. Find a "romantic hideaway" bed-and-breakfast to call your own
3795. Buy him a T-shirt picturing his favorite rock group
3796. Read aloud to each other
3797. Give him a cap from his favorite football team
3798. Go for a midnight stroll on the beach

3799. Jump-start your creativity: Read *The New Drawing on the Right Side of the Brain*, by Betty Edwards
3800. "The giving of love is an education in itself."
~ Eleanor Roosevelt
3801. "When you look for the good in others, you discover the best in yourself." ~ Martin Walsh
3802. Teach your children everything you know about love

3803. Discuss what each of you finds *erotic*
3804. Discuss what each of you finds *sexy*
3805. What would you be willing to *try?*

3806. Give her a stuffed animal with a note attached...
3807. Teddy bears: "I can't bear being away from you"
3808. Stuffed lions: "I'm roarin' to get you"
3809. Stuffed pigs: "I'm hog wild over you"
3810. Stuffed tigers: "You're grrrrrreat!"
3811. Stuffed monkeys: "Let's monkey around"

3812. Gals: Get a classic, matching set of bra, panties, garter belt, and stockings—in *black*
3813. Gals: Get a classic, matching set of bra, panties, garter belt, and stockings—in *white*

3814. Great inspiration and great motivation come from the *heart*, not from the *head*
3815. "The only true gift is a portion of yourself." ~ Ralph Waldo Emerson
3816. The Truly Romantic "Wedding Rededication" Coupon: Good for a small ceremony in which you renew your wedding vows

Favorite Love Songs from 1946

3817. "Come Rain or Come Shine"
3818. "Doin' What Comes Natur'lly"
3819. "Prisoner of Love," Perry Como
3820. "I Dream Of You," Archie Lewis and The Geraldo Strings

3821. Update your ideas of gender differences
3822. Integrating your mind and body will help your heart. Learn about "Awareness Through Movement" at The Feldenkrais Guild: www.feldenkrais.com
3823. Eat in the most romantic villa in Venice: Academia

An A to Z List to Inspire Your Love

Ask your partner to pick a letter. He or she has twenty-four hours in which to perform a loving gesture based on any of the key words below:

3824. **A** is for Attitude, Available, Accept, Ardor, Accolades, Admire, A' La Mode, Anniversary, Ambrosia, Ardent, Athens, Australia
3825. **B** is for Boudoir, B&Bs, Buttercups, Beaches, Blue, Boston, Bicycling, Broadway, Brandy, Bubblebaths, Bahamas
3826. **C** is for Champagne, Creativity, Candlelight, Candy, Chocolate, Convertibles, Casablanca, Cognac, Caviar, Chivalry, Crabtree & Evelyn
3827. **D** is for Diamonds, Dinner, Daffodils, Dancing, Dating, Dolls, Dirty dancing
3828. **E** is for Enthusiasm, Energy, Excitement, Emeralds, Earrings, Elvis, Exotic, Expensive

3829. **F** is for Flirting, Fantasies, Feminine, Faithful, France, Fruits, Frenching, Foreplay

3830. **G** is for Gardenias, Godiva, Get-aways, Glenn Miller, Gourmet, Greece

3831. **H** is for Hearts, Humor, Hugs, Hide-aways, Horses, Hershey's Kisses, Hyatt

3832. **I** is for Intimacy, Intrigue, Italy, Inns, Ingenuity, Ice cream, Ice skating, Interdependent, Imaginative

3833. **J** is for Java, Jasmine, Jell-O, Journey, Joyful, Jingle bells

3834. **K** is for Kissing, Kinky, Kittens, Koala Bears

3835. **L** is for Love, Laughing, Love Letters, Lilacs, Lace, Leather, Leo Buscaglia, Lobsters, Lovemaking

3836. **M** is for Monogamy, Marriage, Masculine, M&M's, Massage, Movies, Mistletoe, Mozart

3837. **N** is for Negligee, Naughty, Nibble, Nighttime, Nubile, Novelty, Nurture, Nymph, Naples, Nightcap

3838. **O** is for Orgasm, Opera, Oprah, Orchid, Outrageous, Outdoors

3839. **P** is for Passion, Poppies, Poetry, Persimmons, Paris, Polkas, Panties, Pizza, Photos, Pearls, Picnics, Playfulness, Purple

3840. **Q** is for Quaint, Quality, Queen, Quebec, Question, QE2, Quiche, Quiver

3841. **R** is for Rendezvous, Roses, Rubies, Red, Reading, Rome, Rituals, Riviera, Restful, Rapture, Rio

3842. **S** is for Sex

3843. **T** is for Talking, Teasing, Tulips, Titillating, Theater, Togetherness, Toasts, Toys, Trains, Trinidad

3844. **U** is for Uxorious, Undress, Undulate, Urges, Unexpected, Union, Under the Spreading Chestnut Tree, Unabashed feelings

3845. **V** is for Violets, Venice, Venus, Valentines, Vegetables
3846. **W** is for Wine, Wisteria, Weddings
3847. **X** is for X-Rated, Xerographic, Xylophones, Xmas
3848. **Y** is for Yes, Yellow, Yin & Yang, Young-at-heart
3849. **Z** is for Zany, Zeal, Zings, Zodiac, Zurich

3850. Get in touch with your own body—it will enhance your enjoyment of sex
3851. Beware of "relationship entropy": The tendency of couples to drift apart if energy isn't added to the relationship
3852. For coffee lovers: Buy a variety of coffee beans
3853. Pledge your love in writing
3854. Practice "emotional foreplay"

3855. A "Professional Sporting Event" Coupon: You are entitled to two tickets to any professional sporting event taking place within 100 miles
3856. "The way to love anything is to realize that it might be lost" ~ G.K. Chesterton
3857. Prepare a bucket of steaming water so he can soak his aching feet
3858. Massage her neck muscles
3859. The "Weekend Movie Marathon" Coupon: You choose a theme, and the coupon-issuer will rent six movies that fit the theme, pop the popcorn, and be your weekend movie date

Lists for Lovers

A+ Couples don't leave things to *chance*, they write things down
3860. A "Wish List"—For *things* you want

3861. A "Dream List"—For *places* you want to visit

3862. A "Fantasy List"—For sensual and sexual desires

3863. A "Date List"—For activities, restaurants

3864. A "Hollywood List"—For films you want to see

3865. A "Home Improvement List"—For ways to enhance your environment

3866. A "Self-Improvement List"—For ways in which you want to grow

3867. Admit it when you're wrong

3868. Love with all your heart

3869. Remember and re-create the feeling of passion you had for your partner when you first met

3870. "The object of love is to serve, not to win."
~ Woodrow Wilson

3871. Love Coupon: Good for a $100 shopping spree in the nearest lingerie shop (or lingerie catalog)

3872. Take the day off work—and spend most of the day in bed together

3873. Give him a tie that illustrates his favorite sports team

3874. Fill her jewelry box with tiny love notes

3875. The "Shoot Your TV" Coupon: You are entitled to one week in which your partner devotes all of his or her TV time to *you*

3876. Learn what he/she considers *touching*

Ways to Earn Your "MBA"
(Masters of Bedroom Amore)

3877. Focus on fondling

3878. Ask your partner to direct you—*very specifically*—in how she likes to be touched

3879. Talk candidly about the differences between *sexy* and *sensual*

3880. Read one book by Dr. Ruth

3881. Guys: Talk more

3882. Gals: Touch more

3883. Practice: Talking "dirty" while making love

3884. Practice: Talking *seductively* in bed

3885. Experiment with fantasies

3886. Experiment with reading erotica

3887. Experiment with sensual, sexy, and outright X-rated movies

3888. Try putting yourself in your partner's shoes (figuratively *and* literally!)

3889. Spend one solid hour exploring various kissing techniques

3890. Guys: Be *vulnerable*—without being a *wimp*

3891. Gals: Be *confident*—without being *overbearing*

3892. Turn your "bedroom" into a "boudoir"

3893. Remember: Practice makes perfect

3894. Try loosening up those vocal cords during sex

3895. Try loosening up those inhibitions during sex

3896. Celebrate New Year's Eve with good friends

3897. Go to Las Vegas for the great entertainment

3898. "Where there is great love there are always great miracles." ~ Willa Cather

3899. Mind-set: Love is a matter of *skills*, not a matter of luck or fate

3900. Eat dinner at the best French restaurant around

3901. Have lunch at the best local dive
3902. For your movie buff: An endless supply of popcorn
3903. Bring dinner home when he/she's really busy

Ways to Put the *Zing* Back in Your Relationship

3904. Give her a bottle of champagne as a "Thank You" for doing some everyday chore
3905. Gals: Promise him a week of ESPN (Exceptional Sex Practiced Nightly)
3906. Revive chivalry
3907. Place a romantic message on a local billboard
3908. Locate a copy of the 1935 hit song "Zing! Went the Strings of My Heart"
3909. Dress to please your partner—while in public
3910. Seduce him
3911. Dress to please your partner—while home alone
3912. Make a giant greeting card from a large cardboard box
3913. Write a note: "My sexiest memory of you is…"
3914. Fly to Paris for the weekend
3915. Leave written clues that lead him to a hidden gift
3916. Rent a Harley motorcycle for a freewheeling vacation
3917. Leave a subtly suggestive voicemail

3918. Simple Sex Rule #1: Guys are fast, gals are slow
3919. Simple Sex Rule #2: Guys are visual—*show* him
3920. Simple Sex Rule #3: Gals are auditory—*tell* her

3921. Create a sexy "Five-Sense Evening," during which you and your lover stimulate all five of each other's senses
3922. Make love to her *the way she wants to be made love to*
3923. Make his/her friends *your* friends

3924. Create a memento wall: Paste up favorite mementos, movie stubs, programs, etc.
3925. "Life for every person should be a journey in jubilance!" ~ Charles Fillmore
3926. Make love in a semi-public place
3927. Expand your definition of love every year
3928. Daily affirmation: "I will appreciate what I have"

3929. Throw *great* parties together...
3930. Become famous for your Halloween costume balls
3931. Host wine tasting parties
3932. Host beer tasting parties
3933. Have a summertime beach party
3934. Gather good friends for dinner once a month
3935. Host a New Year's Eve costume ball
3936. Have monogrammed place mats made
3937. Host an elegant garden party
3938. Host an Academy Awards party

3939. When traveling apart, write one paragraph expressing how much you miss him/her; email it
3940. Rent an RV for a cross-country road trip
3941. When traveling, mail a different postcard every day you're gone
3942. "When you've exhausted all possibilities, remember this: you haven't." ~ Robert Schuller
3943. Wear matching Japanese kimonos

Romantic Movies Starring the All-Time Great Romantic Couples

3944. *Red Dust* (Gable & Harlow)

3945. *Hold Your Man* (Gable & Harlow)
3946. *Flying Down to Rio* (Astair & Rogers)
3947. *Top Hat* (Astaire & Rogers)
3948. *Maytime* (MacDonald & Eddy)
3949. *Sweethearts* (MacDonald & Eddy)
3950. *Love Finds Andy Hardy* (Garland & Rooney)
3951. *Girl Crazy* (Garland & Rooney)
3952. *That Forsyte Woman* (Garson & Pidgeon)
3953. *Scandal at Scourie* (Garson & Pidgeon)
3954. *To Have and Have Not* (Bogart & Bacall)
3955. *Fire Over England* (Leigh & Olivier)
3956. *21 Days Together* (Leigh & Olivier)
3957. *Cleopatra* (Taylor & Burton)
3958. *The Sandpiper* (Taylor & Burton)
3959. *The Long, Hot Summer* (Newman & Woodward)
3960. *Paris Blues* (Newman & Woodward)
3961. *Woman of the Year* (Hepburn & Tracy)
3962. *Without Love* (Hepburn & Tracy)

3963. Learn what he/she considers *exciting*
3964. Eat dinner at the restaurant with the best wine list
3965. Save your love letters in a shoebox
3966. Fall in love all over again
3967. "There is no greater invitation to love than loving first." ~ St. Augustine
3968. The Sweets-for-the-Sweet Coupon: You are entitled to a twelve-pound pile of any three kinds of candy that you specify
3969. Write a tiny note somewhere on your skin with ink, and ask your lover to look for it!

3970. Make a birthday song list
3971. *Happy Birthday*, Stevie Wonder
3972. *Happy Birthday*, New Kids on the Block
3973. *Happy Birthday*, Altered Images
3974. *Birthday*, The Beatles
3975. *Happy Birthday to You*, Bing Crosby
3976. *Happy Birthday to You*, Eddy Howard
3977. *Happy Birthday to You*, Sunsetters
3978. *Happy, Happy Birthday, Baby*, Tune Weavers
3979. *I Wish I Were 18 Again*, George Burns
3980. *When I'm Sixty-Four*, The Beatles
3981. *Young at Heart*, Frank Sinatra

Quirky Questions That Open a
Window into Your Lover's Personality

Sometimes the best route into the psyche is a roundabout
route. Ask your lover these questions:

3982. If you could be a comic strip character, who would
you be?
3983. If you had three wishes, what would they be?
3984. If you could create the perfect job for yourself, what
would it be?
3985. Who are your heroes? (Fictional *and* real)
3986. If your name were to appear in the dictionary, how
would you define yourself?
3987. Could you live for a year in a tent with your partner
(without going crazy)?
3988. How many self-help books have you read?
3989. If you could accomplish one crazy stunt that would
land you in the Guinness Book of World Records,
what would it be?

3990. Would you rather be really, really smart, or really, really good looking?

3991. If you could be a super hero, who would you be?

3992. If you were Rick, in the movie *Casablanca*, would you have let Ilsa leave at the end?

3993. If you had just one more day to live, how would you live that day?

3994. What one thing did your parents *always* yell at you for?

3995. What one part of your body would you like to change?

3996. Would you ever go skinny-dipping?

3997. What three historical figures would you like to have a conversation with?

3998. Did Francesca do the right thing in *The Bridges of Madison County*?

3999. Give a case of his/her favorite wine

4000. "The art of being wise is the art of knowing what to overlook." ~ William James

4001. Give him rock concert tickets taped to the group's latest CD

4002. For your movie buff: His/her favorite movie

4003. "The best proof of love is trust." ~ Dr. Joyce Brothers

4004. Have a love quote embroidered on her pillowcase

4005. A "Coffee, Tea & Me" Coupon: Good for coffee or tea served to you anywhere in your home, at a time of your choosing

4006. Learn to polka

4007. **Stop** complaining!

4008. **Look** lovingly into your lover's eyes

4009. **Listen** attentively

4010.   Buy a box of kids' valentines
4011.   Mail *hundreds* of them to your lover
4012.   Mail one a day for several months
4013.   Mail them all at once
4014.   Fill his briefcase with them
4015.   Tape them all over her car
4016.   Fill the sink with them
4017.   Fill her pillow with them

4018.   Prescription for romance: Compliment him/her
4019.   Repeat every four to six hours

4020.   "There is no remedy for love but to love more."
        ~ Henry David Thoreau
4021.   Drip honey on your lover's body; lick it off
4022.   Give him balloons to match his age
4023.   "A man is never so weak as when a woman is telling
        him how strong he is." ~ Anonymous
4024.   Take a walk in the park
4025.   Spoil him for a solid week

4026.   Learn to square dance (not just for squares)
4027.   Eat in the most romantic inn in Copenhagen:
        Skovshoved
4028.   Give him Godiva Chocolates
4029.   Make a life-sized cardboard cut-out of yourself

Sexy Tips—For Gals Only
4030.   On *his* birthday, give *yourself* some lingerie
4031.   Read a few men's magazines—for some insight into
        the male psyche

4032. Greet him at the door wearing sexy lingerie

4033. Wear a red bow tie and matching heels—and nothing else

4034. Mail him a pair of your sexiest panties and attach a sexy note

4035. Never, never, *never* fake it

4036. Pose on a bed of black silk sheets wearing white silk lingerie

4037. Pose on a bed of white silk sheets wearing black silk lingerie

4038. Seduction music: "I Wanna Be Loved By You," by Marilyn Monroe

4039. Reminder: Most mens' sex hormone levels are highest in the morning

4040. Greet him at the front door wearing your wedding gown

4041. Be his "Calendar Girl": Paste pictures of yourself in a swimsuit calendar

---

4042. Romantic music alert: Earl Klugh CDs: *Heartstrings; Love Songs; Ballads*

4043. French kiss

4044. "Where love is concerned, too much is not even enough." ~ P.A.C. de Beaumarchais

4045. Great relationships require equal parts of passion, commitment, and intimacy

4046. Commission a custom quilt to include a variety of designs symbolizing your life together

4047. Send him a perfumed love letter

4048. Learn to like your in-laws!

4049. Spend a weekend on Nantucket Island

4050. Collect soundtracks from romantic movies…
4051. *Against All Odds*
4052. *Doctor Zhivago*
4053. *Out of Africa*
4054. *Romeo and Juliet*
4055. *Sleepless in Seattle*
4056. *Somewhere in Time*
4057. *The Bodyguard*
4058. *Titanic*
4059. *Top Gun*

Songs to Help You Express Your Feelings: *New Love*

4060. "We've Only Just Begun," The Carpenters
4061. "(I've Been) Searchin' So Long," Chicago
4062. "Puppy Love," Paul Anka
4063. "The First Time Ever I Saw Your Face," Roberta Flack
4064. "All My Loving," The Beatles

4065. Tease
4066. But don't mock
4067. Tickle
4068. But don't torture

4069. Take a moonlit stroll
4070. Give a sexy massage
4071. "Therefore encourage one another and build each other up." ~ 1 Thessalonians 5:11
4072. Have sex on the big boardroom table in the executive conference room of your mate's office
4073. Practice yoga together

4074. Read *The Secret Language of Birthdays*, by Gary Goldschneider and Joost Elffers

4075. A "Quickie" Coupon: This rare and highly-prized coupon entitles you to sex with the coupon-giver *immediately* (No excuses accepted)

4076. Drop into a card shop once a month

Favorite Love Songs from 1947

4077. "A Fellow Needs a Girl"

4078. "Almost Like Being in Love"

4079. "But Beautiful You," Tex Beneke

4080. "Everything I Have Is Yours," Billy Eckstine

4081. "Near You," Francis Craig

4082. "That's My Desire," Frankie Laine

4083. "A kiss is an application for a better position." ~ Jeff Rovin

4084. The Joy of Sex Coupon: The coupon-giver provides the book. You choose the page. You both enjoy yourselves and each other as you follow the instructions on that page

4085. Surprise her with a crystal vase full of flowers

4086. Enemy of Love: Lack of understanding

4087. For your bird lover: *Bird Talk Magazine:* www.birdchannel.com for info

4088. Pinch his butt when no one is looking

Love Songs Recorded by Frank Sinatra

4089. "Almost Like Being in Love"

4090. "At Long Last Love"

4091. "Can I Steal a Little Love"

4092. "Crazy Love"
4093. "Don't Take Your Love From Me"
4094. "End of a Love Affair"
4095. "Everybody Ought to Be in Love"
4096. "Everybody Love Somebody"
4097. "Falling in Love With Love"
4098. "Farewell, Farewell to Love"
4099. "Give Her Love"
4100. "Half as Lovely"
4101. "Hallelujah, I Love Her So"
4102. "Hello Young Lovers"
4103. "Hey Jealous Lover"
4104. "How Are You Fixed for Love"
4105. "I Am Loved"
4106. "I Believe I'm Gonna Love You"
4107. "I Can't Believe That You're in Love with Me"
4108. "I Can't Stop Falling in Love with You"
4109. "I Fall in Love Too Easily"
4110. "I Fall in Love With You Ev'ry Day"
4111. "I Got a Gal I Love"
4112. "I Love My Wife"
4113. "I Love Paris"
4114. "I Love You"
4115. "I Love You (Version #1)"
4116. "I Love You (Version #2)"
4117. "I Loved Her"
4118. "I Wish I Were in Love Again"
4119. "I Wish You Love"
4120. "I Would Be in Love Anyway"
4121. "If I Ever Love Again"
4122. "If I Loved You"

4123. "It's a Lovely Day Tomorrow"
4124. "I've Got a Love to Keep Me Warm"
4125. "I've Never Been in Love Before"
4126. "Just One Way to Say I Love You"
4127. "The Last Call for Love"
4128. "Let's Fall in Love"
4129. "Like Someone in Love"
4130. "Look of Love"
4131. "Love and Marriage"
4132. "Love Is a Many Splendored Thing"
4133. "Love Is Here to Stay"
4134. "Love Is Around The Corner"
4135. "Love Isn't Just for the Young"
4136. "Love Lies"
4137. "Love Locked Out"
4138. "Love Looks So Well on You"
4139. "Love Me"
4140. "Love Me As I Am"
4141. "Love Me Tender"
4142. "Love Means Love"
4143. "Love Walked In"
4144. "A Lovely Moonlit Night"
4145. "Lovely Way to Spend an Evening"
4146. "Lover"
4147. "Love's Been Good to Me"
4148. "Melody of Love"
4149. "Mind If I Make Love To You"
4150. "Moon Love"
4151. "My Love For You"
4152. "My One and Only Love"
4153. "Once I Loved"

4154. "Once in Love with Amy"
4155. "The One I Love"
4156. "One Love"
4157. "One Love Affair"
4158. "P.S.: I Love You"
4159. "People Will Say We're in Love"
4160. "Prisoner of Love"
4161. "Secret Love"
4162. "So in Love"
4163. "So Long My Love"
4164. "Somewhere My Love"
4165. "Take My Love"
4166. "Taking a Chance on Love"
4167. "Tell Her You Love Her"
4168. "Tell Her You Love Her Each Day"
4169. "That's How Much I Love You"
4170. "Then Suddenly Love"
4171. "This Is My Love"
4172. "This Love of Mine"
4173. "This Was My Love"
4174. "To Love and Be Loved"
4175. "Two in Love"
4176. "What Is This Thing Called Love"
4177. "What Now My Love"
4178. "When I Stop Loving You"
4179. "When I'm Not Near the Girl I Love"
4180. "When Somebody Loves You"
4181. "When Your Lover Has Gone"
4182. "Wives and Lovers"
4183. "You Brought a New Kind of Love to Me"
4184. "You My Love"

4185.   "You'd Be So Easy to Love"
4186.   "You'll Always Be the One I Love"
4187.   "Your Love for Me"
4188.   "You're Nobody 'Til Somebody Loves You"

4189.   The "Lazy Love" Coupon: This coupon entitles you to a sensuous, luxurious, extended lovemaking session with the coupon-issuer. Time requirement: At least 3 hours
4190.   Write a *really* sexy, suggestive personal ad in the newspaper—in code!
4191.   Rent every movie that stars his favorite actress
4192.   Love Coupon: Entitling you to an afternoon of watching clouds together
4193.   Wear matching bathrobes
4194.   Take a cooking class together
4195.   Give a subscription to a favorite magazine
4196.   Extend your vacation budget by staying in cheap motels
4197.   Keep every love letter and note from your lover
4198.   Decorate with stuffed Poohs, Piglets, and Tiggers
4199.   Rewrite "The Twelve Days of Christmas"—and give *all* the gifts!

4200.   Copy a romantic poem onto fancy parchment paper
4201.   Have it framed
4202.   Hang it on the wall and wait for your partner to notice it

4203.   Have dinner at home by candlelight
4204.   Heck, have *breakfast* by candlelight!

4205. Make every Monday "Extra Kisses Day"
4206. Make every Tuesday "Gift Day"
4207. Make every Wednesday "Partner Appreciation Day"
4208. Make every Thursday "Love Is About the Little Things Day"
4209. Make every Friday evening "Date Night"
4210. Make every Saturday "Sexual Exploration Day"
4211. Make every Sunday "Spiritual Connection Day"

4212. Take a massage class: Learn to do it *right*
4213. Vacuum kiss (suck the air out of your mouths; separate with a "pop")
4214. "Grow old with me! The best is yet to be." ~ Robert Browning
4215. Have breakfast at the best diner
4216. Daily affirmation: "I will be aware of my feelings of love"
4217. Run a race together for charity
4218. Browse in a lingerie shop once a season

4219. Take a drawing class together
4220. Pose nude for each other
4221. Act out a sexy artist/model fantasy

4222. Pray together
4223. Play together

4224. When traveling, hide a love letter under his/her pillow and tape a photo of yourself to the TV screen
4225. Leave three greeting cards hidden around the house
4226. Mail a greeting card on your way to the airport

4227.   Mail another greeting card as soon as you arrive at your destination

4228.   "Men are all alike in their promises. It is only in their deeds that they differ." ~ Molière

4229.   Clip ads that show possible gift ideas

4230.   FYI: While men aren't typically as *verbal*, they are often more *action-oriented* than women

4231.   Bury an (edible) present in a cake; don't let your partner use hands to find it

4232.   Make romance a *habit*

4233.   "To fall in love is awfully simple, but to fall out of love is simply awful." ~ Anonymous

Favorite Love Songs from 1948

4234.   "A-You're Adorable"

4235.   "It's Magic," Doris Day

4236.   "My Darling, My Darling," Jo Stafford

4237.   "My Happiness," Ella Fitzgerald

4238.   "So in Love"

4239.   "Love Somebody," Doris Day & Buddy Clark

4240.   Remember, a little exhibitionism never hurt

4241.   Turn the *ordinary* into the *special*

4242.   Take turns shooting portrait photos of each other; try to capture the true *essence* of each other's personality

4243.   Send teddy bears

4244.   Surprise your partner at work with flowers

4245.   Explore Greek temples

4246.   Learn to sing a love song duet

4247. When traveling, mail a little love note every day you're gone

4248. A "Dancing Lesson" Coupon: Good for one dancing lesson given by a professional at a dance studio. The coupon-giver must participate.

4249. Go to popular vacation spots off-season

7 Songs to Help You Express Your Feelings: *Suggestive*

4250. "In the Mood," Glenn Miller

4251. "Lay Lady Lay," Bob Dylan

4252. "Light My Candle," from the Broadway musical *Rent*

4253. "Makin' Whoopee!" Gus Kahn

4254. "Physical," Olivia Newton-John

4255. "So Deep Within You," Moody Blues

4256. "We've Got Tonight," Kenny Rogers & Sheena Easton

4257. Learn to disco

4258. Turn everyday events into "little celebrations"

4259. Name your computer hard drive after her

4260. Planning doesn't destroy spontaneity, it creates opportunity

4261. The "Saturday Night Date" Coupon: Where? Wherever you want. When? You decide. The coupon-giver guarantees a great time.

4262. "Vulnerability is always at the heart of love." ~ Leo Buscaglia

4263. Write little love notes

4264. Write long, passionate love letters to one another

4265. Write poetry

4266. Write a "Thank You" note for something your partner's done for you
4267. Write notes on Post-It Notes and stick them around the house
4268. Write notes on rolls of toilet paper
4269. Write a list of ten gifts your partner would love
4270. Write a list of ten places your partner would love to go
4271. Write a list of ten places where you'd like to take your partner
4272. Write a list of ten activities you know your partner would enjoy
4273. Write a note using candy conversation hearts
4274. Write love notes on the refrigerator using Magnetic Poetry
4275. Write a love note using a Scrabble game

4276. Give your partner a *gift* that he or she *wants*
4277. Give your partner a *present* that *you* want him or her to have

4278. "The only love worthy of the name, ever and always uplifts." ~ George MacDonald
4279. Send a Valentine's Day card in *August*

4280. Lingerie, lingerie, lingerie!
4281. A satin camisole and matching tap pants
4282. Matching bra and panty sets
4283. An elegant peignoir
4284. Teddies
4285. Boxer shorts with big red hearts on them
4286. Garter belts and stockings

4287. A bustier
4288. Silk pajamas
4289. An outfit like the one worn by this month's Playmate of the Month

---

4290. Use "multi-tasking" as a strategy to save time
4291. But be totally focused on your mate during intimate times

---

4292. Go for it in a BIG way: Be *outrageously* romantic!
4293. Take a ride in a convertible together
4294. Don't *ever* give your partner reason to be jealous

Favorite Love Songs from 1949

4295. "Candy Kisses," George Morgan
4296. "Diamonds Are a Girl's Best Friend"
4297. "Lovesick Blues," Hank Williams
4298. "Mona Lisa"
4299. "My Foolish Heart"
4300. "Someday (You'll Want Me to Want You)," The Mills Brothers
4301. "Baby, I Need You," Frankie Laine

4302. Write a letter saying you're a researcher for the new edition of *The Joy of Sex*, and you need her help with your studies
4303. Surprise her with sachets for her lingerie drawers
4304. Write a list: "33 Romantic Things I'm Going to Do for You This Year"

4305. Take a romantic cruise…

4306. Abercrombie & Kent Int'l.:
www.abercrombiekent.com

4307. American Canadian Caribbean Line:
www.accl-smallships.com

4308. American Hawaii Cruises:
www.hawaiicruiseoutlet.com

4309. Bergen Line: www.bergenline.com

4310. Carnival Cruise Lines: www.carnival.com

4311. Celebrity Cruises: www.celebrity-cruises.com

4312. Travel Dynamics International:
www.traveldynamicsinternational.com

4313. Clipper Cruise Line: www.clippercruise.com

4314. Club Med Cruises: www.clubmed.com

4315. Princess Cruises: www.princess.com

4316. Silversea Cruises: www.silversea.com

4317. Crystal Cruises: www.crystalcruises.com

4318. Cunard Line: www.cunardline.com

4319. Disney Cruise Line: www.disneycruise.com

4320. The Yachts of Seabourn: www.seabourn.com

4321. Holland America Line: www.hollandamerica.com

4322. Norwegian Cruise Line: www.ncl.com

4323. Orient Lines: www.orientlines.com

4324. Premier Cruises:

4325. Regal Cruises: www.regalcruiseline.com

4326. Royal Caribbean Int'l.: www.royalcaribbean.com

4327. Regent Seven Seas Cruises: www.rssc.com

4328. Star Clippers: www.star-clippers.com

4329. Imperial Majesty Cruise Line:
www.imperialmajesty.com

4330. Residential Cruise Line:
www.residentialcruiseline.com/index.htm

4331. Windstar Cruises: www.windstarcruises.com

4332. Re-create the fun and excitement you had in early stages of your relationship

4333. Secretly place a "Valentine ad" in a theater playbill for a show you're going to attend

4334. Mind-set: "Couple-Thinking": View yourself primarily as a member of a couple

4335. "Respect is love in plain clothes." ~ Frankie Byrne

4336. Buy her a T-shirt picturing her favorite movie star

4337. Enemy of Love: Repetition

4338. Plan a picnic in a garden

4339. Send a written invitation inside a picnic basket

4340. Include the CD *In the Garden*, by Eric Tingstad & Nancy Rumbel

Reasonable and Unreasonable
Expectations for Couples

4341. Don't expect perfection

4342. Do expect honesty

4343. Don't expect him/her to read your mind

4344. Do expect him/her to anticipate you

4345. Don't expect infatuation to last forever

4346. Do expect true love to last forever

4347. Don't expect to live happily ever after without working at it!

4348. Do expect to live lovingly ever after

4349. Don't expect him/her to be reasonable all the time

4350. Do expect him/her to control his/her emotions most of the time

4351. Don't expect to be "in sync" all of the time
4352. Do expect to forgive one another regularly

4353. "If you can dream it you can do it." ~ Walt Disney
4354. Identify your dreams…what do you *want*? (To live happily ever after? To create a loving family?)
4355. Share your dreams with your mate
4356. Focus your love, your energy, and your intentions on your dream

4357. Guys: Buy her an *entire* outfit.
4358. Include: Elegant lingerie, a gorgeous dress, a matching scarf, a piece of jewelry, and shoes
4359. (Have her best girlfriend advise you!)
4360. Make sure you get all the sizes *perfect*
4361. Spread the outfit on the bed
4362. Along with a written invitation to dinner

4363. Retain your personal style while accommodating your mate
4364. Recognize that one mode of expression isn't enough
4365. When he gets up in the middle of the night: Roll onto his side of the bed, then demand a sexual favor before you'll move over

Ways to Love a Virgo
(24 August–23 September)

4366. Virgo is an *earth* sign: Cater to his/her grounded, practical nature
4367. Gift tip: Natural and elegant
4368. Objects made of wood

4369. Plants and flowering bushes make great gifts
4370. Gardening tools and books
4371. Prefers natural foods to sweets
4372. Buttercups; hazelnut trees
4373. Visually-appealing foods
4374. The elegance of Paris
4375. Wrap gifts in blue for your Virgo

4376. "Why it is better to love than be loved? It is surer."
~ Sacha Guitry
4377. Place a *standing order* with a florist: Never forget another anniversary!
4378. A "Wednesday Night Date" Coupon: Renewable every week for 2 years
4379. Start some *good* habits: Read *Habits of the Heart*, by Robert Bellah

---

4380. Write a list: "12 Things About You That Make Me Smile"
4381. Type it up on your computer using fancy fonts
4382. Give it to him/her along with a photo of you

Ways to Affair-Proof Your Relationship

4383. Be best friends as well as lovers
4384. Don't nag
4385. Laugh together often
4386. Make love often
4387. Don't wear sloppy clothes to bed
4388. Don't let problems go unresolved
4389. Keep your partner among your top three priorities
4390. Let the infatuation fade, but keep the *passion* alive

4391. Never relinquish your role as your mate's "lover"
4392. Make some sacrifices but don't martyr yourself for his/her sake
4393. Weave love, sex, and romance into the fabric of your daily lives

Places to Take Your Water-Loving Lover Snorkeling

4394. Bahamas, Out Islands
4395. Bonaire Marine Park, Netherlands Antilles
4396. Delos, Greece
4397. Gulf of Aqaba, Red Sea
4398. Heron Island, Australia
4399. La Jolla, California
4400. Looe Key, Florida
4401. Madang, Papua, New Guinea
4402. Providentiales, Turks and Caicos
4403. Santa Barbara Island, California
4404. Stingray City, Grand Cayman

4405. Cater to the kid in him...
4406. Go to an amusement park together
4407. Vacation at a dude ranch in the American West
4408. Go to a pro baseball game together

4409. "On life's vast ocean diversity we sail, Reason the card, but passion is the gale." ~ Alexander Pope
4410. The "Hero" Coupon: Redeemable for two hero sandwiches (also known as "grinders" and "submarine sandwiches") and two sodas
4411. Keep two lovebirds—named after the two of you
4412. Visit a spiritually meaningful place, like Jerusalem

4413. Listen closely for the song in her heart
4414. Learn to sing that song of love together
4415. Sing that song back to her when she forgets

4416. Don't buy her cheap lingerie—
4417. Unless you plan to rip it off her body during passionate lovemaking

4418. Enemy of Love: Mismatched partners
4419. Begin each day with a prayer
4420. "I am, in every thought of my heart, yours."
~ Woodrow Wilson
4421. "Service isn't a big thing. It's a million little things."
~ Anonymous
4422. Take an extra five minutes to give thanks for each other at the end of the day

4423. Brainstorm as many romantic ideas as you can in fifteen minutes
4424. Generate ideas that are serious and silly
4425. Practical and ridiculous
4426. Expensive and cheap
4427. Meaningful and sexy
4428. Generate ideas for gifts and gestures…
4429. And places to go and things to do

4430. Admit it when you're wrong
4431. Do-It-Yourself Romantic Afternoon: 1 canoe, 1 lazy day, 2 star-struck lovers

4432.   Be patient with each other's style of communication...

4433.   Some people (typically men) communicate *to get information*

4434.   Some people (typically women) communicate *to make emotional connection*

4435.   Some people (typically men) use communication as a way to *compete*

4436.   Some people (typically women) use communication as a way to *cooperate*

4437.   For parents only: Enough already! Escape from your kids for five hours!

4438.   "Remember when you were at your best? Now be there again!" ~ Anonymous

4439.   Identify the worst "Relationship Rut" you are in—and resolve to get *out*!

4440.   Mind-set: Love is an *art*, not a *science*

4441.   Quit trying to do it *perfectly*! Just keep trying!

Great Date Movies

4442.   *9 1/2 Weeks* (♥ ♥ ♥ ♥ ♥ Romance Moving Rating) (Erotic)

4443.   *40 Days and 40 Nights* (♥ ♥)

4444.   *The African Queen* (♥ ♥ ♥)

4445.   *Aladdin* (♥ ♥)

4446.   *American Pie* (trilogy) (♥ ♥)

4447.   *The American President* (♥ ♥ ♥)

4448.   *America's Sweethearts* (♥ ♥)

4449.   *Angel Eyes* (♥ ♥)

4450.   *Anna Karenina* (♥ ♥)

4451. *A Place in the Sun* (♥ ♥ ♥)
4452. *Basic Instinct* (♥ ♥ ♥ ♥ ♥) (Erotic)
4453. *Beauty and the Beast* (♥ ♥ ♥ ♥)
4454. *Braveheart* (♥ ♥)
4455. *The Break-Up* (♥ ♥ ♥)
4456. *Breakfast at Tiffany's* (♥ ♥ ♥ ♥)
4457. *Butch Cassidy and the Sundance Kid* (♥ ♥ ♥ ♥)
4458. *Camelot* (♥ ♥ ♥)
4459. *Carlito's Way* (♥ ♥)
4460. *Circle of Friends* (♥ ♥)
4461. *Color of Night* (♥ ♥) (Erotic)
4462. *Dance with Me* (♥ ♥)
4463. *Dances with Wolves* (♥ ♥ ♥)
4464. *Don Juan DeMarco* (♥ ♥)
4465. *Down to Earth* (♥ ♥ ♥)
4466. *Dying Young* (♥ ♥ ♥ ♥ ♥)
4467. *Empire Records* (♥ ♥ ♥)
4468. *The English Patient* (♥ ♥ ♥)
4469. *Ever After* (♥ ♥ ♥)
4470. *The Family Stone* (♥ ♥ ♥ ♥)
4471. *Fever Pitch* (♥ ♥)
4472. *For the Love of the Game* (♥ ♥ ♥)
4473. *Forget Paris* (♥ ♥)
4474. *Four Weddings and a Funeral* (♥ ♥ ♥)
4475. *French Kiss* (♥ ♥ ♥)
4476. *Gigi* (♥ ♥ ♥)
4477. *Grease* (♥ ♥ ♥)
4478. *Great Expectations* [with Paltrow & Hawke] (♥ ♥ ♥)
4479. *The Holiday* (♥ ♥ ♥ ♥)
4480. *It Could Happen to You* (♥ ♥)
4481. *Kate and Leopold* (♥ ♥)

4482. *Keeping the Faith* (♥ ♥)
4483. *The King and I* (♥ ♥ ♥ ♥ ♥)
4484. *The Lake House* (♥ ♥ ♥)
4485. *Last of the Mohicans* (♥ ♥ ♥)
4486. *Legends of the Fall* (♥ ♥)
4487. *Like Water for Chocolate* (♥ ♥ ♥ ♥)
4488. *Lonesome Dove* (♥ ♥)
4489. *The Long Hot Summer* (♥ ♥ ♥ ♥)
4490. *Maid in Manhattan* (♥ ♥ ♥)
4491. *Message in a Bottle* (♥ ♥ ♥)
4492. *The Mirror Has Two Faces* (♥ ♥ ♥)
4493. *Moonstruck* (♥ ♥ ♥ ♥ ♥)
4494. *Music & Lyrics* (♥ ♥)
4495. *Never Been Kissed* (♥ ♥)
4496. *Nine Months* (♥ ♥)
4497. *The Notebook* (♥ ♥ ♥ ♥)
4498. *Notting Hill* (♥ ♥ ♥)
4499. *Office Space* (♥ ♥ ♥)
4500. *Oklahoma!* (♥ ♥ ♥)
4501. *On Golden Pond* (♥ ♥ ♥)
4502. *One Fine Day* (♥ ♥ ♥)
4503. *Only You* (♥ ♥)
4504. *Out of Africa* (♥ ♥ ♥ ♥)
4505. *The Philadelphia Story* (♥ ♥ ♥ ♥)
4506. *Picture Perfect* (♥ ♥)
4507. *Pretty Woman* (♥ ♥ ♥)
4508. *Reality Bites* (♥ ♥ ♥)
4509. *Rebel Without a Cause* (♥ ♥)
4510. *Return to Me* (♥ ♥ ♥ ♥)
4511. *Roman Holiday* (♥ ♥ ♥)
4512. *Rumor Has It* (♥ ♥ ♥)

4513. *Sabrina* [with Bogart & Hepburn] (♥ ♥ ♥)
4514. *Sabrina* [with Julia Ormand & Harrison Ford] (♥ ♥ ♥)
4515. *Saturday Night Fever* (♥ ♥)
4516. *Scent of a Woman* (♥ ♥)
4517. *Sense and Sensibility* (♥ ♥ ♥)
4518. *She's All That* (♥ ♥ ♥)
4519. *Singin' in the Rain* (♥ ♥ ♥ ♥)
4520. *Six Days, Seven Nights* (♥ ♥ ♥)
4521. *Sleepless in Seattle* (♥ ♥ ♥ ♥ ♥)
4522. *Sliding Doors* (♥ ♥ ♥ ♥)
4523. *Sommersby* (♥ ♥ ♥ ♥)
4524. *Splendor in the Grass* (♥ ♥ ♥ ♥)
4525. *Star Wars* (♥ ♥)
4526. *The Thornbirds* (♥ ♥ ♥ ♥)
4527. *To Have and Have Not* (♥ ♥ ♥)
4528. *The Truth About Cats and Dogs* (♥ ♥)
4529. *Two Weeks Notice* (♥ ♥)
4530. *Up Close and Personal* (♥ ♥)
4531. *A Walk to Remember* (♥ ♥ ♥ ♥)
4532. *The Wedding Date* (♥ ♥ ♥)
4533. *The Wedding Singer* (♥ ♥ ♥)
4534. *West Side Story* (♥ ♥ ♥ ♥ ♥)
4535. *What Women Want* (♥ ♥)
4536. *While You Were Sleeping* (♥ ♥)
4537. *Wuthering Heights* (♥ ♥ ♥ ♥)

4538. If you live in the city, take a drive in the country
4539. If you live in the country, visit the nearest city
4540. If you're landlocked, visit the coast
4541. If you're coastal, find a mountain to hike
4542. If you're shy, join Toastmasters together

4543.　If you have two left feet, take dance lessons
4544.　If you're afraid of flying, take a cross-country trip by train

4545.　Listen better
4546.　Call often
4547.　Play more
4548.　Work less
4549.　Talk quietly

4550.　Check out netflix.com
4551.　The Splash-Filled "Bubblebath-For-Two" Coupon: Included: Candlelight, champagne, bubblebath, and one wet and willing partner

Favorite Love Songs from 1950

4552.　"A Bushel and a Peck"
4553.　"Be My Love," Mario Lanza
4554.　"I Wanna Be Loved," The Andrews Sisters
4555.　"It's So Nice to Have a Man Around the House"

4556.　Feel more alive: Read *Keep Your Brain Alive: 83 Neurobic Exercises*, by Lawrence Katz and Manning Rubin
4557.　Buy him a new set of tires for his car
4558.　Arrange Sunday brunch at home (serve a *gourmet feast* for your partner)

4559.　Clip newspaper comics that reflect your relationship
4560.　A "Peanuts" comic about Charlie Brown's unrequited love
4561.　A "Blondie" comic about Dagwood's bumbling but true love

4562. A "Rose Is Rose" comic about making daily life romantic
4563. A "Single Slices" comic about the adventures of singledom
4564. A "Zippy" comic about some bizarre aspect of love
4565. Mail one of these comics to your partner
4566. Tape some comics to the refrigerator door
4567. Fold a comic into his/her wallet

Relationship Skills to Master
If You Want an A+ Relationship

Take the "Relationship Report Card": Grade yourself and your partner (A+ through F, like in school):

4568. Affection _____
4569. Arguing skills _____
4570. Attitude _____
4571. Commitment _____
4572. Communication _____
4573. Considerate _____
4574. Couple thinking _____
4575. Creativity _____
4576. Empathy _____
4577. Flexibility _____
4578. Friendship _____
4579. Generosity _____
4580. Gift-giving skills _____
4581. Honesty _____
4582. Household management _____
4583. Listening skills _____
4584. Lovemaking _____
4585. Patience _____

4586. Playfulness _____
4587. Romance _____
4588. Self-awareness _____
4589. Self-esteem _____
4590. Sense of humor _____
4591. Sensitivity _____
4592. Spontaneity _____
4593. Tolerance _____

Guide to Grading:
A = Passionate, exciting, fulfilling; not perfect but clearly excellent
B = Very good, solid, better-than-most, consistent
C = Average, adequate, acceptable, okay, ho-hum, static
D = Below average, bad but not hopeless
F = Hopeless, dangerous; tried, didn't work
♥ You grade yourself and your partner
♥ Get your partner to grade him/herself and you
♥ Compare and discuss your grades; you'll gain great insight into your relationship
♥ Celebrate everything from a B- to an A+
♥ Work to improve your C's and D's

4594. "There is need for variety in sex, but not in love."
~ Theodor Reik
4595. Overlook your partner's faults
4596. Toss a coin in a fountain and make a romantic wish together

4597. The note: "You are the light of my life"

4598. The songs: "You Are the Sunshine of My Life," by
Stevie Wonder (1973)
4599. "Sunrise Serenade," by Glenn Miller (1939)
4600. "You Are My Sunshine," by Jimmie Davis (1940)
4601. "Sunshine of Your Love," by Cream (1968)

4602. A gift women want: *Elegant* lingerie
4603. A present men want to give women: *Sexy* lingerie

4604. Never, never, *never* nag. Use positive reinforcement.
It really works
4605. Eat dinner at the best Chinese restaurant around
4606. Play Glenn Miller's "In the Mood" to let him know
you're in the mood
4607. Enemy of Love: Boredom

Favorite Love Songs from 1951
4608. "Because of You," Tony Bennett
4609. "I Get Ideas"
4610. "My Heart Cries for You," Mitch Miller
4611. "The Glory of Love," Five Keys
4612. "Would I Love You (Love You, Love You)," Patti Page
4613. "Pretty-Eyed Baby," Jo Stafford & Frankie Laine

4614. Climb Mount Washington
4615. Hire a pianist to play during dinner at home
4616. Give a bouquet of *edible* flowers! (Tiger lilies, zucchini
flowers, marigolds)
4617. "Whatever our souls are made of, his and mine are
the same." ~ Emily Bronte

4618.   Gift & Date Idea: Get the song "Endless Love," by
         Diana Ross & Lionel Richie—
4619.   And rent the movie *Endless Love*, featuring the song

Classic Love Songs

4620.   "All of Me" (1931)
4621.   "As Time Goes By" (1943)
4622.   "I Can't Give You Anything but Love" (1928)
4623.   "I Love You for Sentimental Reasons" (1945)
4624.   "I'm Getting Sentimental Over You" (1932)
4625.   "I'm in the Mood for Love" (1935)
4626.   "Love Is a Many Splendored Thing" (1955)
4627.   "Love Me Tender," (1956)
4628.   "The Man I Love" (1924)
4629.   "Moon River" (1961)
4630.   "My Funny Valentine" (1937)
4631.   "Some Enchanted Evening" (1949)

4632.   Try being *totally positive* for one entire week
4633.   No complaining allowed
4634.   Read *A Complaint-Free World*, by Will Bowen

4635.   Prove your love through your actions—not your
         words
4636.   "Look at a person's light, not their lampshade."
         ~ Jerry Jampolsky
4637.   Keep a stash of her favorite candy hidden from the kids
4638.   Go to one of Emeril Lagasse's restaurants:
         www.emerils.com

4639.   Eskimo kiss (rub noses)

4640. The only time "getting the last word in" works is when those words are "I love you"

4641. Spend a second honeymoon at a picturesque Italian villa

4642. For parents only: Spend an entire afternoon photographing your family

4643. Teach your kids about love through the example of your own relationship

4644. Go camping instead of taking an expensive vacation

4645. Create public signals to let your lover know you're hot for him/her...

4646. Hum "your song" in her ear

4647. Say, "It's getting *awfully hot* in here..."

4648. Scratch your left ear with your right index finger

4649. Quote a Shakespearian sonnet

4650. Or have one rendered in calligraphy

4651. Sonnet 18 begins, "Shall I compare thee to a summer's day?"

4652. Re-write the sonnet to reflect the two of you

Love Tips for *Parents*

4653. Don't refer to each other as "Mom" and "Dad"

4654. Remember: You're still *lovers*, as well as parents

4655. Do make time for each other—At least two dates per month

4656. Don't turn yourself into a martyr for the sake of your kids

4657. Remember: Parents have a *right* to privacy from their kids

4658. Do learn from your children: The joy and wonder of life!

4659. Don't feel guilty for wanting to escape from your kids occasionally
4660. Do find great babysitters: Train 'em, and pay 'em well!
4661. Do find someone who can babysit on *school nights*, too
4662. When out on a date together, refrain from talking about the kids
4663. Don't smother your kids—They need space, too
4664. Take brief vacations away from the kids
4665. Do make more time by *streamlining* household chores
4666. Have a "quickie" while your kids watch TV
4667. Make love while your kids nap
4668. Don't live your life *for* your kids, but *with* them
4669. Do be loving role models for your children

4670. Treat your partner like royalty
4671. Treat her to her favorite sundae
4672. Treat him to his favorite sweet treat
4673. Treat your partner with a sexual surprise

4674. Rollerblade
4675. Stay at the fanciest hotel in Budapest: Gellert
4676. Never, never, *never* forget your partner's birthday
4677. Don't hold your frustrations inside until they explode all at once
4678. Compare your stated priorities with how you actually spend your time
4679. "One advantage of marriage is that, when you fall out of love with her or he falls out of love with you, it keeps you together until you fall in again." ~ Judith Viorst
4680. Play in a playground

4681. Play a romantic fantasy character
4682. Mold Play-Doh into a heart

4683. Count shooting stars together
4684. Count the number of days you've been married
4685. Count the number of days you've been a couple
4686. Count your blessings
4687. Count the number of times you've made love

4688. Togetherness = One milkshake, two straws
4689. Go on a *third* honeymoon

4690. Fly to Hawaii
4691. Fly to Venice
4692. Fly to Paris
4693. Let your imagination fly
4694. Fly in a glider
4695. Fly in a blimp
4696. Fly a kite

Favorite Love Songs from 1952

4697. "Hold Me, Thrill Me, Kiss Me," Karen Chandler
4698. "How Do You Speak to an Angel"
4699. "Wish You Were Here," Eddie Fisher
4700. "You Belong to Me," Jo Stafford

4701. Give him a cap from his favorite hockey team
4702. "And yet, a single night of universal love could save everything." ~ Roland Giguere
4703. Buy the ingredients and plan a sushi night
4704. Celebrate with a special bottle of *expensive* wine

4705. Fill a bag of M&M's with all green ones—seal it up and give it to your partner

4706. Give fine Belgian chocolate

4707. Get a poster in her favorite artistic style for her

4708. Upgrade his favorite software

Dos and Don'ts of Sexual Fantasies

Exploring sexual fantasies is a great way to spice up your love life

4709. Do go all out—costumes, props, etc.

4710. Don't take it too seriously

4711. Do "stay in character"

4712. Don't share your fantasy with *anyone*!

4713. Do go along with your partner's imagination

4714. Don't break the mood

4715. Do plan "story lines"

4716. Don't push your shy partner too far or too fast

4717. Do stretch your "comfort zone"

4718. Ask him/her to pick a number between one and ten thousand—then consult this book, and *do* that item!

4719. (If the chosen item is impossible, subtract his/her age from the number and perform *that* number!)

4720. Learn from your mistakes

Best Love Songs by The Beatles

4721. "All My Loving"

4722. "And I Love Her"

4723. "I Want to Hold Your Hand"

4724. "P.S. I Love You"

4725. "She's a Woman"
4726. "Something"
4727. "The Long and Winding Road"

4728. Have breakfast in front of a roaring fire
4729. The "Weekend Getaway" Coupon: Here's the deal: You get to choose the weekend, and the coupon-issuer gets to choose the location
4730. Women: Remember, men like flowers, too!
4731. Sexy movie alert: *The Unbearable Lightness of Being*
4732. Do something wonderful and out of character
4733. Thank God for bringing the two of you together
4734. Attend Bible classes together
4735. Once you've mastered foreplay, add "afterplay" to your repertoire
4736. Sleep in a feather bed with a down comforter
4737. Give him hockey tickets taped to a puck

4738. Buy a case of champagne. Label each of the twelve bottles…
4739. "His birthday"
4740. "Her birthday"
4741. "Christmas/Hanukkah/Holidays"
4742. "Anniversary (of meeting)"
4743. "Anniversary (of wedding)"
4744. "Groundhog Day"
4745. "For a midnight snack"
4746. "Before making love"
4747. "Celebrate a work achievement"
4748. "The first snowfall of the year"
4749. "For making up after a fight"

4750.   "The first day of Spring"

4751.   "We are shaped and fashioned by what we love."
~ Johann Wolfgang von Goethe

4752.   See your relationship as a place to exercise your creativity

4753.   Use a flower on the pillow as a signal that you want to make love

4754.   Learn a *great* dance routine á la Fred Astaire and Ginger Rogers

4755.   Write "I love you" in skywriting

4756.   Get a vanity license plate with a secret love code

4757.   The "101 Kisses" Coupon: Redeemable for 101 Hershey's Kisses. Coupon-giver's treat!

4758.   View rainbows by moonlight at Cumberland Falls State Park in Kentucky

4759.   Secretly save money for your 50th anniversary celebration

4760.   Leave *clues* about where and when you'll meet for a special date

4761.   "Actions speak louder than words"

4762.   Take action right now—don't wait another five minutes!

4763.   Turn off the TV, turn on the radio, and dance in your living room

4764.   Pop open a bottle of cheap champagne—*right now*—just to celebrate your love

4765.   Include one romantic gesture on your To Do List every week

4766.   Act like you did when you first fell in love

4767. Take a walk together after dinner every evening

Your 3 Resources for Expressing Love

4768. Time—A very limited resource; this is why it's so precious
4769. Money—Also a limited resource; handy for gifts, travel, etc.
4770. Creativity—Your *unlimited* resource; fun and often makes up for lack of time and money

Favorite Love Songs from 1953

4771. "And This Is My Beloved"
4772. "My Love, My Love"
4773. "No Other Love," Perry Como
4774. "Secret Love"
4775. "That's Amore," Dean Martin

4776. On your anniversary, create a sexual gift based on the number of years you've been together
4777. On your 3rd anniversary—take a three-day "Sexual Holiday"
4778. On your 10th anniversary—give her ten "Orgasm Coupons"
4779. On your 16th anniversary—give him sixteen kisses— on sixteen different body parts

Ways to Really Be a *Couple* in Public

4780. Always make your "entrance" arm-in-arm
4781. Wear outfits that match in a subtle way
4782. Compliment her in front of her friends
4783. Hold her chair for her at the table
4784. Whisper your pet name to her

4785. Public Displays of Affection
4786. Wear matching baseball caps
4787. Brush against him in a sexually suggestive way
4788. Open doors for her with an extra little *flourish*
4789. Hold hands
4790. Give him a seductive smile
4791. Order for her when dining out
4792. Wink at him from across the room
4793. Blow her a kiss
4794. Buy her one rose from a street vendor

4795. Give your partner room to breathe, but always be there for him/her
4796. Unlearn: Your superior attitude about being logical and reasonable
4797. Call her at work and say, "Is this the office of the most beautiful woman in the world?"
4798. Remember: Being happy together is a *decision*

Ways to Take Care of His Heart

4799. Send him a photo of the two of you that will bring a smile to his face
4800. Make love so vigorously that you give him an aerobic workout!
4801. Give him *low-fat* chocolates
4802. Learn CPR together
4803. Watch a movie that you know will touch him
4804. Exercise with him—and wear a skimpy spandex outfit to get his heart racing!
4805. Read *The Marriage Benefit: The Surprising Rewards of Staying Together*, by Mark O'Connell

4806. Read *Eatingwell's Comfort Foods Made Healthy: The Classic Makeovers Cookbook*, by Jessie Price and The EatingWell Editors

4807. Have him reduce the fat in his diet by 75%

4808. "Husbands are like fires—they go out when unattended." ~ Zsa Zsa Gabor

4809. Attend to his wants, his needs, his quirky uniqueness

4810. Don't let your kids consume all of your time and energy

4811. Tonight: Do one little thing that you know would *delight* him

Listening Skills for Lovers

4812. Give your lover your *undivided* attention

4813. Read between the lines

4814. Eliminate the phrase "Yes, but…"

4815. Don't interrupt your partner

4816. Practice empathy

4817. Suspend judgment

4818. Make lots of eye contact

4819. Listen for the *emotional* content—

4820. As well as the *informational* content of what's said

4821. Give the benefit of the doubt

4822. Listen to *understand*—not to *rebut*

4823. Listen with patience

4824. Allow there to be silences in your conversations

4825. Listen with your heart, not your head

4826. Listen carefully to the *tone* of your partner's voice

4827. Pay attention to *body* language

4828.   Review your priorities monthly: Make sure love is in the top three
4829.   Attend the Valentine's Day/mid-winter carnival in St. Paul, Minnesota
4830.   "Self-love is not only necessary and good, it is a prerequisite for loving others." ~ Rollo May
4831.   Take care of your partner's physical, emotional, and spiritual needs
4832.   Celebrate holidays together
4833.   Dab his favorite perfume between your breasts

Qualities That 5,000 Women
Want *Most* in Husbands

4834.   Sensitivity
4835.   Romantic
4836.   Good listener
4837.   Strong character
4838.   Empathy
4839.   Intelligence
4840.   Shares his feelings
4841.   Sense of humor
4842.   Understanding
4843.   Responsiveness

4844.   Dads: Add Mother's Day to your list of Obligatory Romance Days
4845.   Moms: Make him "King for a Day" on Father's Day

4846.   Favorite gifts for men: Big-screen TVs
4847.   Favorite gifts for men: Leather briefcases
4848.   Favorite gifts for men: Hobby-related stuff

4849. For your golf nut: You caddy for him/her!

4850. Rent a canoe

4851. Give her symphony tickets taped to the CD of the featured selection

4852. "See everything; overlook a great deal; correct a little." ~ Pope John XXIII

4853. Go camping with rented equipment

4854. Collect mementos of your honeymoon

4855. Create a collage of menus, tickets, postcards, etc., from your honeymoon

4856. Spend a *second* honeymoon in the same place you visited on your *first*

4857. (Same hotel—same *room*!)

4858. Tell the hotel manager: You'll receive extra special treatment!!

4859. Guys: Remember—Cuddling is just as important as sex

4860. Gals: Remember—Sex is just as important as cuddling

4861. Be your mate's biggest fan: Write him/her a fan letter

4862. "Real love begins where nothing is expected in return." ~ Antoine de Saint-Exupery

4863. Visit the New England Carousel Museum: www.thecarouselmuseum.org

---

4864. Become famous for your *oddball* parties…

4865. Throw a "scavenger hunt" party

4866. Dress as football players and cheerleaders for a Super Bowl party

4867. Invite friends over to watch *The Wizard of Oz*
4868. Throw Solstice parties in the Summer and Winter

4869. English: "I want to make love with you"
4870. French: "Je voudrais faire l'amour avec toi"
4871. Italian: "Vorrei far l'amore con te"
4872. German: "Ich möchte mit dir schlafen"
4873. Spanish: "Quiero hacer el amor contigo"
4874. Portugese: "Eu quero fazer amor con você"

4875. Designate one week to improving your communication skills…
4876. Monday: Get *You Just Don't Understand*, by Deborah Tannen
4877. Tuesday: Do two exercises from the book
4878. Wednesday: Talk about the times you felt most connected
4879. Thursday: Identify your biggest communication problem as a couple
4880. Friday: Reverse roles: What insights arise?
4881. Saturday: Practice patience!
4882. Sunday: Communicate with body language only

4883. Buy her turquoise jewelry
4884. Purchase an automatic car starter for her for those cold days & nights
4885. Buy two Snuggies and spend the rest of the day cuddling: www.getsnuggie.com

4886. Be her hero
4887. Be his playmate

4888. Be her friend
4889. Be his confidante
4890. Be her servant
4891. Be his gopher
4892. Be her cheerleader
4893. Be his caddy
4894. Be her fantasy
4895. Be his support

Romantic Tips for Guys Only

4896. Let her warm her cold feet on you in bed
4897. Treat her like a *queen* while she's pregnant
4898. Wear a bow tie and cummerbund—and nothing else
4899. Put the toilet seat down!
4900. Hold her face gently in your hands when you kiss
4901. Don't just roll over after making love
4902. Never, never, *never* give her *practical* gifts
4903. Read a few women's magazines—for some insight into the female psyche
4904. If you want her to wear nice lingerie to bed, *you start* by wearing silk boxers
4905. Shave on Saturday night
4906. Be her birth coach
4907. Share the TV remote control with her
4908. Get her her *own* TV remote control
4909. Don't be a slob in the bathroom
4910. Rinse the sink after you shave
4911. *Never* compare her to past girlfriends
4912. When dining out, *always* order dessert, and let her nibble off your plate
4913. Read *Cuddle Sutra*, by Rob Grader and imitate the poses

4914. Send a clever email to her parents, asking permission to marry their daughter
4915. Never, never, *never* joke about her PMS
4916. Quit the macho act when you're with your mate
4917. Be her "Calendar Boy": Paste pictures of yourself on a Chippendale calendar for her
4918. Bring her the little soaps and shampoos from hotels

4919. Gals: Get a "fantasy photo" taken of yourself
4920. Lingerie portraits are most popular
4921. Followed by "fantasy outfit" and nude poses
4922. (This experience may boost your self-esteem, as you'll experience how *made-up* those fashion models are!)
4923. Have a large print made and framed
4924. Present it to him with a grand unveiling ceremony
4925. (Give him a small print to carry in his wallet!)

Favorite Love Songs from 1954

4926. "Answer Me, My Love," Nat King Cole
4927. "If I Give My Heart to You," Doris Day
4928. "Little Things Mean A Lot," Kitty Kallen

4929. Acknowledge when your partner is right
4930. Enjoy a sunrise picnic
4931. The Bubblebath-For-Two Coupon: You know what to do.
4932. "The heart has its reasons which reason knows nothing of." ~ Blaise Pascal
4933. Enemy of Love: Lack of respect

Fun & Quirky Ways to
Get to Know Each Other Better

4934. Share favorite childhood memories
4935. Visit your childhood home together
4936. "Fantasy Window Shopping:" Talk about *why* you'd buy various items
4937. Play "Show and Tell" using a beloved item from your childhood
4938. Have your astrological charts analyzed
4939. See what a Ouija Board has to say about your relationship
4940. Learn to read Tarot Cards together
4941. Visit a gypsy fortune teller together
4942. Learn to analyze horoscopes, and do readings for the two of you
4943. Have your handwriting analyzed
4944. Learn the art of handwriting analysis
4945. Visit sites of special meaning to you
4946. Share stories of the childhood objects you still own
4947. Study and compare your anagrams
4948. Share stories from grammar school
4949. Share stories from college
4950. Share stories about your first job
4951. Tell your funniest stories
4952. Share your most embarrassing moments
4953. Share your moments of great insight
4954. Share your most painful moments
4955. Share the milestones of your life
4956. Talk about your favorite teacher
4957. Talk about your heroes
4958. Talk about your real-life role models

4959.   Talk about your fictional role models

4960.   On a whim, get a discount fare to Paris for the weekend

4961.   Experiment: Dress as sexy as you *dare*, for a date out with him

4962.   Use chocolate body paint

4963.   "Love is always revolutionary." ~ Andrei Voznesensky

4964.   Make love on the kitchen table

4965.   Enemy of Love: Prudishness

4966.   Classic Gift #1: Flowers

4967.   Classic Gift #2: Perfume

4968.   Classic Gift #3: Jewelry

4969.   Classic Gift #4: Champagne

4970.   Classic Gift #5: Chocolate

4971.   Classic Gift #6: Lingerie

4972.   Classic Gift #7: Dinner

4973.   Classic Gift #8: Music

4974.   Classic Gift #9: Theater

4975.   Classic Gift #10: Art

4976.   Classic crooning from Johnny Mathis…

4977.   Selected CDs: *All About Love; Wonderful*

4978.   *Too Much, Too Little, Too Late*

4979.   *In the Still of the Night*

4980.   Guys: Do something *for* her that you hate to do

4981.   It only counts as a loving gesture if you do it cheerfully and without complaint

4982.   Go grocery shopping, wash the dishes, weed the garden

4983. When traveling, give a rose for each day you'll be away
4984. Write down your dreams and wishes for your future together
4985. Splurge at Crabtree & Evelyn
4986. Be patient
4987. Stay in a restored palace in Madrid: Santa Mauro

4988. Treat your lover to Cedar Point, the rollercoaster capital of the world (Ohio), and the following ones
4989. "Thunderbolt" at Kennywood in Pittsburgh, Pennsylvania
4990. "Magnum XL-200" at Cedar Point in Sandusky, OH
4991. "Cyclone" at Astroland in Brooklyn, New York
4992. "Megafobia" at Oakwood Coaster Country in Pembrokeshire, Wales
4993. "The Beast" at Paramount's Kings Island in Kings Island, OH

4994. Gift & Date Idea: Get the song "When Doves Cry," by Prince—
4995. And rent the movie *Purple Rain*, featuring the song
4996. And let yourselves be inspired to create a night of hot sex

The 12 Birthflowers—and Their Symbolic Meanings

Accompany the bouquet with a note about the symbolic meaning of his/her birthflower:

4997. January: Snowdrop—*purity*
4998. February: Carnation—*courage*
4999. March: Violet—*modesty*

5000. April: Lily—*virtue*
5001. May: Wisteria—*hope*
5002. June: Rose—*simplicity*
5003. July: Daisy—*innocence*
5004. August: Poppy—*peace*
5005. September: Morning Glory—*contentment*
5006. October: Cosmos—*ambition*
5007. November: Chrysanthemum—*cheerfulness*
5008. December: Holly—*foresight*

5009. Spread suntan lotion on her back for her—*slowly and sensuously*
5010. Togetherness = One iPod, two headsets
5011. "There isn't any formula or method. You learn to love by loving." ~ Aldous Huxley
5012. Center yourself, both physically and emotionally: Take an "Awareness Through Movement" Feldenkrais class: www.feldenkrais.com

---

Things You Should
Know About Your Partner

Exploring these topics will help you get to know your partner's likes and dislikes a little bit better. Knowing these things will bring you closer together and help you express your love more effectively and buy more appropriate gifts

5013. Favorite color
5014. Lucky number
5015. Favorite flower
5016. Favorite author
5017. Favorite book (fiction)
5018. Favorite book (non-fiction)

5019. Favorite fairy tale
5020. Favorite children's book
5021. Favorite Bible passage
5022. Favorite saying
5023. Favorite proverb
5024. Favorite poem
5025. Favorite poet
5026. Favorite song
5027. Favorite singer
5028. Favorite musical band
5029. Favorite *kind* of music
5030. Favorite dance tune
5031. Favorite romantic song
5032. Favorite slow dance tune
5033. Favorite rock 'n roll song
5034. Favorite ballad
5035. Favorite country song
5036. Favorite Gospel song
5037. Favorite jazz number
5038. Favorite R&B tune
5039. Favorite songwriter
5040. Favorite magazine
5041. Favorite meal
5042. Favorite food
5043. Favorite vegetable
5044. Favorite fruit
5045. Favorite cookie
5046. Favorite ice cream
5047. Favorite kind of chocolate
5048. Favorite snack food
5049. Favorite restaurant (expensive)

5050. Favorite restaurant (cheap)
5051. Favorite fast food joint
5052. Favorite TV show (current)
5053. Favorite TV show (old)
5054. Favorite comedian
5055. Favorite actor (living)
5056. Favorite actor (of any era)
5057. Favorite actress (living)
5058. Favorite actress (of any era)
5059. Favorite movie of all time
5060. Favorite adventure movie
5061. Favorite erotic movie
5062. Favorite romantic comedy
5063. Favorite comedy film
5064. Favorite action movie
5065. Favorite Broadway play
5066. Favorite musical
5067. Favorite show tune
5068. Favorite breed of dog
5069. Favorite breed of cat
5070. Favorite animal
5071. Favorite comic strip
5072. Favorite comic character
5073. Favorite TV cartoon
5074. Favorite TV cartoon character
5075. Favorite artist
5076. Favorite style of artwork
5077. Favorite painting
5078. Favorite sculpture
5079. Favorite hero/heroine/role model
5080. Favorite heroine

5081. Role model (actual person)
5082. Role model (fictional)
5083. Favorite athlete
5084. Favorite sport (to watch)
5085. Favorite Olympic sport
5086. Favorite sports teams
5087. Favorite board game
5088. Favorite foreplay activity (to receive)
5089. Favorite foreplay activity (to perform)
5090. Favorite lovemaking position
5091. Favorite sexy outfit (for partner)
5092. Favorite sexy outfit (for self)
5093. Favorite erotic fantasy
5094. Favorite time of day to make love
5095. Favorite place on your body to be touched erotically
5096. Favorite music to make love to
5097. Favorite season
5098. Favorite time of day
5099. Favorite holiday
5100. Favorite hobby
5101. Favorite type of jewelry
5102. Preferred jewelry (silver or gold?)
5103. Preferred clothing (for yourself)
5104. Preferred clothing (for your partner)
5105. Favorite designer
5106. Favorite erotic clothing (for yourself)
5107. Favorite erotic clothing (for your partner)
5108. Dream vacation spot
5109. Favorite vacation activity
5110. Favorite foreign city
5111. Favorite foreign country

5112.   Favorite wine
5113.   Favorite champagne
5114.   Favorite beer
5115.   Favorite soft drink
5116.   Favorite way to spend an afternoon
5117.   Favorite room in your home
5118.   Favorite woman's perfume
5119.   Favorite men's cologne
5120.   Favorite brand of make-up
5121.   Favorite aroma
5122.   Favorite fictional character
5123.   Favorite historical personality
5124.   Best gift you've ever received
5125.   Favorite way to relax
5126.   Favorite way to get energized
5127.   Favorite store
5128.   Favorite side of the bed
5129.   Favorite TV sitcom
5130.   Favorite TV drama
5131.   Favorite joke
5132.   Favorite classical composer
5133.   Favorite symphony
5134.   Favorite opera
5135.   Favorite album
5136.   Favorite car (make & year)
5137.   Favorite *color* for a car
5138.   Favorite country
5139.   Favorite city
5140.   Favorite clothing designer
5141.   Favorite dance
5142.   Favorite gemstone

5143. Favorite pet
5144. Best subject in school
5145. Favorite Girl Scout cookie
5146. Favorite day of the week
5147. Favorite month of the year

5148. Give a movie poster of his/her favorite actor
5149. "Perform random acts of kindness and senseless acts of beauty." ~ Anne Herbert
5150. Visit a gift shop once every two months
5151. Consciously *choose* to be in a good mood: They're contagious
5152. Every year, get a Christmas tree ornament with special meaning

5153. When she's eight months pregnant, have a professional portrait taken of the two of you
5154. When your baby is six, twelve, and eighteen months old, have family portraits taken

5155. Vacation in spots inspired by his/her favorite books and films
5156. If your partner is a fan of *Midnight in the Garden of Good and Evil* visit Savannah, Georgia
5157. Take your *Braveheart* to Scotland
5158. Fans of *Somewhere in Time* vacation at the Grand Hotel, on Mackinac Island, Michigan
5159. Visit the *Anne of Green Gables* house on Prince Edward Island
5160. Fans of Disney, see *Toy Story* come to life on the Disney Cruise ship: http://disneycruise.disney.go.com

5161. Tour the covered bridges in Madison County, Iowa
5162. Take a Mediterranean *Odyssey*, and visit many of the Greek islands
5163. Take inspiration from the film *Casablanca*—and take an exotic vacation to Casablanca, Moracco

5164. Write a love poem in haiku style
5165. Set her ringtone to a song that reminds her of you
5166. "Happiness is not a state to arrive at, but a manner of traveling." ~ Samuel Johnson
5167. Eat dinner at the best restaurant in the state
5168. Give diamonds!
5169. On a whim, get a discount fare to *somewhere* for the weekend

Favorite Love Songs from 1955

5170. "Earth Angel," Penguins
5171. "Only You," The Platters
5172. "Unchained Melody," Al Hibbler & Les Baxter
5173. "Yellow Rose of Texas," Mitch Miller

5174. Never go to bed mad
5175. Never part without kissing
5176. Never insult your partner
5177. Never complain to your family about your mate
5178. Never betray a confidence
5179. Never criticize your partner in public
5180. Never say never

Best Love Songs by Diana Ross & The Supremes

5181. "Ain't No Mountain High Enough"

5182. "Baby Love"
5183. "When You Tell Me That You Love Me"
5184. "I'm Gonna Make You Love Me" (with the Temptations)
5185. "Stop! In the Name of Love"
5186. "Touch Me in the Morning"
5187. "You Can't Hurry Love"

5188. "You cannot do a kindness too soon—for you never know how soon it will be too late." ~ Ralph Waldo Emerson
5189. Love: Say it, express it, do it—*now!*
5190. *Carpe diem*—"Seize the day"
5191. Mail confetti in an envelope along with a note that simply says, "Let's celebrate!"
5192. Hide a love note in his pants pockets

5193. Close your eyes and imagine what your lover looks like
5194. Close your eyes to your partner's shortcomings

5195. Say this: "I love you"
5196. Repeat four times daily for the rest of your life

5197. Write a one-stanza love poem
5198. Give it to your partner on your anniversary
5199. Add one new stanza every year
5200. On your 25th anniversary, have it rendered in calligraphy
5201. On your 50th anniversary, have it set to music and recorded!

5202.   Open your heart and soul to each other

5203.   Learn to play "Heart and Soul" on the piano

5204.   Go to Rome for dinner

5205.   Remember: People do what they do out of either love or fear

---

The Most Romantic Broadway Musicals of All Time

5206.   *A Little Night Music*

5207.   *Aspects of Love*

5208.   *Brigadoon*

5209.   *Carousel*

5210.   *Fiddler on the Roof*

5211.   *Funny Girl*

5212.   *Grease*

5213.   *Guys and Dolls*

5214.   *Hello Dolly*

5215.   *Kiss Me Kate*

5216.   *Man of La Mancha*

5217.   *My Fair Lady*

5218.   *Oklahoma*

5219.   *Phantom of the Opera*

5220.   *Show Boat*

5221.   *Sound of Music*

5222.   *South Pacific*

5223.   *Sweet Charity*

5224.   *The Fantastics*

5225.   *The King and I*

5226.   *West Side Story*

5227.   Present her with a fine gold locket with your photo inside

5228. Blindfold her and make slow, sensual love to her
5229. Enemy of Love: Generic gestures

5230. Give your heart
5231. Give it a chance
5232. Give her your entire income tax refund
5233. Give him your best sexy smile
5234. Give in to your feelings
5235. Give without expecting anything in return
5236. Give in during an argument
5237. Give up your inhibitions
5238. Give your partner the benefit of the doubt
5239. Give all you've got

Sexy Games for Lovers to Play

5240. Strip poker
5241. Strip chess
5242. Nude Twister
5243. I Dare You
5244. Scrabble Sex
5245. One-A-Day
5246. Naughty Charades
5247. Talk Dirty to Me
5248. Elevator Challenge
5249. Taking Turns
5250. In Public
5251. Instant Gratification
5252. Delayed Gratification

5253. Create "signals" to let your lover know you're in the mood for love…

5254. Play anything by Billie Holiday on the stereo
5255. Have "your song" playing when he/she returns home
5256. For men: Casually say, "I think I'll shave tonight…"
5257. A pillow that says "TONIGHT" on one side, and "LATER" on the other

5258. Start with Elizabeth Browning's poem, "How do I love thee, let me count the ways"
5259. Re-write it in your own words
5260. Write a numbered list of all the ways you love your partner

5261. "Love is a talkative passion." ~ Bishop Wilson
5262. Spend a lazy Sunday afternoon together
5263. "You never know till you try to reach them how accessible men are; but you must approach each man by the right door." ~ Henry Ward Beecher

Ways to Love a Libra
(24 September–23 October)

5264. Libra is an *air* sign: Cater to his/her light, funloving nature
5265. Gift tip: Romantic and elegant
5266. Libras love games
5267. Lingerie
5268. Get a wide selection of romantic music
5269. Hydrangeas; apple trees
5270. Delicate or sweet foods
5271. The exotic beauty of Egypt
5272. Wrap gifts in bright blue and pink

5273. Go horseback riding together
5274. Listen to the CD *Amore: The Great Italian Love Arias*
5275. Rent a yacht and crew for a Caribbean cruise
5276. For your golf nut: A dozen new golf balls

5277. Take your mate somewhere *special*...
5278. Has she seen all of her favorite singers *in concert*?
5279. Has he heard all of his favorite symphonies played *live*?
5280. Has she been to the *best* restaurant in her *favorite* city?
5281. Has he seen his favorite team play *live*?
5282. Has she been to the *Broadway opening* of a new play?
5283. Has he been to the birthplace of his favorite actor?

5284. Overwhelm him/her
5285. Honor him/her
5286. Romance him/her
5287. Woo him/her
5288. Date him/her
5289. Feed him/her
5290. Stimulate him/her
5291. Nurture him/her
5292. Understand him/her
5293. Support him/her
5294. Calm him/her
5295. Surprise him/her
5296. Delight him/her

5297. Favorite gifts for women: Bath oils
5298. Favorite gifts for women: Scented lotions
5299. Favorite gifts for women: Potpourri
5300. Favorite gifts for women: Designer purses

Funniest (Yet True!) Things Ever Said About Love

5301. "People who throw kisses are hopelessly lazy."
~ Bob Hope

5302. "It all comes down to who does the dishes."
~ Norman Mailer

5303. "Love is the triumph of imagination over intelligence." ~ H. L. Mencken

5304. "Why does a woman work ten years to change a man's habits, and then complain that he's not the man she married?" ~ Barbra Streisand

5305. For your beach bunny: Vacations at America's best beaches...

5306. Cannon Beach, Oregon

5307. Kapalua Beach, Maui, Hawaii

5308. Main Beach, East Hampton, New York

5309. East Beach, Santa Barbara, California

5310. Grayton Beach, Florida

5311. Sandspur, Bahia Honda Key, Florida

5312. Get to know your partner better by asking quirky questions—like, "If you were stranded on a desert island..."

5313. What three music CDs would you most like to have with you?

5314. What would you miss the most?

5315. How long do you think you would survive?

5316. Would you wear clothes?

5317. What three books would you want to bring?

Favorite Love Songs from 1956

5318. "After the Lights Go Down Low," Al Hibbler
5319. "Memories Are Made of This," Dean Martin
5320. "Mr. Wonderful," Peggy Lee
5321. "Since I Met You Baby," Ivory Joe Hunter
5322. "Tonight You Belong to Me," Patience & Prudence
5323. "You're Sensational"

5324. Enemy of Love: Bad attitude
5325. Rent a big screen TV for watching *Casablanca*
5326. Give him a truly wild tie
5327. Remember: A vacation is just a trip, but a honeymoon is a state-of-mind

---

5328. Giftwrap a wishbone in a jewelry box
5329. The note: "Wish you were here."

5330. Be curious
5331. Be kind
5332. Be giving
5333. Be courteous
5334. Be generous
5335. Be creative
5336. Be spontaneous
5337. Be funloving

5338. Give your partner choices:
5339. Classic or avant-garde?
5340. Conservative or outrageous?
5341. Public or private?
5342. Expensive or cheap?

5343. Modern or antique?
5344. Here or there?
5345. Loud or soft?
5346. Big or small?
5347. Light or dark?
5348. Fast or slow?
5349. Today or tomorrow?
5350. Active or lazy?
5351. One or many?
5352. Gold or silver?
5353. Now or later?
5354. Right or left?
5355. Red or blue?
5356. Day or night?

5357. Cover the entire floor of your living room with balloons
5358. Play "footsie" under the table
5359. Enemy of Love: Lack of role models
5360. Spend an entire *day* in bed together
5361. "To love is to receive a glimpse of heaven." ~ Karen Sunde

---

5362. While on vacation, tell everybody that you're *newlyweds* (You'll be treated *extra* special)
5363. In Italy, point to yourselves and say "Novelli sposi"
5364. In China, say "Xin hun"
5365. In Denmark, say "Nygifte"
5366. In France, say "Nouveaux mariés"
5367. In Germany, say "Hochzeitspaar"
5368. In Greece, say "Nionymphi"
5369. In Japan, say "Shin kon"
5370. In Portugal, say "Récem casados"

5371. In Russia, say "Novobrachnoe"
5372. In Spain, say "Recién casados"
5373. In Sweden, say "Nygifta"

5374. Pick seven random dates throughout the year, and make them *special* in a unique or odd way
5375. Label Day #1: "Play Day"
5376. Label Day #2: "Music Day"
5377. Label Day #3: "Food Day"
5378. Label Day #4: "Sex Day"
5379. Label Day #5: "Red Day"
5380. Label Day #6: "Humor Day"
5381. Label Day #7: "Surprise Day"
5382. Create three more "special days" that cater to your lover's interests

5383. Make reservations at a local bed-and-breakfast for Valentine's Day *a year in advance*
5384. The "Ultimate Full-Body Massage" Coupon: The coupon-issuer will give you a *one-hour, professional-style, full-body* massage
5385. Return to the spot with the most romantic view you've ever experienced
5386. "The loving are the daring." ~ Baynard Taylor
5387. Call him at work and tell him *in explicit detail* how you're going to make love to him tonight

5388. Be prepared! Always have on hand:
5389. A bottle of champagne
5390. Some candles
5391. A little "trinket gift"

5392. A romantic greeting card
5393. A humorous greeting card
5394. A lingerie gift
5395. A CD of romantic music

5396. Take a horse-drawn carriage ride through Central Park in New York
5397. "Love is the silent saying and saying of a single name." ~ Mignon McLaughlin
5398. Fall asleep holding hands
5399. Visit www.hahaha.com for info on the Montreal comedy festival
5400. Give him mud flaps for his truck featuring his favorite cartoon character
5401. For parents only: Read a book on parenting together
5402. Mail him a pack of matches. Attach a note: "I'm hot for you"
5403. Whenever you buy new lingerie, model it for him

Songs to Help You Express Your Feelings: *Loneliness & Missing You*

5404. "Far Away," Carole King
5405. "I Miss You," Klymaxx
5406. "I Miss You Like Crazy," Natalie Cole
5407. "Missing You Now," Michael Bolton
5408. "Missing You," Jim Reeves
5409. "Wishing You Were Here," Chicago
5410. "You've Lost That Lovin' Feeling," Daryl Hall & John Oates

5411. Lower your inhibitions

5412. Raise your expectations of yourself

5413. Make time to be alone together
5414. Turn off the TV, phone, and pager
5415. Escape from work, chores, and the computer
5416. Isolate yourselves from kids and pets

5417. Try being *totally accepting* of your partner for one entire week—
5418. No criticizing allowed
5419. Try being completely *non-judgmental* for one entire week—
5420. No preaching allowed

5421. If your mate is "past-oriented," he/she appreciates the sentimental and nostalgic—
5422. Save things, find mementos, focus on *meaning*
5423. If your mate is "now-oriented," he/she appreciates spontaneity and creativity—
5424. Be adventurous, be flexible, do lots of *little* things
5425. If your mate is "future-oriented," he/she appreciates planning and anticipation—
5426. Create surprises, plan ahead, make grand gestures

Ways to *Overdo It* for Your Lover

5427. Write a love poem—and compose one new stanza *every week*
5428. Get *every recording ever made* by his favorite musical group
5429. Make a little loving gesture *every day for a solid year*
5430. Get *every book* ever written by her favorite author

5431. Get *every movie* starring his favorite actor
5432. Get twenty-five pounds of her favorite candy
5433. Take her to see the movie *Titanic*—fifteen times
5434. Make love to him every night—until he asks you to stop
5435. Give her twelve dozen roses on Valentine's Day
5436. Write a list: "101 Reasons Why You're the Best"
5437. Write each reason on a separate square of paper
5438. Wrap them in a fancy gift box

5439. Remember: Your friendship will get you through when the love falters
5440. A "Quickie Back Massage" Coupon: Performed by the coupon-giver. Must be performed *immediately* upon relinquishment of this coupon
5441. Loosen up! Have *fun* in your relationship

5442. "The smallest good deed is better than the grandest good intention." ~ Duguet
5443. Wear scented body lotion
5444. Write a letter together to be opened by your children when they're fifty years old
5445. Make a distinction between "making love" and "having sex"—and make sure you do *both*
5446. Enemy of Love: Stinginess in general
5447. Serve breakfast in bed
5448. Send her a menu from the fancy restaurant you're taking her to

Ways to "Get It" by Mail

While you do have to shop, you don't necessarily have to go "shopping"

5449. African Market Catalog (arts, clothing): www.bestafricanmarket.com
5450. Comedy gifts: www.comedycentral.com/
5451. Elegant Beeswax Candles: www.elegantcandles.net
5452. For Counsel (for lawyers!): www.forcounsel.com
5453. Official PGA gifts: www.tourstop.com/
5454. Official hockey gifts: www.shop.nhl.com
5455. Into the Wind (kites 'n stuff): www.intothewind.com
5456. Levinger (reader's tools): http://www.levenger.com/
5457. The Lighter Side (funny stuff): www.lighterside.com
5458. ThinkGeek: http://www.thinkgeek.com/
5459. The Nature Store: www.naturestore.com
5460. Neiman Marcus (clothing & related): www.neimanmarcus.com
5461. Recollections (nostalgic): www.recollections.biz
5462. Rick's Movie Graphics (posters 'n stuff): www.ricksmovie.com
5463. Littleton Coin Company (¢): www.littletoncoin.com
5464. Sexy Shoes (*high* heels): www.sexyshoes.com
5465. The Smithsonian (curious items): www.si.edu
5466. Sporty's Catalog (sports-related): www.sportys.com
5467. Stave Puzzles (jigsaw puzzles): www.stavepuzzles.com
5468. Sundance (western & rustic): www.sundancecatalog.com
5469. Tailwinds (aviation): www.tailwinds.com
5470. Vermont Teddy Bear Co. (hand-made!): www.vermontteddybear.com
5471. Victorian Papers (elegant papers): victoriantradingco.com
5472. Williams-Sonoma (cook's tools): www.williams-sonoma.com
5473. Wireless (cool stuff): www.thewirelesscatalog.com

5474. The Wood Workers' Store (practical tools):
http://www.woodworkersshop.com/
5475. Worldwide Games (games & puzzles):
www.worldwidegames.com

5476. Catch her eye—and tell her you adore her
5477. "Can't Take My Eyes Off You," Frankie Valli
5478. "These Eyes," The Guess Who
5479. "For Your Eyes Only," Sheena Easton

Favorite Love Songs from 1957

5480. "All Shook Up!" Elvis Presley
5481. "An Affair to Remember"
5482. "April Love," Pat Boone

5483. Use her favorite stuffed animal in a romantic gesture
5484. Put love notes in a teddy bear's paws
5485. Put new jewelry on it
5486. Secretly pack it in her suitcase
5487. Mail it to her at work
5488. Hold it hostage for romantic favors

His Name in a Song: 12 Hits Named for Guys

5489. "Arthur's Theme (Best That You Can Do),"
Christopher Cross
5490. "Bennie and the Jets," Elton John
5491. "Big Bad John," Jimmy Dean
5492. "Bobby's Girl," Marcie B
5493. "Daniel," Elton John
5494. "Danny's Song," Anne Murray
5495. "Frankie," Connie Francis

5496. "Hats Off to Larry," Del Shannon
5497. "Johnny Angel," Shelley Fabares
5498. "Louie Louie," The Kingsmen
5499. "Michael," The Highwaymen
5500. "Mickey," Toni Basil

5501. *Fighting for Your Marriage: Positive Steps for Preventing Divorce and Preserving a Lasting Love (New & Revised)*, by Howard J. Markman, Scott M. Stanley, and Susan L. Blumberg
5502. *Do I Have to Give Up Me to Be Loved By You?* by Jordan & Margaret Paul
5503. *Is There Really Sex After Kids?* by Jill Savage
5504. *His Needs, Her Needs* by William F. Harley Jr.
5505. *Manslations: Decoding the Secret Language of Men*, by Jeff Mac
5506. *Do You Know Your Husband*, by Dan Carlinsky
5507. *Do You Know Your Wife*, by Dan Carlinsky

5508. Kiss hello
5509. Kiss goodbye
5510. Kiss a message in Morse Code
5511. Kiss a part of his/her body you've never kissed before
5512. Kiss in public
5513. Kiss and make up
5514. Kiss and "get down"

5515. Surf: http://www.foreignfilms.com/
5516. Hire a professional photographer to take tasteful-yet-sexy photos of you for your mate
5517. Start with the romantic basics, then *give 'em a twist!*

5518. Coordinate background music and special events
5519. Play Glenn Miller's "String of Pearls" when giving a string of pearls
5520. Play Barry Manilow's "Looks Like We Made It" when you've come through a rough time
5521. Play Simon and Garfunkel's "Bridge Over Troubled Waters" to thank your partner for being there for you
5522. Play Bad Company's "Feel Like Makin' Love" when…well, *you* know
5523. Play Kenny Rogers' "Through the Years" during a special anniversary celebration
5524. Play Harry Connick, Jr.'s version of "It Had to Be You" during an engagement party

5525. Write love notes on the kitchen blackboard
5526. Go on a picnic
5527. The "Multiple-Choice" Coupon: Choose one: 1) One soothing massage, 2) One romantic movie date, or 3) Dinner for two

5528. Give her perfume—
5529. And create a date to match its name:
5530. "Passion" perfume: Be passionate—And plan an evening of lovemaking
5531. "Tropics" perfume: Be exotic—Plan a vacation to tropical Trinidad
5532. "Destiny" perfume: Be prophetic—Write a poem about why it's your *destiny* to be together

5533. Splurge on a shopping spree at www.wbshop.com

5534. Give a balloon in his/her favorite color
5535. Kiss her gently to wake her
5536. Hire a local performer to serenade her
5537. "Love at the lips was touch as sweet as I could bear."
~ Robert Frost
5538. Enemy of Love: Selfishness
5539. Send an envelope full of nothing but love stamps
5540. Live *passionately* (*work* passionately, *play* passionately, *love* passionately)
5541. Take a holistic look at your lives and your love at the Chopra Center for Well Being, in La Jolla, California: www.chopra.com

***

5542. Themed gifts & date: A bottle of "Incognito" perfume
5543. And a CD by the group Incognito: *Positivity* or *Beneath the Surface*
5544. And create a *mysterious* date: Wear a disguise and go to a dim restaurant

***

"His" and "Hers" Ideas
5545. "His" and "Hers" matching motorcycles
5546. "His" and "Hers" matching T-shirts
5547. Have "His" and "Hers" overnight bags packed at all times
5548. "His" and "Hers" matching coffee mugs
5549. "His" and "Hers" monogrammed bath towels
5550. Carve "His" and "Hers" jack-o-lanterns at Halloween
5551. "His" and "Hers" rocking chairs
5552. "His" and "Hers" bicycles
5553. Get "His" and "Hers" mobile phones
5554. "His" and "Hers" Porsches (Millionaires need love, too)

5555. "His" and "Hers" VW Bugs (Love for the rest of us)
5556. "His" and "Hers" tennis rackets
5557. "His" and "Hers" matching silk pajamas
5558. "His" and "Hers" matching heart-shaped tattoos!
5559. "His" and "Hers" ornaments
5560. "His" and "Hers" monogrammed towels
5561. "His" and "Hers" bottles of red and white wine
5562. "His" and "Hers" matching beach towels

5563. Don't mistake lust for love
5564. (There's nothing *wrong* with lust; just recognize the difference)
5565. When you feel *love*, act on it
5566. Likewise, when you feel *lust*, act on *that!*

5567. Forgive
5568. Forget

5569. Have the courage to open up to your partner
5570. Have the courage to work through your tough issues
5571. Read *Freedom from Fear: Finding the Courage to Act, Love, and Be*, by Forrest Church
5572. Read *Love and Courage*, by Hugh Prather
5573. Read *The Courage to Create*, by Rollo May
5574. Remember: Love just *happens*, but your have to *create* a relationship

5575. Write a love poem that uses her *name* as the major rhyme

Favorite Love Songs from 1958

5576. "All I Have to Do Is Dream," Everly Brothers
5577. "Devoted to You," Everly Brothers
5578. "Do You Want to Dance," Bobby Freeman
5579. "To Know Him Is to Love Him," Teddy Bears
5580. "Volare," Domenico Mudugno
5581. "There's Only One of You," The Four Lads
5582. "You Are My Destiny," Paul Anka

5583. Write a *hot-hot-hot* note to him; seal it in three envelopes; place it under his windshield wiper
5584. Celebrate birthdays
5585. Blindfold him and make wild love to him
5586. "I'd rather have roses on my table than diamonds on my neck." ~ Emma Goldman
5587. Make reservations at the best restaurant in town for Valentine's Day *a year in advance*
5588. Surprise him with candy conversation hearts

5589. From a pack of playing cards, give her the Two of Hearts, along with a note: "Our two hearts beat as one."
5590. Give him the Three of Hearts: "Three reasons why I gave my heart to you…"
5591. Give her the Four of Hearts: "Here's where we're going on our next four dates…"
5592. Give him the Five of Hearts: "I'll pick you up promptly at five tonight for a little surprise…"
5593. Give her the Queen of Hearts, and make her Queen for a Day

5594. Put a dollar in a jar every time you make love

5595. Use the money on your 50th wedding anniversary

Red Hot Books to Set Your Sex Life Ablaze

5596. *101 Nights of Grrreat Sex*, by Laura Corn

5597. *269 Sex Games*, by Hugh de Beer

5598. *For Each Other: Sharing Sexual Intimacy*, by Lonnie Barbach

5599. *Daily Sex: 365 Positions and Activities for a Year of Great Sex!* by Jane Seddon

5600. *Kama Sutra*, DK Publishing

5601. *The Passion Parties Guide to Great Sex: Secrets and Techniques to Keep Your Relationship Red Hot*, by Pat Davis

5602. *What Men Really Want In Bed: The Surprising Secrets Men Wish Women Knew About Sex*, by Cynthia W. Gentry and Nima Badiey

5603. *Wicked Quickies: 52 Ways to Get It On Anytime, Anywhere*, by Audacia Ray

5604. *Cosmo's Aqua Kama Sutra: 25 Sex Positions for the Tub, Shower, Pool and more*

5605. *Position of the Day*, by Nerve.com

5606. *269 Amazing Sex Tips and Tricks for Her*, by Anne Hooper and Philip Hodson

5607. *269 Amazing Sex Tips and Tricks for Him*, by Anne Hooper and Philip Hodson

5608. Buy her favorite candy bar

5609. Create a traffic ticket: A citation for "speeding away" with your heart

5610. Practice: The philosophy of "Walk a mile in his/her shoes"; learn empathy

5611.   "Kissing power is stronger than will power."
        ~ Abigail Van Buren
5612.   Rent a cabin in the woods

Insights About Arguing

5613.   Become more aware of what's really going on, and
        you'll both benefit greatly
5614.   Arguing about money is rarely about money—It's
        about *power*
5615.   Arguing about sex is rarely about sexuality—It's about
        intimacy
5616.   Arguing about chores is rarely about chores—It's
        about *fairness*
5617.   Arguing about the kids is rarely about the kids—It's
        about *control*
5618.   Arguing about jealousy is rarely about fidelity—It's
        about *maturity*
5619.   Arguing about work is rarely about the work—It's
        about *time*
5620.   Arguing about relatives is rarely about them—It's
        about *expectations*

5621.   If she's very practical-minded, *don't* send cut flowers
5622.   Send *silk* flowers instead
5623.   Or flowering plants
5624.   Or give her a gift certificate to her favorite shop
5625.   Or just give her cash

Favorite Love Songs from 1959

5626.   "Dedicated to the One I Love," Shirelles
5627.   "Donna," Ritchie Valens

5628. "Dream Lover," Bobby Darin
5629. "I Only Have Eyes for You," Flamingos
5630. "Venus," Frankie Avalon

5631. Prescription for romance: Say "I love you" three times in the morning, and three times in the evening
5632. Repeat dosage every day for the rest of your life

5633. Always have a stash of wrapping paper
5634. And matching bows
5635. And a selection of cool boxes

The 12 Star Signs of the Zodiac and Their Basic Personality Traits

Knowing your partner's attributes will let you show your love in a custom-made way

5636. Aries (20 March–20 April): Courageous, energetic, loyal
5637. Taurus (21 April–21 May): Sensible, peaceful, stable
5638. Gemini (22 May–21 June): Unpredictable, lively, charming, witty
5639. Cancer (22 June–22 July): Secure, home-loving, graceful
5640. Leo (23 July–23 August): Idealistic, honorable, loyal
5641. Virgo (24 August–23 September): Shy, sensitive, values knowledge
5642. Libra (24 September–23 October): Diplomatic, charming, stylish
5643. Scorpio (24 October–22 November): Compassionate, proud, determined
5644. Sagittarius (23 November–21 December): Bold, impulsive, adventurous

5645. Capricorn (22 December–20 January): Resourceful, self-sufficient, responsible

5646. Aquarius (21 January–18 February): Bold, emotional under cool exterior

5647. Pisces (19 February–19 March): Imaginative, sympathetic, romantic

5648. The "Delicious Midnight Snack" Coupon: The coupon-giver will fix you a snack of your choosing and serve it to you no matter how late

5649. Togetherness = Sitting side-by-side in diner booths

5650. "A wedding anniversary is the celebration of love, trust, partnership, tolerance, and tenacity. The order varies for any given year." ~ Paul Sweeney

5651. Serve dessert in bed

5652. *Massage (101 Essential Tips)*, by Nitya LaCroix

5653. Learn what he/she considers *scandalous!*

5654. Have a "love note conversation" consisting entirely of song titles!

5655. Him: "I'm in the mood for love"

5656. Her: "Some enchanted evening"

5657. Him: "I want to hold your hand"

5658. Her: "I can't give you anything but love"

5659. Him: "Why do I love you?"

5660. Her: "Opposites attract"

5661. Don't get stuck in any *one* mode of expressing your love…

5662. You need both communication *and* quiet times

5663. Be *spontaneous* sometimes, and *well-planned* other times

5664.   Celebrate your *similarities* and honor your *differences*
5665.   Use *surprises* as well as *rituals*

Qualities That 5,000 Men *Dislike* Most in Wives

5666.   Nagging
5667.   Overly emotional
5668.   Dogmatic
5669.   Fickle
5670.   Not enough sex
5671.   Procrastinating
5672.   Manipulative
5673.   Angry
5674.   Siding with the kids
5675.   Talking too much

Songs to Help You Express Your Feelings: *Anniversaries & Celebrations*

5676.   "Always and Forever," Heatwave
5677.   "The Anniversary Song," Richard Tucker
5678.   "Celebration," Kool & The Gang
5679.   "Forever and Ever, Amen," Randy Travis
5680.   "More Today Than Yesterday," Spiral Staircase
5681.   "Our Love Is Here to Stay"

5682.   The gift: A poster of her dream vacation location
5683.   The note: "Some day, my love"
5684.   Take a walk on the beach
5685.   Celebrate Valentine's Day *one day early*

5686.   English: "You're so sexy"
5687.   French: "Tu es très sexy"

5688. Italian: "Sei molto sexy"
5689. German: "Du bist sehr sexy"
5690. Spanish: "Eres muy sexy"
5691. Portugese: "Você é muito sexi"

5692. Buy him a puppy
5693. Go away on vacation
5694. "Where we do not respect, we cease to love."
~ Benjamin Disraeli
5695. The "Completely Caffeinated Coffee Date" Coupon:
Choose your favorite café and get ready to put on a buzz

5696. Dedicate one week to exploring your emotions.
5697. Sunday: Tenderness
5698. Monday: Joy
5699. Tuesday: Nostalgia
5700. Wednesday: Wonder
5701. Thursday: Peace
5702. Friday: Passion
5703. Saturday: Love

5704. On his 32nd birthday: Bake and number 32
chocolate chip cookies
5705. Invite 32 people to his birthday party
5706. Give him 32 kisses
5707. Give him a 32-minute-long backrub
5708. Call him at 32 minutes past the hour, every hour, to
say "I love you"
5709. Give him a sports jersey with the number 32
5710. Present him with a list of "32 Reasons Why You're
the Best"

5711. The gift: An elegant wristwatch
5712. The inscription: "I always have time for you"

Favorite Love Songs from 1960

5713. "Are You Lonesome To-night," Elvis Presley
5714. "Baby You Got What It Takes," Brook Benton & Dinah Washington
5715. "Georgia on My Mind," Ray Charles
5716. "It's Now or Never," Elvis Presley
5717. "Save the Last Dance for Me," Drifters

5718. Make a sudden, radical change in how you express your love ("Quantum Romance")
5719. Make small, gradual changes in your love style ("Process Romance")

5720. Dedicate yourself to improving your relationship skills:
5721. Create your own *personalized* Couples Curriculum
5722. Get your lover to join you in this year-long experiment in life improvement
5723. Create a one-year course by choosing twelve topics (Communication, Sexuality, Creativity, etc.) and focus on one topic each month
5724. Find books that address these topics and read them together
5725. Create your own "homework" assignments
5726. You may want to repeat the "Sexuality" segment *several* times

5727.   Try a little foot reflexology on your lover: Read
        The Complete Guide to Foot Reflexology, by Kevin &
        Barbara Kunz

5728.   Hold a surprise birthday party for your partner
5729.   And for the truly adventurous: Hold a surprise wedding

5730.   Choose gemstones according to their *color*, to help
        express your feelings:
5731.   Choose a gemstone to match his/her eyes
5732.   Choose a *combination* of different gems in his/her
        favorite color
5733.   Write a poem that incorporates the symbolism of
        the gem
5734.   Get jewelry that incorporates his/her birthstone
5735.   Custom-design a piece of jewelry that combines *your*
        birthstone and your *lover's* birthstone
5736.   Use the birthstones of all of your *children*
5737.   Red: Ruby, garnet, tourmaline, spinel, red beryl, coral
5738.   Blue: Sapphire, tanzanite, topaz, zircon, tourmaline,
        spinel, aquamarine
5739.   Green: Emerald, garnet, peridot, sapphire, jade
5740.   Purple: Amethyst, sapphire, tanzanite, spinel
5741.   Pink: Tourmaline, sapphire, spinel, kunzite,
        morganite, pearl, coral
5742.   Yellow: Citrine, topaz, opal, garnet, tourmaline
5743.   Brown: Topaz, andalusite, smoky quartz
5744.   White: Moonstone, pearl, diamond

5745.   Words that *men* love to hear: "You're the *greatest*"
5746.   Words that *women* love to hear: "I *adore* you"

5747. If your partner is a perfectionist, identify *specific things* you're willing to do *perfectly*—if he/she will stop expecting you to be perfect all the time

5748. Host an at-home movie film festival

Creative Ways to Celebrate Valentine's Day

5749. Devote yourself 100% to each other on Valentine's Day

5750. Rent a local hotel's Honeymoon Suite

5751. Take the day off work on Valentine's Day

5752. One day simply *isn't* enough! Celebrate for a *week!*

5753. Buy *several boxes* of kids' valentines, and *flood* your partner with them!

5754. Give your partner one card *every hour on-the-hour*

5755. Make a batch of heart-shaped cookies

5756. Make a giant Valentine card on the back of a travel poster—

5757. And have vacation travel tickets taped to the poster

5758. Plan *a solid day's worth* of romantic music

5759. Stay at a local bed & breakfast

5760. Send *ten* Valentine's Day cards

5761. Send a *hundred* Valentine's Day cards!

5762. Spend the *entire day* watching romantic movies

5763. Give your modern gal a piece of antique jewelry

5764. Bake a heart-shaped cake—

5765. And decorate it with red frosting and heart-shaped sprinkles

5766. Spend *every* Valentine's Day together

5767. Send a Valentine's Day card each day for a week

5768. Send a Valentine's Day card each day for a month

5769. Find the best "Lovers' Package" at a local hotel
5770. Spend the *entire day* in bed together

Favorite Love Songs from 1961

5771. "Blue Moon," Marcels
5772. "I Like It Like That," Chris Kenner
5773. "Stand By Me," Ben E. King
5774. "Tonight My Love, Tonight," Paul Anka

5775. Hold a picnic by starlight *and* candlelight—outside at midnight
5776. Gals: Practice that sultry, throaty voice that guys like so much

Ways to Love a Scorpio
(24 October–22 November)

5777. Scorpio is a *water* sign: Cater to his/her dreamy, romantic nature
5778. Gift tip: Natural and sensuous
5779. Bath accessories and scented items
5780. Quality leather items and adornments
5781. Honeysuckle; hawthorn
5782. Sharp and tangy foods
5783. The jazz and passion of New Orleans
5784. Wrap gifts in maroon for your Scorpio

5785. Give two red roses
5786. Secretly fill a bottle of 7-Up with champagne
5787. Write "I love you" in the dust on the coffee table

Best Ski Resorts

Skiing: The only relationship activity where it's acceptable to go *downhill*

5788. Aspen, Colorado

5789. Bear Mountain, California

5790. Big Sky, Montana

5791. Jackson Hole, Wyoming

5792. Mammoth Mountain, California

5793. Mont Tremblant, Quebec, Canada

5794. Purgatory Resort, Durango, Colorado

5795. Sierra-At-Tahoe, California

5796. Snowbird, Utah

5797. Snowmass, Colorado

5798. Steamboat, Colorado

5799. Sugarbush, Vermont

5800. Sun Valley, Idaho

5801. Telluride, Colorado

5802. Vail, Colorado

5803. Whistler/Blackcomb, British Columbia, Canada

5804. Go to a carnival or fair together

5805. Take a roll of quarters for playing games

5806. Win a teddy bear for her

5807. Declare a moratorium on your diet—have some cotton candy

---

5808. Guys: Exchange a little of your rugged individualism for relationship building

5809. Gals: Trade some of your empathy for assertiveness

5810. Fill her purse with bubble gum

5811. Start the day in a special way: Recite a prayer or affirmation together
5812. Use a portable reading light when reading in bed
5813. Enemy of Love: Rigid attitudes
5814. Get her some Jimmy Buffett tunes to prepare for a Florida Keys vacation

5815. Enjoy a week in Acapulco
5816. Put your feelings on paper
5817. Declare *peace* in the "Battle of the Sexes"

Best Love Songs by Celine Dion

5818. "Beauty and the Beast" (with Peabo Bryson)
5819. "Because You Loved Me"
5820. "If You Asked Me"
5821. "Let's Talk About Love"
5822. "Tell Him"
5823. "The Power of Love"
5824. "When I Fall in Love" (with Clive Griffin)

5825. Dote on your dog lover
5826. Get a subscription to *Dog World Magazine*: www.animalnetwork.com/dogworldmag
5827. Visit the Dog Museum, near St. Louis: www.museumofthedog.org

Love Tips for Business Executives

5828. For salesmen in love: Treat her better than your best customer
5829. For VPs in love: Prepare a "Relationship Annual Report" for your mate

5830. For advertising execs in love: Create an ad campaign that expresses your love

5831. For stockbrokers in love: How well are your "relationship stocks" doing?

5832. For PR execs in love: Create a love-related "PR stunt" for your partner

5833. For managers in love: Are you managing your *relationship* as well as you're managing your *career*?

5834. For Regional Managers: If your partner were in charge of giving bonuses for your "performance" at home, how big would this quarter's bonus be?

5835. For Junior VPs: Are you practicing your *relationship* skills as diligently as your *golf* skills?

5836. For CPAs in love: Conduct a cost-benefit analysis of love in your life

5837. For engineers in love: Increase your expression of affection by 23%

5838. For job hunters: Create a Relationship Resume that lists your qualifications

5839. For company presidents: Are you providing adequate leadership and inspiration at *home*?

5840. For CEOs in love: Are you keeping your most important "shareholder" happy?

5841. For Big Shot Board Members: Are your daily activities in sync with your "Mission Statement"?

5842. For CFOs in love: Review your emotional "investment" in your partner

5843. For marketing managers: Identify and meet the Strategic Objectives of your relationship

5844. For supervisors in love: Delegate *more*—and get home *earlier*

5845. For manufacturing execs: Do you have your suppliers of romantic gifts lined-up?

5846. For bankers in love: You don't give cheap toasters to your most important customers, do you? Well?

5847. For sales managers in love: Focus 10% more effort on your most important customer—and watch your "bonus" increase proportionally

5848. For computer programmers: Work the "bugs" out of your relationship

5849. For quality control execs: Ensure the level of "quality time" spent at home

5850. For HR managers in love: Take one of your corporate "Personality Profiles" together—Use the results to improve your relationship

5851. For entrepreneurs in love: You're creating something new and valuable. Go for it!

5852. For workaholics in all fields: It's a cliché, but it's *true*: No one, on his deathbed, *ever* said, "I wish I'd spent *more* time *working*"

5853. Use Morse Code to tap out messages

5854. Use foreign languages to say "I love you"

5855. Use foreign languages to say explicit sexy things!

5856. Use your creativity to be romantic every day

5857. Use your inborn talents to help express your love

5858. Use your time wisely

5859. Call just to say "I love you"

5860. Call from your mobile phone

5861. Call from an airplane phone

5862. Call from work, just to say "Hi"

5863. Call every hour, *on the hour* with reasons why you're in love

5864. Entertain your spouse's friends even if you're not *crazy* about them

Favorite Love Songs from 1962

5865. "Can't Help Falling in Love," Elvis Presley

5866. "I Can't Stop Loving You," Ray Charles

5867. "Sherry," Four Seasons

5868. Write a love letter to your partner every day for a month and tell him/her how you love them

5869. Write a love letter to your partner—every day for the rest of your life

5870. Take turns writing love letters to each other

5871. Have a conversation with your partner—in writing

5872. Write a love note, then fashion it into an exotic origami shape

5873. "Just one great idea can completely revolutionize your life." ~ Earl Nightingale

5874. Find *one* great idea in this book and practice it intensely for one solid month

5875. Choose a *second* great idea to focus on during the next month

5876. The "Tea For Two" Coupon: Good for a quiet afternoon tea, English style. No kids allowed

5877. "There is only one happiness in life, to love and be loved." ~ George Sand

5878. Watch a dramatic thunderstorm together

5879. Give him a Craftsman tool

5880. Take your Elvis fan to Graceland: www.elvis.com
5881. Hire an Elvis impersonator to entertain at a birthday party
5882. Use *only* Elvis stamps when mailing love letters
5883. Watch all thirty-three movies that Elvis starred in
5884. Complete your lover's collection of Elvis albums

5885. Believe in the power of love
5886. Note: You need *power* to bring love alive
5887. Read *The Power Is Within You*, by Louise Hay
5888. "Loving, like prayer, is a power as well as a process. It's curative. It is creative." ~ Zona Gale
5889. Read *Unlimited Power*, by Anthony Robbins
5890. "Love Power," by Dionne Warwick & Jeffrey Osborne
5891. Read *The Power of Positive Thinking*, by Norman Vincent Peale
5892. Utilize Flower Power: Order a bouquet (or two)
5893. Read *Real Love: The Truth About Finding Unconditional Love and Fulfilling Relationships*, by Greg Baer
5894. Read *The Power of Infinite Love & Gratitude: An Evolutionary Journey to Awakening Your Spirit*, by Darren R. Weissman
5895. *Tantra for Erotic Empowerment: The Key to Enriching Your Sexual Life*, by Mark A. Michaels, Patricia Johnson, and Tristan Taormino

5896. *The Seduction Cookbook: Culinary Creations For Lovers*, by Diane Brown

5897. "No one should be allowed to die before he has loved." ~ Saint-John Perse
5898. Serve champagne in crystal goblets *tonight*
5899. Love Coupon: Entitles you to three full hours of uninterrupted peace and quiet. The coupon-issuer removes all distractions
5900. Give forget-me-nots. Attach a note: "Don't forget me!"
5901. Attend a Tony Robbins seminar together: www.tonyrobbins.com

5902. Pick him up at the airport in a limousine
5903. Have champagne in the limo
5904. Dress provocatively for him
5905. Make love in the back seat on the way home!

5906. Make an effort
5907. Make a homemade greeting card
5908. Make out
5909. Make it work
5910. Make your partner feel *special*
5911. Make the most of your potential
5912. Make love
5913. Make your weekends *special*
5914. Make believe
5915. Make every minute count
5916. Make time
5917. Make up

Ways to Turn a C- Relationship into an A+ Relationship

5918. Guys: Don't equate *romance* and *sex*

5919. Gals: Modernize your concept of "Cupid." (Guys don't relate to naked cherubs)

5920. If you tend to be *action*-oriented, try being more *verbal*

5921. If you tend to be *verbal*, try being more *action*-oriented

5922. Even though "actions speak louder than words," you *still* need to say "I love you" often

5923. Unwind together

5924. Make a "Commemorative Scroll" to celebrate a special day

5925. Create a "Romantic Idea Jar": 100 ideas on slips of paper; choose one each week

5926. Read *Romantic Questions: Growing Closer Through Intimate Conversation*, by Gregory J.P. Godek

5927. Have an affair—with your wife

5928. Sing a romantic song on your partner's voicemail

5929. Call and make up a song on the spot

5930. Watch the sunrise from Cape Cod

5931. Propose with a message on a scoreboard at a major league ballpark

5932. Read *The Smart Girl's Guide to the G-Spot*, by Violet Blue

5933. "When love and skill work together, expect a masterpiece." ~ John Ruskin

5934. For nurses in love: Take the "pulse" of your relationship; apply appropriate therapy

5935. Decorate with balloons picturing her favorite cartoon character

5936. Towel her dry after she showers

5937. Gals: Sit in his lap and "make out"

5938. Go out on an extravagant date
5939. Go out on a cheap date
5940. Go out on a limb—express yourself
5941. Go out on a fantasy date
5942. Go out on a dancing date
5943. Go out on a dinner date

5944. Talk, talk, talk
5945. Listen, listen, listen
5946. Read *The Lost Art of Listening*, by Michael Nichols

Different Ways of Viewing Romance

Everyone has a natural inclination: Your easiest inspiration will come from *one*—But interesting surprises will come from the *other*!

5947. Gifts vs. Gestures
5948. Obligatory vs. Optional
5949. Spontaneous vs. Planned
5950. Simple vs. Complicated
5951. Time Spent vs. Money Spent
5952. Micro vs. Macro
5953. Public vs. Private
5954. Items vs. Experiences
5955. Sexy vs. Lovey
5956. Fancy vs. Plain
5957. Fun and Light vs. Deep and Meaningful
5958. Weekday vs. Weekend
5959. Daily vs. Weekly vs. Monthly vs. Yearly
5960. Little Passions vs. Big Passions

5961. Past vs. Now vs. Future
5962. Surprises vs. Expected
5963. Quick vs. Time Consuming
5964. Practical vs. Frivolous
5965. Periodic vs. One-Time

5966. Pay attention when your partner is talking to you
5967. Pay *close* attention to the emotional contents, not merely the words
5968. Pay *really* close attention when your partner is distressed or crying

---

Favorite Love Songs from 1963

5969. "Be My Baby," Ronettes
5970. "Candy Girl," Four Seasons
5971. "He's So Fine," The Chiffons
5972. "So Much in Love," Tymes

5973. Send your kids out to the movies with a babysitter—
5974. Spend some uninterrupted time at home alone

5975. Guys: Love her for who she *is*—not for who you wish her to be
5976. Gals: Love him for who he *is*—not for who he used to be

---

5977. Hang a hotel "Do Not Disturb" sign on your bedroom door
5978. Hang in there—through thick and thin
5979. Hang out together—a *lot*

5980.   Arrange for your favorite restaurant to play "your song" during dinner

5981.   Speak from the heart, but don't leave the head behind

5982.   Create a collage of your family photos

5983.   Be honest about whatever *rut* your relationship is stuck in—

5984.   And take *specific steps* to escape from that rut

5985.   Never throw away the Sports Section before your partner has read it

5986.   Never throw away the Victoria's Secret catalog without ordering one item from it!

5987.   Never throw a temper tantrum

Gift Ideas for 23 Different Kinds of Fanatics

5988.   For Beatles fanatics: Attend The Fest for Beatles Fans. Visit: www.thefestforbeatlesfans.com

5989.   Also, for Beatles fanatics: Take the "Magical Mystery Tour" in Liverpool: www.cavernclub.org/mystery_tour.com

5990.   For tea lovers: Tea Lovers Club, http://www. teacuppa.com/Tea-of-the-Month-Club.asp

5991.   For baseball card collectors: Rare cards! From Goodwin & Co.: www.goodwinandco.com

5992.   For Monty Python aficionados: All forty-five episodes of *Monty Python's Flying Circus*

5993.   For Barbie Doll collectors: Treat her to something worthwhile at http://www.barbiecollector.com

5994.   For lovers of spicy food: *The Red Hot Cookbook: Create a Culinary Inferno with Flaming Good Recipes from Around the World*, by Ruby Le Bois

5995. For funny folks: International Clown Hall of Fame. In Milwaukee, Wisconsin: www.theclownmuseum.org

5996. For a football fanatic: Get Superbowl tickets

5997. For math mavens: *Math Appeal (Mind-Stretching Math Riddles)*, by Gregory Tang and Harry Briggs

5998. For history buffs: Get original newspapers dating back to 1880. The Historic Newspaper Archives: www.historicnewspaper.com

5999. For computer fanatics: *PC Mod Projects: Cool It! Light It! Morph It! (Consumer)*, by Edward Chen, Carl Mixon, Philip Mansfield, and Grace Punska

6000. For horse lovers: *The Horse Lover's Bible: The Complete Practical Guide to Horse Care and Management*, by Tamsin Pickeral

6001. For horse lovers: A trip to see the Kentucky Derby

6002. For garden guys and gals: Jackson & Perkins Roses & Gardens catalog: www.jacksonandperkins.com

6003. For your fish aficionado: *Aquarium Fish Magazine:* www.fishmagazine.com

6004. For floating fanatics: Bombard Balloon Adventures: www.buddybombard.com

6005. For autograph hounds: http://www.authenticsportscollectibles.com/

6006. For Japanese anime enthusiasts: The Right Stuff International: www.rightstuf.com

6007. For jazz fans: Vacation in New Orleans

6008. Also, for jazz fans: Attend the Montreal Jazz Festival, in early July: www.montrealjazzfest.com

6009. For golf fanatics: Get seats at the U.S. Open

6010. Also, for golf fanatics: A new Ping putter

6011. For Oprah oglers: Get tickets to be in the audience

6012.   For classical music fans: All nine Beethoven symphonies
6013.   Also, for classical music fans: All forty-two Mozart symphonies
6014.   And more for classical music fans: All ten Haydn symphonies
6015.   For space nuts: Plan a trip to watch a launch: www.nasa.gov/
6016.   The Crossword Club: http://www.thecrosswordclub.co.uk/

6017.   Change one bad habit that drives your partner crazy—
6018.   In exchange for your partner changing one bad habit that drives *you* up the wall

Ways to Move from *Practical* to *Elegant*

Add a little spice to your lover's life

6019.   Replace her cheap pens with a fabulous fountain pen
6020.   Travel first class instead of coach
6021.   Replace your plain bed with a classic canopy bed
6022.   Replace the cookie jar with an antique tin
6023.   Replace his/her paper bookmarks with *meaningful* markers
6024.   Give Godiva instead of cheaper chocolate
6025.   Add a feather bed to your mattress
6026.   Get her some expensive French lace lingerie
6027.   Serve breakfast using your best china and crystal

6028.   Remember: Romance is *always* about love, but only *sometimes* about sex
6029.   Replace the little strips of paper in Hershey's Kisses with your own little love notes

6030. Send a love letter that you've cut into jigsaw puzzle pieces
6031. Send the puzzle pieces all at once in a jumble
6032. Leave out one *critical* puzzle piece—and send it the next day
6033. Send the puzzle pieces one-a-day for two weeks

6034. Observe "Obligatory Romance Days" (Valentine's Day, birthdays, anniversaries)
6035. Focus attention on "Optional Romance"—every *other* day of the year!

6036. Remember: Romance is a state of mind
6037. But: Romance is *also* a state of being

6038. Listen for the feelings between the words
6039. Listen for the meaning behind the actions

Songs to Help You Express Your Feelings: *Devotion & Commitment*

6040. "Ain't No Mountain High Enough," Diana Ross
6041. "An Everlasting Love," Andy Gibb
6042. "As Long as He Needs Me," Shirley Bassey
6043. "Hopelessly Devoted to You," Olivia Newton-John
6044. "I Just Want to Be Your Everything," Andy Gibb
6045. "I'll Cover You," from the Broadway musical *Rent*
6046. "I'll Never Leave You," Harry Nilsson
6047. "Love of My Life," Abba
6048. "The Right Thing to Do," Carly Simon
6049. "Say You'll Be Mine," Christopher Cross
6050. "You're My Everything," The Temptations

6051. "Tune-in" to romantic opportunities: They're all around you!
6052. In articles and ads
6053. In newspapers and magazines
6054. On TV and radio
6055. In shop windows and billboards
6056. Share your most vivid dream
6057. Share your recurring dreams
6058. Interpret each other's dreams

6059. Keep love at the top of your list!
6060. Give 24-karat gold *anything*
6061. Gals: Act out the classic "Sexy Nurse Fantasy"
6062. Give yourself permission to express your emotions
6063. Learn more about the physiological side of sex
6064. Buy your partner *one* share of stock in his/her favorite company!
6065. For singles only: Ask his/her friends for insights into his/her personality
6066. Write a "Declaration of *Interdependence*"
6067. For your Romantic Music Library: Suzanne Ciani's *The Velocity of Love*
6068. Give her an umbrella of her favorite flowers

Relationship Questions
(For Married Couples Only)

Maintaining an A+ Marriage requires knowing each other *really* well

6069. Before anything was "official," how did you *know* you were going to marry each other?

6070. Where were you when you proposed (or were proposed to)? *Exactly* what was said?

6071. What are your goals as a couple?

6072. As you were growing up, what kind of person did you imagine you'd marry?

6073. What is the most memorable thing that happened during your wedding?

6074. Do you believe that you and your spouse were *destined* to be together?

6075. How many children do you want to raise?

6076. How do you plan to celebrate your 50th wedding anniversary?

6077. Should a husband and wife be each other's best friend?

6078. Do you believe that romance can be kept alive between two people for a *lifetime*?

6079. Have a picnic in the nude

6080. Have each piece of your silverware engraved with a different love quote

6081. Give her a box of elegant stationery

6082. "It's kind of fun to do the impossible." ~ Walt Disney

6083. Play "romantic-words-only" Scrabble

6084. An "Old-Fashioned Bowling Date" Coupon: Included: Shoe rental, all bowling fees, soda, and popcorn.

6085. Go lingerie shopping together

6086. Save time by recording *all* your favorite TV shows— so you can skip all the commercials

6087. You could easily save fifteen to thirty minutes a day— which you could devote to love

6088.   Write a list: "33 Reasons I Love You"
6089.   Make it into a scroll
6090.   Give it to your partner tied with a red ribbon

6091.   Hide a small note under the pillow…
6092.   Or in the medicine cabinet
6093.   Or under a dinner plate
6094.   Or in the refrigerator
6095.   Or in a pizza box
6096.   Or between the pages of a book she's reading

6097.   "It is when you give of yourself that you truly give."
         ~ Pierre Corneille
6098.   Give one hour of uninterrupted time to your partner
6099.   Use your unique creativity to express your love
6100.   Go out of your way, go above and beyond, for your mate

Ways to Use the Heart Shape

6101.   Make a heart-shaped pizza
6102.   Your initials in a heart—in *skywriting*
6103.   Cut the kitchen sponges into heart shapes
6104.   While out at a formal dinner, nonchalantly draw a
         heart on the back of his hand with a pen
6105.   Have a heart-shaped pool built
6106.   Your initials in a heart—on wet cement in a sidewalk
6107.   Trace a heart-shape in fogged-up windows
6108.   Your initials in a twenty-foot heart in the snow
6109.   A quilt with a heart motif
6110.   Your initials in a heart—etched on a brick in your patio
6111.   Pepperoni in the shape of a heart on the pizza

6112. Trace a fifty-foot heart in the sand on a beach
6113. Grill burgers in the shape of a heart
6114. Heart-shaped sandwiches
6115. For math nuts: r = a(1-cosA)
6116. Use heart-shaped stickers
6117. Band-Aids with heart designs
6118. Heart-shaped place mats
6119. Trace a heart on the ice when ice skating
6120. A silk tie with hearts on it
6121. A heart-shaped chunk of cheese
6122. A mug with hearts on it
6123. A heart-shaped mug
6124. A heart-shaped door mat
6125. Socks with heart designs on them
6126. Heart-shaped doilies
6127. Heart-shaped eyeglasses
6128. A front-yard flag with hearts on it
6129. Poke holes in the shape of a heart in the crust of a freshly baked pie
6130. Make heart-shaped chocolate chip cookies
6131. Heart-shaped confetti
6132. The classic heart-shaped box of chocolates
6133. Individual chocolate treats that are heart-shaped
6134. Carve a heart—with your initials in it—in a tree
6135. Get a heart-shaped tattoo with her initials in it
6136. Greeting cards with hearts
6137. Fold the dinner napkins into heart shapes
6138. Silk boxer shorts with a heart motif
6139. Draw hearts on the mirror with lipstick
6140. Use only love stamps with heart shapes on them
6141. Find a wine with a heart motif on the label

6142.   Heart-shaped rubber stamps

6143.   Heart-shaped cakes

6144.   Heart designs in icing on a cake

6145.   Heart-shaped candles

6146.   Heart-shaped appetizers

6147.   Heart-shaped picture frames

6148.   Heart-shaped wreaths

6149.   Heart-shaped ice cubes

6150.   A heart-shaped rug

6151.   Find a heart-shaped Jell-O mold

6152.   Cut banana slices into heart shapes and put them in Jell-O

6153.   Shape pancakes into heart shapes

6154.   Cut toast into heart shapes

6155.   Cut a heart shape out of toast and fry an egg in the center

6156.   Heart-shaped Rice Krispy Treats

6157.   Slice strawberries into heart-shapes

6158.   A heart-shaped pendant

6159.   A heart-shaped pin

6160.   Heart-shaped earrings

6161.   Heart-shaped pasta

6162.   Heart-shaped red balloons

6163.   Heart-shaped cookie cutters

6164.   Heart-shaped key rings

6165.   Heart-shaped candy conversation hearts

6166.   Cut the lawn into the shape of a giant heart

6167.   Make a heart-shaped kite together!

6168.   Get a *humongous* heart-shaped box of candy

6169.   Heart-shaped shrubbery/topiary

6170.   A big, heart-shaped ice sculpture

6171.   Send an envelope filled with heart-shaped glitter

6172. While tanning, place a small, heart-shaped piece of cardboard on your body

6173. Cut a piece of paper into a heart shape, then write a love letter on it

6174. Scrape the ice off his windshield—in the shape of a heart

6175. Enemy of Love: Apathy

6176. For couples only: Go out to a singles bar together; talk about how lucky you are to have found each other!

6177. Give her a *variety* of jewelry...

6178. Rings

6179. Bracelets

6180. Necklaces

6181. Earrings

6182. Watches

6183. Pins

6184. Ankle bracelets

6185. Toe rings

6186. Belly button rings

6187. Time yourselves: How *fast* can you make love?

6188. Time yourselves: How *long* can you make sex last?

6189. Lose yourself in long, lazy lovemaking

6190. Lose track of time during a long, lazy afternoon together

6191. Lose your (emotional) inhibitions when talking with your partner

6192. Lose your (sexual) inhibitions when making love

6193. Write "I love you" on fifty Post-It notes
6194. Post them all over the house

6195. Learn all the verses to "L Is for the Way You Look at Me"
6196. Sing it to him/her
6197. Make up *additional* verses for the song
6198. Write verses that spell-out your partner's name
6199. On Valentine's Day give her a *real arrow* with a note attached: "To [the two of you], From Cupid"

Favorite Love Songs from 1964

6200. "Chapel of Love," Dixiecups
6201. "Love Me Do," The Beatles
6202. "She Loves You," The Beatles
6203. "Under the Boardwalk," Drifters
6204. "Understand Your Man," Johnny Cash
6205. "My Guy," Mary Wells

6206. Dress in formal wear for a picnic in the park
6207. Dare to express your deepest feelings
6208. Make love on your couch
6209. Don't confuse the size of the love with the size of the price tag
6210. "I've decided to stick with love." ~ Martin Luther King Jr.

6211. Learn all the verses to "Singin' in the Rain"
6212. Rent the romantic movie classic *Singin' in the Rain*

6213. During the next rainstorm: Go for a walk and sing "Singin' in the Rain"

6214. Call your spouse to arrange a "date"

6215. In a love note, tell her: "My *concupiscent* feelings for you can no longer be contained"

CDs of Instrumental Music
Hand-Picked for Romantic Evenings

6216. *Breakin' Away*, by Al Jarreau

6217. *Feels So Good*, by Chuck Mangione

6218. *Livin' Inside Your Love*, by George Benson

6219. *Suite for Flute & Jazz Piano*, by Jean-Pierre Rampal and Claude Bolling

6220. *Touch*, by John Klemmer

6221. *Twin Sons of Different Mothers*, by Dan Fogelberg and Tim Weisberg

6222. *Silk Road II*, by Kitaro

6223. *Solo Flight*, by Markus Allen

6224. *Textures*, by Greg Joy

6225. *Angel Love*, by Aeoliah

6226. A "Love Code": 1-4-3 means "I love you"

6227. Squeeze your partner's hand, 1-4-3

6228. While in adjacent public restrooms, pound 1-4-3 on the wall

6229. Send a postcard, with the message: "1-4-3"

6230. Send one birthday card for each year of his/her age— one-a-day

6231.   Send one birthday card for each year of his/her age—
        all at once!

Proverbs of Love from Around the World

6232.   "If you would understand men, study women."
        ~ French proverb

6233.   "The heart that loves is always young."
        ~ Greek proverb

6234.   "A man is not where he *lives*, but where he *loves*."
        ~ Latin proverb

6235.   "He who is impatient is not in love."
        ~ Italian proverb

6236.   "Where love reigns the impossible may be attained."
        ~ Indian proverb

6237.   "He gives double who gives unasked." ~ Arab proverb

6238.   "Try to reason about love and you will lose your
        reason." ~ French proverb

6239.   "There is no one luckier than he who thinks himself
        so." ~ German proverb

6240.   "An old man in love is like a flower in winter."
        ~ Portuguese proverb

6241.   "Married couples who love each other tell each
        other a thousand things without talking."
        ~ Chinese proverb

6242.   "Not the lover, but his language, wins the lady."
        ~ Japanese proverb

6243.   Support your partner *emotionally*

6244.   Support your partner *financially*

6245.   Support your partner's beliefs and values

6246.   Support your partner through a tough time at work

6247. Support your partner through family difficulties
6248. Support your partner *always and forever*

"Photo Fantasies" for Lovers

Cameras have inspired many fantasies

6249. He's a *Playboy* photographer, she's a model. Scene 1: He seduces her
6250. He's a *Playboy* photographer, she's a model. Scene 2: *She* seduces *him*
6251. Variation: A *sizzling, bold* seduction
6252. Variation: A *slow, subtle, flirty* seduction
6253. Question: How would you pose for *different* magazines?
6254. Variation: She's a *Playgirl* photographer, and *he's* the model
6255. Posing for the *Sports Illustrated* "Swimsuit Issue"
6256. "Victoria's Secret catalog photo shoot"
6257. How would you pose *differently* for the "Frederick's of Hollywood" catalog?

6258. Live as lovers
6259. Remember: Medical studies show that people in better relationships live longer, healthier lives!
6260. Live this day as if it were your last
6261. Daily affirmation: "I will be patient with my mate"
6262. Let your children see you kissing
6263. "The most important thing a father can do for his children is to love their mother." ~ Theodore Hesburgh
6264. Pile onto the couch and cuddle with the whole family while watching TV

6265. Share stories with your kids about how the two of you met

6266. Give your *wife* a gift on the *kids'* birthdays

6267. Gals: Make room for his buddies (It will take pressure off your relationship)

6268. Guys: Don't resent her girlfriends (It will help keep her sane)

Questions to Determine Your "Sex Style"

Very often, a person's "personality style" doesn't match his/her "sex style"

6269. When it comes to sex, do you stick to the basics?

6270. Do you explore a lot?

6271. Are you creative?

6272. What are your patterns?

6273. Are you spontaneous? Are you habitual?

6274. Are you verbal?

6275. Do you act out?

6276. Are you predictable?

6277. Do you adjust your style based on your mood?

6278. Do you change your style based on your mate's moods?

6279. What are your favorite positions?

6280. How important are *setting* and *mood* to you?

6281. Take your movie-loving lover to film-oriented theme parks...

6282. Universal Studios in Orlando, Florida

6283. Universal Studios Hollywood in Universal City, California

6284. Disney-MGM Studios at Walt Disney World in Lake Buena Vista, Florida

6285. Parents: Present a "united front" to your kids
6286. Don't let them play you off one another

6287. "Never cut what you can untie." ~ Joseph Joubert
6288. Most all arguments can be untangled without unraveling the relationship
6289. Hang in there. Have faith. Have hope
6290. Try *everything* to make it work

6291. Pamper him
6292. Give him a foot massage
6293. Wash (and wax) his car
6294. Do his weekend chores for him
6295. Serve his favorite snacks while watching TV

6296. Always be available
6297. Via phone or fax
6298. Via pager or email

6299. Guys: You need to know her dress size
6300. Her shoe size and stocking size
6301. Her blouse size and nightgown size
6302. Her bra size and panty size
6303. Her pants size and coat size
6304. Her finger size (for rings that fit)

6305. Be passionate
6306. Write a book together

6307. Warm up with an electric blanket
6308. Eat dinner at the best Indian restaurant around

6309. Accompany your partner on a business trip
6310. Take an extra day and turn it into a mini-vacation

6311. English: "Hold me"
6312. French: "Prends-moi dans tes bras"
6313. Italian: "Abbracciami"
6314. German: "Halt mich fest"
6315. Spanish: "Abrázame"
6316. Portugese: "Me abrace"

6317. Send a love letter in the mail
6318. Send the kids away for the evening
6319. Send the kids away for the weekend
6320. Send your kids to summer camp
6321. Send a taxi to pick him up at work and drop him off at your favorite restaurant
6322. Send your prayers to your partner
6323. Send away for lots of gift catalogs

6324. Gift & Date Idea: Get the song "Some Enchanted Evening," by Jay & the Americans—
6325. And rent the movie *South Pacific*, featuring the song
6326. Or—surprise your partner with tickets to the musical, live on stage

6327. Dare to fondle each other under a blanket at a football game
6328. Splurge on a $1,000 shopping spree in Tiffany's

6329. Enemy of Love: Stinginess with *time*
6330. Put a penny in a jar every time you make love
6331. Play duets together on the piano

Visual Puns to Use in Love Notes

Use actual *items* as part of your love notes

6332. "We're quite a (pear)"
6333. "You're the (apple) of my eye"
6334. "We're a (match) made in heaven"
6335. "(Honey), I'm yours"
6336. "I'm your biggest (fan)"
6337. "Please don't (squash) my hopes"
6338. "You're the (toast) of the town!"
6339. "Sweetheart, you're a (peach)"
6340. "I (wood) do anything for you"
6341. "Please go out on a (date) with me!"
6342. "(Peas) be mine!"
6343. "(Olive) you!"

6344. Create a weekend of romance with a "theme song"
6345. Give a copy of the song "Thank God It's Friday," by Love & Kisses—
6346. And go on a date this Friday to a restaurant you've never visited before
6347. Give a copy of the song "Saturday in the Park," by Chicago—
6348. And pack a picnic lunch for a lazy Saturday afternoon together
6349. Give a copy of the song "Sunday Mornin,'" by Spanky & Our Gang—
6350. And share a romantic Sunday brunch

Favorite Love Songs from 1965

6351. "Eight Days a Week," The Beatles
6352. "I Got You Babe," Sonny & Cher
6353. "It's Not Unusual," Tom Jones
6354. "My Girl," Temptations
6355. "You Were on My Mind," We Five

6356. Give her one *beautiful* red rose—
6357. And the song "Roses Are Red (My Love)," by Bobby Vinton

6358. Create a collage of memorabilia from your life together
6359. Don't cramp your partner's style
6360. Gals: *Stop* communicating with him! (Take *action* instead)
6361. Take an inventory of your personal talents, interests, skills, aptitudes, and passions—and use them to generate ideas for expressing your love
6362. Write postcards in code: "I.L.Y." etc.
6363. Create a custom bookmark by laminating a favorite comic strip
6364. Write love notes on 1 dozen eggs
6365. For last minute Broadway seats, call Tickets on Request: www.ticketsonrequest.aceder.info
6366. Re-define yourself: From "spouse" to "lover"
6367. Go out to a movie

6368. Attend a pro basketball game
6369. Attend a Broadway show

6370. Attend a pro football game
6371. Attend to your partner's needs
6372. Attend to your partner's *wants*
6373. Attend your children's soccer games—*together*
6374. Attend an event that you've never attended before
6375. Attend a lecture
6376. Attend a pro baseball game
6377. Attend a pro hockey game
6378. Attend to your partner's secret desires
6379. Attend a religious service together
6380. Attend the ballet
6381. Attend a symphony
6382. Attend an opera
6383. Attend a jazz concert
6384. Attend a rock concert
6385. Attend a big band concert

6386. Splurge on a $50 shopping spree in the Sears Tool Department
6387. "Love is blind." ~ Geoffrey Chaucer

17 Books on Marriage

6388. *The Proper Care and Feeding of Marriage*, by Dr. Laura Schlessinger
6389. *Sacred Marriage*, by Gary L. Thomas
6390. *Keeping the Love You Find*, by Harville Hendrix
6391. *Passionate Marriage: Keeping Love and Intimacy Alive in Committed Relationships*, by David Schnarch
6392. *How to Improve Your Marriage Without Talking About It*, by Patricia Love and Steven Stosny
6393. *The Four Seasons of Marriage*, by Gary Chapman

6394. *Saving Your Marriage Before It Starts: Seven Questions to Ask Before and After You Marry*, by Les and Leslie Parrott

6395. *The New Rules of Marriage: What You Need to Know to Make Love Work*, by Terrence Real

6396. *The Secrets of Happily Married Men*, by Scott Haltzman

6397. *Devotions for a Sacred Marriage: A Year of Weekly Devotions for Couples*, by Gary L. Thomas

6398. *Starting Your Marriage Right: What You Need to Know in the Early Years to Make It Last a Lifetime*, by Dennis Rainey and Barbara Rainey

6399. *Why Marriages Succeed or Fail*, by John Gottman

6400. *The Ten Commandments of Marriage*, by Ed Young and Beth Moore

6401. *Marriage, a History: How Love Conquered Marriage*, by Stephanie Coontz

6402. *Secrets of a Passionate Marriage*, by David Schnarch

6403. *Extraordinary Relationships*, by Roberta Gilbert

6404. *Couples Companion: Meditations and Exercises for Getting the Love You Want*, by Harville Hendrix, PhD

6405. An Ice Cream Sundae Coupon: This coupon includes a one hour reprieve from any diets

6406. Text him LMLT ("Let's Make Love Tonight")

6407. "Life is a flower of which love is the honey." – Victor Hugo

6408. Keep one fresh rose in the house *at all times*

6409. Rent matching motorcycles for a road trip

6410. Share a piece of your wedding cake on your first anniversary

6411. Gift & Date Idea: Get the song "Summer Nights," by John Travolta & Olivia Newton-John—And rent *Grease*, featuring the song

6412. Or—surprise your partner with tickets to the musical, live on stage

---

6413. "A man is already halfway in love with any woman who listens to him." ~ Brendan Francis

6414. This reflects the truth that men *do* desire deep communication (not *just* sex!)

6415. Gals: Listen to him with *renewed attention*—and watch him respond

---

6416. Don't buy roses on Valentine's Day! (It's expensive and expected)—

6417. Do buy *different* flowers

Ways to Give Money As a Gift in a Creative Way

6418. A bouquet of long-stemmed twenty dollar bills

6419. A Christmas tree decorated with silver dollar ornaments

6420. Origami money

6421. A one hundred-dollar-bill single rose

6422. A wine bottle filled with cash

6423. A toilet paper roll of dollar bills

6424. A twenty pound sack o' quarters

6425. A money wreath

6426. Streamers made of one dollar bills taped together

6427. A cereal box bursting with pennies

6428. A large box filled with lots of crumpled-up bills

6429. A tiny little box filled with a folded-up one hundred dollar bill
6430. A "salad" made of money "greens"
6431. An elegantly framed one hundred dollar bill
6432. A giant glass jar filled with cash

6433. Never fake interest in his hobbies—
6434. Be genuine about it or don't bother
6435. Never fake orgasms—It's insulting to him and frustrating for you

6436. Your job is to support your partner in his/her changes and challenges—
6437. Not to stand back, point them out, and analyze

Favorite Love Songs from 1966

6438. "A Groovy Kind of Love," Mindbenders
6439. "Good Lovin'," Young Rascals
6440. "My Love," Petula Clark
6441. "Strangers in the Night," Frank Sinatra
6442. "What Now, My Love," Sonny & Cher
6443. "You Are My Soul & Inspiration," Righteous Brothers
6444. "Working My Way Back to You," The Four Seasons
6445. "My World Is Empty Without You," The Supremes
6446. "I Got You (I Feel Good)," James Brown
6447. "You Don't Have to Say You Love Me," Dusty Springfield

6448. Respect each other's privacy…
6449. Don't listen to her phone conversations

6450. Don't go through his wallet

6451. When your partner is feeling low, your job is to lift him/her up
6452. Not to label and analyze the problem

6453. Cater to the kid in her...
6454. Get a copy of her favorite book from childhood
6455. Buy her favorite flavor of bubble gum
6456. Spring a surprise birthday party for her

6457. Respond with love—*regardless* of what your partner says or does
6458. (All negative behaviors are *disguised calls for love*)
6459. Respond to what's *really* going on—not simply to what's on the surface

6460. Massage Coupon #1: The Soothing Foot Massage. Administered by the coupon-giver. At least twenty minutes in duration
6461. Massage Coupon #2: The Stress-Releasing Back Massage. Includes scented body lotion and thirty minutes of deep muscle massage.
6462. Massage Coupon #3: The Erotic Massage. Location: Bedroom. Clothing: Optional.

6463. Give 100% to your relationship
6464. Don't fall into the trap of "giving 150%"
6465. It's *impossible* to give more than you have; it will just frustrate you and make you feel guilty

6466. Hang a flag from the country of his/her ancestors
6467. Treat yourselves to breakfast at a local diner
6468. Visit www.libidomag.com—"Erotica for people who like to read"
6469. "Man makes love by braggadocio, and woman makes love by listening." ~ H. L. Mencken
6470. Unlearn your superior attitude about being in touch with your feelings
6471. Toss coins in a wishing well together and share the same wish
6472. Stay young at heart while growing old together
6473. Get a funny or sexy or romantic temporary tattoo

Ways to Love a Sagittarius
(23 November–21 December)

6474. Sagittarius is a *fire* sign: Cater to his/her passionate, sexual nature
6475. Gift tip: Travel-related
6476. Travel accessories, maps, travel books
6477. Anything—or anywhere—exotic
6478. Take an adventurous trekking vacation
6479. Carnation; oak trees
6480. Nutty flavors, spicy foods
6481. The open spaces of Australia
6482. Wrap gifts in deep purple for your Sagittarius

6483. Don't complain about your work as soon as you return home
6484. "Shared laughter is erotic too." ~ Margie Percy
6485. Enjoy a lazy Sunday afternoon canoe ride on a beautiful pond

6486. Give him a T-shirt picturing his favorite cartoon character

6487. A song for the engaged: "I Do, I Do, I Do," by ABBA

6488. When playing tennis, refuse to use the word "Love" to mean "Zero"

6489. "Everything belonging to a loved one is precious." ~ P.A.C. de Beaumarchais

6490. For your Romantic Music Library: Acoustic Alchemy's *Reference Point*

6491. Practice your relationship skills as often as you practice your golf swing

6492. Remember: You can fall in love with the same person over and over again!

6493. Write, inscribe, text, engrave coded messages on all your gifts

6494. A.T.S.B.O. (And They Shall Be One)

6495. Y.A.M.O.A.O. (You Are My One and Only)

6496. A.A.F. (Always and Forever)

6497. Y.A.M.S. (You Are My Sweetie)

6498. H.D.I.L.T. (How Do I Love Thee)

6499. I.L.Y.M.T.T.Y. (I Love You More Today Than Yesterday)

6500. Y.A.M.A.T.W. (You and Me Against the World)

6501. T.H.B.A.O. (Two Hearts Beating As One)

6502. Y.A.M.—L.F. (You and Me—Lovers Forever)

6503. L.O.M.L. (Love of My Life)

6504. T.L.A. (True Love Always)

6505. M.Y.A. (Miss You Already)

6506. G.M.F.L. (Geese Mate for Life)

6507. Gals: Quit using "feminine wiles" on him—
6508. Be honest and straightforward (Otherwise you'll wear a mask your entire life together)
6509. Guys: Quit the macho posturing with her—
6510. Be yourself and share yourself (Otherwise you'll have to keep up that macho act throughout your entire life together)

6511. English: "Kiss me"
6512. French: "Embrasse-moi"
6513. Italian: "Baciami"
6514. German: "Küß mich"
6515. Spanish: "Bésame"
6516. Portugese: "Me beija"

6517. Never let jealousy get the better of you
6518. Write "I love you" on his rearview mirror with lipstick
6519. Choose little tables-for-two at restaurants
6520. Defy superstition: Celebrate your luck in finding each other every Friday the 13th
6521. Visit "Honeymoon Island": Kauai, Hawaii
6522. For engaged couples only: Find a couple happily married for more than fifty years; take them to lunch and learn their secrets

Romantic Things to Do in Small Spaces

6523. Go through revolving doors together
6524. Take a road trip in a VW "Love Bug"
6525. Take silly pictures in a photo booth
6526. Join her in the dressing room while lingerie shopping
6527. Make love in a restroom aboard a plane in flight

6528. Relax together in a Jacuzzi
6529. Make love in a closet at a friend's party
6530. Sleep spoon-style in a single bed
6531. Squeeze into an oversize recliner for a cozy night at home
6532. Wrap yourselves together in a cruise ship cabin
6533. Make love in the back seat of a car
6534. Travel in a train's sleeper car
6535. Attend movie theaters that have "loveseats"
6536. Sit side-by-side in booths at little diners
6537. Make love in an elevator
6538. Go on vacation aboard an RV
6539. Hold a picnic in a tree fort
6540. Make love in the back of a limousine
6541. Take a relaxing bubblebath together
6542. Make love in a sleeping bag

6543. "Remember that happiness is a way of travel—not a destination." ~ Roy M. Goodman
6544. Read *The Portable Romantic*, by Gregory J.P. Godek
6545. Hike the Grand Canyon
6546. Make love on a deserted beach
6547. Give a gentle massage
6548. Get an original magazine from the year and month of his/her birthday
6549. Share a midnight snack
6550. For your car nut: Have a tiny love note etched in his car's dipstick

6551. Compliment her on her sparkling eyes…
6552. "Pretty Blue Eyes," Steve Lawrence
6553. "Brown-Eyed Girl," Van Morrison

6554. "Green-Eyed Lady," Sugarloaf
6555. "Blue Eyes," Elton John
6556. "Sexy Eyes," Dr. Hook

Favorite Love Songs from 1967

6557. "All You Need Is Love," The Beatles
6558. "Baby I Love You," Aretha Franklin
6559. "Make Me Yours"
6560. "Daydream Believer," Monkees
6561. "Happy Together," Turtles
6562. "I Never Loved a Man," Aretha Franklin
6563. "To Sir with Love," Lulu

6564. "Great thoughts come from the heart." ~ Luc de Clapiers
6565. Plan a *great* romantic surprise to take place one month from today
6566. Think with your *heart*, not just your *head*
6567. Use your heart—instead of your head—to re-evaluate your priorities

6568. Explore the unusual, unfamiliar, and unknown
6569. Pursue the extraordinary and extravagant
6570. Practice forgiveness, forethought, and foreplay
6571. Pay attention to your intuition and insights

States with Romantic and Curious Town Names

Just think of all the romantic possibilities! Travel cross-country and stay only in "romantic" towns. Target special towns that match the themes in your life

6572. **Alabama:** Angel, Love Hills
6573. **Alaska:** Utopia, Wiseman
6574. **Arizona:** Dateland, Darling, Date, Love, Eden, Valentine
6575. **Arkansas:** Eros, Delight, Heart, Hon, Romance
6576. **California:** Bridalveil Fall, Happy Camp, Harmony, Newlove, Paradise, Rough and Ready, Tranquility
6577. **Colorado:** Bridal Veil Falls, Climax, Fairplay, Goodnight, Loveland, Loveland Pass, Mutual, Security
6578. **Connecticut:** Pleasure Beach
6579. **Delaware:** Green Acres, Harmony Hills
6580. **Florida:** Lovedale, Romeo, Kissimmee, Venus, Christmas, Honeymoon Island, Venus
6581. **Georgia:** Climax, Ideal, Lovejoy, Sale City, Sparks
6582. **Idaho:** Bliss, Eden, Star, Sweet
6583. **Illinois:** Joy, Fidelity, Love, Lovejoy
6584. **Indiana:** Advance, Hope, Santa Claus, Valentine
6585. **Iowa:** Jewell, Loveland, Lovington, Manly
6586. **Kansas:** Bloom, Climax, Eureka, Gem, Joy, Lovewell, Paradise, Protection
6587. **Kentucky:** Beauty, Goody, Lovely, Number One, Ogle, Pleasureville
6588. **Louisiana:** Eros, Sunset, Valentine
6589. **Maine:** Friendship, Harmony, Tryon, Union
6590. **Maryland:** Darlington, Delight, Golden Beach, Halfway, Love Point, Unity, Welcome
6591. **Massachusetts:** Hopedale, Silver Lake
6592. **Michigan:** Bliss, Charity Island, Climax, Paradise, Romeo
6593. **Minnesota:** Climax, Darling, Fertile, Harmony, Welcome
6594. **Mississippi:** Bond, Darling, Eden, Love, Star

6595. **Missouri:** Belle, Bliss, Eureka, Fair Play, Neck, Paradise

6596. **Montana:** Bond, Eureka, Opportunity, Paradise, Valentine

6597. **Nebraska:** Sparks, Tryon, Valentine

6598. **Nevada:** Contact, Paradise, Sparks

6599. **New Hampshire:** Coos

6600. **New Jersey:** Fellowship, Loveladies

6601. **New Mexico:** Loving, Climax

6602. **New York:** Bliss, Climax, Eden, Swan Lake

6603. **North Carolina:** Climax, Delight, Eden, Lovejoy, Star, Tryon, Welcome, Wise

6604. **North Dakota:** Bloom, Darling Lake, Heart River, Union

6605. **Ohio:** Charm, Climax, Loveland, Loveland Park

6606. **Oklahoma:** Loveland, Loving, Loyal, Sparks

6607. **Oregon:** Diamond, Bridal Veil, Christmas Lake Valley

6608. **Pennsylvania:** Climax, Harmony, Intercourse, Lovejoy, Lover, Paradise, Paris, Venus

6609. **Rhode Island:** Diamond Hill, Harmony, Hope Valley

6610. **South Carolina:** Darlington, Eureka, Union

6611. **South Dakota:** Date, Eden, Eureka, Faith, Ideal, Winner

6612. **Tennessee:** Bride, Love Joy, Lovetown, Sweet Lips

6613. **Texas:** Beaukiss, Blessing, Climax, Comfort, Eden, Eureka, Fort Bliss, Groom, Happy, Lovelady, Loving, Paradise, Poetry, Rising Star, Royalty, Star, Utopia, Valentine, Venus

6614. **Utah:** Eden, Eureka, Paradise, Virgin

6615. **Vermont:** Blissville, Eden

6616. **Virginia:** Casanova, Love, Rose Hill, Valentines, Wise

6617. **Washington:** Eureka, Loveland, Opportunity, Union

6618. **West Virginia:** Belle, Romance, Tango
6619. **Wisconsin:** Friendship, Luck, Moon, Romance
6620. **Wyoming:** Diamondville, Eden, Heart Lake, Heart Mountain, Old Faithful, Reliance

---

6621. Gals: Buy a clingy, elegant 1940s-style evening gown—and greet him at the door wearing it
6622. Ice skate
6623. Wear "Eternity" perfume—To show him that you'll love him for all eternity

---

6624. "Between whom there is hearty truth there is love." ~ Henry David Thoreau
6625. What's the difference between "truth" and "*hearty truth*"?
6626. Confide or confess one secret to your partner today; watch the intimacy increase

---

6627. A list: "21 of My Favorite Memories of You"
6628. Create a collage based on this list
6629. Or create a memory album
6630. Start a new list, beginning today
6631. Present your partner with a new list each time you reach another twenty-one

---

6632. Hide a small gift in a cereal box...
6633. Or in the glove compartment
6634. Or in his golf bag
6635. Or in her desk drawer
6636. Or in a box of Cracker Jacks
6637. Send a formal, printed invitation to have dinner

6638. Send a formal, printed invitation to have sex
6639. Send a ribboned scroll declaring your neverending love
6640. Send a big box via UPS—with a tiny gift packed in the middle
6641. Send a poem via email—send one line per hour

6642. Create "theme gifts": Combine similar items and ideas to create fun and meaningful gifts
6643. *Friends Forever: Great Things Happen When We're Together*, by Susan Winget

The "Dirty Dozen"—Relationship Killers to Watch Out For

6644. Apathy
6645. Cynicism
6646. Immaturity
6647. Stereotyped thinking
6648. Lack of commitment
6649. Poor communication
6650. Lack of empathy
6651. Poor self-esteem
6652. Lack of skills
6653. Unresolved resentments
6654. Lack of creativity
6655. Television

6656. Write a love poem in formal sonnet style
6657. Listen to Gershwin tunes
6658. "Love will make a way out of no way." ~ Lynda Barry
6659. Arrange Sunday brunch at a local fancy restaurant
6660. Spend a wild weekend in Las Vegas together

6661. "At the touch of love, everyone becomes a poet." ~ Plato

6662. Try your hand at writing a love poem

6663. Don't expect your first efforts to be great—but keep at it

6664. Try writing poems for occasions in your life

6665. Practice acts of random kindness…

6666. And senseless loving

6667. And daily politeness

6668. And increased sensitivity

6669. And creative romance

6670. Have realistic expectations of your partner

6671. Have realistic expectations of yourself—

6672. But keep striving to do better!

6673. Write a list: "12 Reasons Why We Should Make a Baby Together"

6674. Create a "First Class Weekend" for your mate

6675. A Zen tip: When you're together, *be* together: "Be here now"

6676. "Love that which will never be seen twice." ~ Alfred de Vigny

6677. Single guys: Show your commitment by ritually burning your *Little Black Book*

6678. Attitude Experiment: Imagine that you have just one month to live: How would you treat your partner differently?

6679. Indulge your romantic whims

6680. Indulge your erotic fantasies

6681. Indulge his/her sweet tooth

6682. Indulge yourself

6683. Indulge your partner

6684. Take your time—love deepens over time

6685. Give your time—it's your most precious resource

6686. Spoon (the sleeping position!)

6687. Be his "Boy Toy"

6688. Label a box "Sweet Nothings" and giftwrap it

6689. Slip a love note into her eyeglasses case

6690. "When you get into a tug-of-war, drop the rope."
~ Bart Jarvis

6691. Return to your favorite romantic beach

6692. Enemy of Love: Grudges

6693. Enlarge to poster-size the best photo of the two of you

6694. Make love on the cellar stairs

6695. Have a limousine pick her up at work on her birthday

6696. Get him *an entire library* of books on his hobby

6697. Decorate Christmas cookies together

6698. Live in the moment

6699. Greet her at the airport with two dozen roses

6700. Banish all "negative talk" at meals

6701. Make a habit of taking leisurely walks together

6702. Make a custom mix of "walking music"; make a mix every two months

6703. "Walkin' My Baby Back Home" (1930)

6704. "Love Walked In," by Kenny Baker (1938)

6705. "Let's Take an Old-Fashioned Walk" (1949)

Songs to Help You Express
Your Feelings: *Longing/Yearning*

6706. "Against All Odds (Take a Look at Me Now),"
Phil Collins
6707. "Ain't No Sunshine," Bill Withers
6708. "Baby Come to Me," Patti Austin & James Ingram
6709. "Closer to Believing," Emerson, Lake & Palmer
6710. "How Can I Tell You," Cat Stevens
6711. "I Need You," America
6712. "If Ever You're in My Arms Again," Peabo Bryson
6713. "If I Can't Have You," Yvonne Elliman
6714. "Need Her Love," Electric Light Orchestra
6715. "Until the Night," Billy Joel
6716. "Watching and Waiting," The Moody Blues
6717. "When I Need You," Leo Sayer
6718. "You Take My Breath Away," Queen

6719. For left-brained, logical folks: Use your *natural* logical
skills in expressing your love
6720. For right-brained, creative folks: Use your *natural*
creativity in expressing your love
6721. For left-brained, logical folks: Practice your
unfamiliar, creative, wacky side
6722. For right-brained, creative folks: Practice your
unfamiliar, logical, rational side

Items for a *Weekly* Romantic Checklist
6723. Bring home one small, unexpected gift or present
6724. Share *some* form of physical intimacy
6725. Share an *entire* afternoon or evening together

6726. Share two insights you gained this week
6727. Write at least one little love note
6728. Mail *something* to your partner
6729. Plan something special for the weekend

Favorite Love Songs from 1968

6730. "A Beautiful Morning," Rascals
6731. "Angel of the Morning," Merrilee Rush
6732. "Honey," Bobby Goldsboro
6733. "Light My Fire," Jose Feliciano
6734. "Love Is All Around," Troggs
6735. "Love Is Blue," Paul Mauriat
6736. "Midnight Confessions," The Grass Roots
6737. "The Look of Love," Sergio Mendes & Brazil 66
6738. "This Guy's in Love with You," Herb Alpert & Tijuana Brass

6739. Wear matching ski caps
6740. Give your *undivided attention*
6741. Play tourist in your own town
6742. "There is no surprise more wonderful than the surprise of being loved." ~ Charles Morgan
6743. Garden together
6744. For sci-fi fans: Films on video from Science Fiction Continuum: www.sfcontinuum.com
6745. Celebrate a "Final Fling" on the last day of Summer

Quotable Quotes on "Love"

6746. "Love demands all, and has a right to it." ~ Beethoven
6747. "Love does not dominate; it cultivates." ~ Johann Wolfgang von Goethe

6748. "Love is a verb." ~ Clare Boothe Luce
6749. "Love is all we have, the only way that each can help the other." ~ Euripides
6750. "Love and emptiness in us are like the sea's ebb and flow." ~ Kahlil Gibran
6751. "Love and food are equally vital to our sanity and survival." ~ Kuo Tzu
6752. "Love conquers all things; let us too surrender to Love." ~ Virgil
6753. "Love and the gentle heart are but a single thing." ~ Dante Alighieri
6754. "Love begets love. This torment is my joy." ~ Theodore Roethke
6755. "Love cannot be commanded." ~ Latin proverb
6756. "Love comes after the wedding." ~ Laplander proverb
6757. "Love dies only when growth stops." ~ Pearl S. Buck
6758. "Love does not—*cannot*—hurt. It is the *absence* of love that hurts." ~ Gregory J.P. Godek
6759. "Love is a fruit in season at all times, and within the reach of every hand." ~ Mother Teresa
6760. "Love is a great beautifier." ~ Louisa May Alcott
6761. "Love is an act of endless forgiveness, a tender look which becomes a habit." ~ Peter Ustinov
6762. "Love is an energy which exists of itself. It is its own value." ~ Anonymous
6763. "Love is an irresistible desire to be irresistibly desired." ~ Robert Frost
6764. "Love is being stupid together." ~ Paul Valery
6765. "Love is blind." ~ Geoffrey Chaucer
6766. "Love is blind; that is why he always proceeds by the sense of touch." ~ French proverb

6767. "Love is its own aphrodisiac and is the main ingredient for lasting sex." ~ Mort Katz

6768. "Love is more easily demonstrated than defined." ~ Anonymous

6769. "Love is never complete in any person. There is always room for growth." ~ Leo Buscaglia

6770. "Love is not love until love's vulnerable." ~ Theodore Roethke

6771. "Love is merely an empty concept *unless* you bring it alive through *action*." ~ Gregory J.P. Godek

6772. "Love is not only something you feel. It is something you do." ~ David Wilkerson

6773. "Love is not ruled by reason." ~ Moliere

6774. "Love is patient and kind; love is not jealous or boastful." ~ 1 Corinthians 13:4

6775. "Love is staying awake all night with a sick child. Or a very healthy adult." ~ David Frost

6776. "Love is supreme and unconditional; like is nice but limited." ~ Duke Ellington

6777. "Love is the active concern for the life and growth of that which you love." ~ Erich Fromm

6778. "Love is the great asker." ~ D. H. Lawrence

6779. "Love is the greatest refreshment in life." ~ Pablo Picasso

6780. "Love is the irresistible desire to be desired irresistibly." ~ Louis Ginsberg

6781. "Love is the only disease that makes you feel better." ~ Sam Shepard

6782. "Love is the only effective counter to death." ~ Maureen Duffy

6783. "Love is the only game that is not called on account of darkness." ~ Anonymous

6784. "Love is the triumph of imagination over intelligence." ~ H. L. Mencken

6785. "Love is trembling happiness." ~ Kahlil Gibran

6786. "Love is what you've been through with somebody." ~ James Thurber

6787. "Love keeps us hopeful, in all situations, against all evidence." ~ Lewis B. Smedes

6788. "Love knoweth no laws." ~ Sir John Lyly

6789. "Love knows not its depth till the hour of separation." ~ Kahlil Gibran

6790. "Love stretches your heart and makes you big inside." ~ Margaret Walker

6791. "Love: the most fun you can have without laughing." ~ Anonymous

6792. "Love thrives on trivial kindnesses." ~ Theodor Fontane

6793. "Love wasn't put in your heart to stay, Love isn't love till you give it away." ~ Anonymous

6794. "Love will find a way." ~ Anonymous

6795. "Love, you know, seeks to make happy rather than to be happy." ~ Ralph Connor

6796. One is the loneliest number—so spend one whole day together

6797. Tea for two

6798. Three's a crowd, so send the kid away for the day!

6799. Highly recommended: *The 7 Habits of Highly Effective People*, by Stephen Covey

6800. Also, *The 7 Habits of Highly Effective Families*, by Stephen Covey

6801. Create your own memorable photo gifts at www. snapfish.com
6802. And Kodakgallery.com

6803. Gift & Date Idea: Watch the movie *Titanic* together
6804. Get her a copy of the movie on DVD
6805. Get her the soundtrack
6806. Get a photo taken of the two of you in a "Rose Pose": On a ship's bow, while standing behind her, hold her arms outstretched and enjoy the sunset (All *Titanic* fans will appreciate this)

Important Questions for Engaged Couples

If you want your relationship to last a lifetime, it will help to look at these issues:

6807. In what ways do you want your marriage to be like your parents' marriage?
6808. In what ways do you want your marriage to be *different* from your parents' marriage?
6809. What is the one thing that the opposite gender simply doesn't "get" about your gender?
6810. What lessons did you learn from your *previous* love relationships?
6811. How much "personal space" do you need?
6812. What is your idea of the "perfect wedding"?
6813. Where do you want to honeymoon?
6814. Under what circumstances would you see a couple's counselor?
6815. How frequently would you like to have sex?
6816. How many children do you want to have?
6817. At what age will you let your children date?

6818. If your children are sexually active at the same age that you were, will that be OK with you?

6819. Do you fold your underwear or just stuff it in the drawer?

6820. When dining out, sit *next to* each other, instead of *across from* each other

6821. Kiss under water

6822. "Love is love's reward." ~ John Dryden

6823. Greet him at the door wearing a jersey from his favorite football team—*and nothing else*

6824. Build a fire in your fireplace in *August*

6825. The Victorian Inn on Martha's Vineyard: http://www.thevic.com/

6826. Celebrate with Dom Perignon

America is a *very* romantic place: Here's how to get vacation info:

6827. Alabama: www.touralabama.org

6828. Alaska: www.travelalaska.com

6829. Arizona: www.arizonaguide.com

6830. Arkansas: www.arkansas.com

6831. California: www.visitcalifornia.com

6832. Colorado: www.colorado.com

6833. Connecticut: www.ctvisit.com

6834. Delaware: www.visitdelaware.com

6835. District of Columbia: www.washington.org

6836. Florida: www.visitflorida.com

6837. Georgia: www.georgia.org

6838. Hawaii: www.gohawaii.com

6839. Idaho: www.visitidaho.org

6840. Illinois: www.enjoyillinois.com
6841. Indiana: www.in.gov/visitindiana
6842. Iowa: www.traveliowa.com
6843. Kansas: www.travelks.com
6844. Kentucky: www.kentuckytourism.com
6845. Louisiana: www.louisianatravel.com
6846. Maine: www.visitmaine.com
6847. Maryland: www.mdisfun.org
6848. Massachusetts: www.mass-vacation.com
6849. Michigan: www.michigan.org
6850. Minnesota: www.exploreminnesota.com
6851. Mississippi: www.visitmississippi.org
6852. Missouri: www.visitmo.com
6853. Montana: www.visitmt.com
6854. Nebraska: www.visitnebraska.gov
6855. Nevada: www.travelnevada.com
6856. New Hampshire: www.visitnh.gov
6857. New Jersey: www.state.nj.us/travel
6858. New Mexico: www.newmexico.org
6859. New York: www.iloveny.com
6860. North Carolina: www.visitnc.com
6861. North Dakota: www.ndtourism.com
6862. Ohio: www.discoverohio.com
6863. Oklahoma: www.travelok.com
6864. Oregon: www.traveloregon.com
6865. Pennsylvania: www.visitpa.com
6866. Rhode Island: www.visitrhodeisland.com
6867. South Carolina: www.discoversouthcarolina.com
6868. South Dakota: www.travelsd.com
6869. Tennessee: www.tnvacation.com
6870. Texas: www.TravelTex.com

6871. Utah: www.utah.com
6872. Vermont: www.travel-vermont.com
6873. Virginia: www.virginia.org
6874. Washington: www.tourism.wa.gov
6875. West Virginia: www.wvtourism.com
6876. Wisconsin: www.tourism.state.wi.us
6877. Wyoming: www.wyomingtourism.com

6878. The gift: Seven bottles of scented bubble bath
6879. The note: "For a week of rest and relaxation"

6880. Give her a second look
6881. Give him a second chance
6882. Make her second-to-none

6883. Guys: Express your masculinity—but don't be *trapped* in it
6884. Gals: Glory in your femininity—but don't be *limited* by it
6885. Guys: Explore your gentle, soft, sensitive side
6886. Gals: Explore your confident, sexy, powerful side

6887. Write a "Self-Improvement Plan" for yourself
6888. Ask for your partner's input

Favorite Love Songs from 1969

6889. "Baby I Love You," Andy Kim
6890. "Love (Can Make You Happy)," Mercy
6891. "Sugar, Sugar," Archies
6892. "To Busy Thinking 'Bout My Baby," Marvin Gaye
6893. "You Make Me So Very Happy," Blood, Sweat & Tears

6894. The gift: Costume jewelry
6895. The note: "The diamond is fake—the love is real"

6896. Surprise your jazz fan with tickets to the New Orleans Jazz Festival: www.nojazzfest.com
6897. Or vacation at the Festival International de Jazz de Montréal: www.montrealjazzfest.com
6898. And add to the ambiance with "Jazz" cologne
6899. And create a jazzy mood with CDs by Louis Armstrong and Count Basie
6900. And by Fats Waller and Paul Desmond

6901. Peruse the many erotic books by Anaïs Nin
6902. You may want to takes notes, and read passages aloud
6903. *Little Birds*
6904. *Delta of Venus*
6905. *Henry and June*
6906. *A Spy in the House of Love*
6907. *A Literate Passion*
6908. *Obnazhennaia Makha*
6909. *Ladders to Fire*
6910. *Paris Revisited*

6911. Gals: Flash him a little cleavage when no one else is looking
6912. Attend the Valentine's Day/mid-winter carnival in Venice, Italy
6913. Use a love stamp *every time* you mail something to your lover
6914. Send a chocolate chip cookie bouquet

6915. "Then I saw you through myself, and found we were identical." ~ Fakhr Iraqi

6916. For your golf nut: 18 holes at the best local course

6917. Sign your love letters: "Your One and Only"

6918. Get fun rubber stamps that reflect his/her hobbies or interests

6919. Give *fragrant* flowers: Daphne, Wisteria, Hyacinth

6920. "There is but one genuine love-potion—consideration." ~ Menander

6921. Cover strategic body parts with whipped cream

6922. Put comics from the *New Yorker* on the fridge

6923. Go on a second honeymoon

6924. Musical lovenote: "Play the CD *Gorilla*, by James Taylor. My message to you is song No. 3"

6925. Divorce. Divorce yourself from your worries—it will make you a better mate

6926. Read *How to Stop Worrying and Start Living*, by Dale Carnegie

---

6927. Plan a vacation that matches your mate's vacation style:

6928. Romantic: Visit Venice, Italy

6929. Adventurous: Go trekking in Peru

6930. Party: Go to Las Vegas, Nevada

6931. Culinary: Tour the great restaurants of France

6932. Shopping: Cruise Fifth Avenue in NYC

6933. Lazing: Sit on the beach in Maui, Hawaii

6934. Curious: Take a self-improvement seminar

6935. Cultural: Tour the museums of Italy

6936. Spiritual: Visit a monastery or retreat house

Romantically *Wet* Things to Do

6937. Dance in the rain together and sing "Singin' in the Rain"
6938. Be *extravagantly* gallant: Toss your coat over a puddle to keep her dry
6939. Go fishing together
6940. Go sailing together
6941. Swim underneath a waterfall
6942. Take a bubble bath together
6943. Go skinny dipping (in a neighbor's pool at midnight)
6944. Go skinny dipping (at a public beach—remove your suits in the water)
6945. Install a hot tub in your back yard
6946. Learn to water ski
6947. Go jet skiing together
6948. Go scuba diving together
6949. Pour Cognac on your partner's body—lick it off
6950. Go to the beach together
6951. Stroll through the fog in San Francisco
6952. Run through a sprinkler together
6953. Go snorkeling together
6954. Melt an ice cube over your lover's body
6955. Go digging for clams
6956. Wash your car—and have a hose battle
6957. Go river rafting
6958. Hold a private Wet T-shirt Contest
6959. Learn to surf together

6960. Renew your wedding vows in a *private* ceremony
6961. Gather meaningful music from your first wedding and from the ensuing years

6962. Gather cherished mementos from your years together

6963. Gals: You need to know: His coat size
6964. Shoe size and hat size
6965. Shirt size and pants size
6966. Finger size (for bowling balls that fit)

Favorite Love Songs from 1970

6967. "ABC," Jackson Five
6968. "Close to You," Carpenters
6969. "Everything Is Beautiful," Ray Stevens
6970. "Green Eyed Lady," Sugarloaf
6971. "I Think I Love You," Partridge Family
6972. "I'll Be There," Jackson Five
6973. "Signed, Sealed, Delivered," Stevie Wonder
6974. "For the Love of Him," Bobbi Martin
6975. "Love on a Two Way Street," The Moments

6976. Locate a new pattern of stars, and name the new constellation after your lover
6977. Enjoy an autumn hayride together
6978. Get a bumper sticker that reflects her hobby
6979. Ritual: Say "God bless you" after he/she sneezes

Love Quotes from Shakespeare

6980. "Love's best habit is a soothing tongue."
6981. "Now join your hands, and with your hands your hearts."
6982. "Speak low if you speak love."
6983. "The course of true love never did run smooth."
6984. "They do not love that do not show their love."
6985. "For stony limits cannot hold love out."

6986. "Love comforteth like sunshine after rain."

6987. "Love sought is good, but giv'n unsought is better."

6988. "If thou dost love, pronounce it faithfully."

6989. "Doubt thou the stars are fire; Doubt that the sun doth move/Doubt truth to be a liar/but never doubt I love."

6990. "Be thou familiar, but by no means vulgar."

6991. "Love's gentle spring doth always fresh remain."

6992. For police officers in love: Drive your squad car to Lover's Lane, scare off the teenagers, then stay and make out with your partner!

6993. Start with *subtle* romantic gestures

6994. "Joy is not in things; it is in us." ~ Richard Wagner

6995. Fill the glove compartment with Hershey's Kisses

6996. Gift & Date Idea: Get the song "Hard to Say I'm Sorry," by Chicago—

6997. And rent the movie *Summer Lovers*, featuring the song

6998. *Living, Loving & Learning*, by Leo Buscaglia

6999. *Personhood*, by Leo Buscaglia

7000. *Born for Love*, by Leo Buscaglia

7001. Make love in the dark

7002. Make love in the dark without speaking a word

7003. Make love in the dark with music on

7004. How would you arouse your partner if you had just ten minutes?

7005. Half an hour? Three hours? All day? All weekend?

7006. The biggest mistake men make in foreplay is that they don't spend enough time doing it!

7007. The biggest mistake women make in foreplay is that they are too timid and conservative

7008. A framed print of his/her favorite work of art

7009. Create a "Count-Down Calendar" anticipating your next big vacation

7010. Make all of her Holiday gifts "Theme Gifts"

7011. Go on an "Escape from the Kids Date"

7012. Cuddle—caress—curl-up

7013. Replace all the artwork in your bedroom with romantic prints

7014. Daily affirmation: "I am *in love* with my partner"

7015. "How much better is thy love than wine." ~ Song of Solomon 4:10

7016. One guy wrote to his wife, "I love you more than I love the Superbowl."

7017. Write *one simple line* about your love

7018. Take a look at your life: Have superficial things become top priorities? Re-dedicate yourself to love

7019. Promise your lover the moon and the stars…

7020. "Fly Me to the Moon" (1962)

7021. "Blue Moon" (1934)

7022. "In the Chapel in the Moonlight," Ruth Etting (1936)

7023. "By the Light of the Silvery Moon," Ray Noble (1941)

7024. "Stairway to the Stars" (1935)

7025. "You Are My Lucky Star" (1935)

7026. "Love in the Starlight," Dorothy Lamour (1938)

7027. "Don't Let the Stars Get in Your Eyes" (1952)

7028. "Good Morning Starshine," Oliver (1969)

7029. "Stardust" (1940)

Questions About Your Beliefs
(That Reveal a *Lot* About You)

A+ Couples share more than a fondness for each other; they share a great many of the same "core beliefs"

7030. Do you believe that opposites attract?

7031. Do you believe that people learn from their mistakes?

7032. Do you believe that two people can be soul mates?

7033. How does one *recognize* soul mates?

7034. Under what circumstances do you believe that therapy is worthwhile?

7035. Do you believe in love at first sight?

7036. Do you believe in the religion you were raised in?

7037. Do you believe in karma?

7038. What do you believe is the biggest difference between men and women?

7039. Do you believe that things "generally turn out for the best"?

7040. Do you believe that "Absence makes the heart grow fonder"?

7041. Do you believe that "It's not whether you win or lose, it's how you play the game"?

7042. Learn French together—

7043. And spend two weeks in Paris to get you started!

7044. Invite your animal-lover to the zoo—

7045. With a note inside a box of Animal Crackers—
7046. Follow up the date with a stuffed animal of his/her favorite animal

7047. Give the gift of time (your time)
7048. Give the gift of time (a wristwatch)
7049. Inscribe on a watch: "I'll always have time for you."

Favorite Love Songs from 1971
7050. "All I Ever Need Is You," Sonny & Cher
7051. "If You Could Read My Mind," Gordon Lightfoot
7052. "Never Can Say Goodbye," Jackson Five
7053. "Temptation Eyes," Grass Roots
7054. "That's The Way I've Always Heard It Should Be," Carly Simon
7055. "Treat Her Like a Lady," Cornelius Brothers & Sister Rose

7056. Whisper "You're the best" while out at a party
7057. Whisper "I love you" while walking
7058. Whisper her name while making love
7059. Whisper erotic suggestions while out in public

7060. Hire a wedding consultant to help you plan an extravagant anniversary
7061. Fold up your love notes like it's high school
7062. If you're basically a shy person, experiment with being sexually demonstrative
7063. Eat dinner at the most elegant restaurant in town

Ways to Love a Capricorn
(22 December–20 January)

7064. Capricorn is an *earth* sign: Cater to his/her grounded, practical nature
7065. Gift tip: Exclusive, quality
7066. Fine pens, quality glassware
7067. Scented candles, unusual picture frames
7068. Pansies; pine trees
7069. Elaborate desserts
7070. Monumental Moscow
7071. Wrap gifts in brown and deep gray

7072. Create a "*perfect* weekend" (your *partner's* definition of perfect)
7073. Toast each other with champagne
7074. Daily affirmation: "I am romantic"
7075. Give greeting cards that are blatantly obscene!
7076. A+ Romance Rating: The musical *Phantom of the Opera*, by Andrew Lloyd Weber

7077. Surprise her with a flower for no specific reason
7078. Surprise him at work with a picnic lunch
7079. Surprise her by running a bubble bath
7080. Surprise him by dressing sexy at home

7081. Listen with your ears, mind, and heart
7082. Listen for the message behind the words your partner says
7083. Balance your head with your heart

7084. Practice feeling your feelings (It's not as easy as it appears to be)

7085. Become familiar with the full range of your feelings

7086. Talk with your partner about your feelings (the good *and* the bad)

7087. "If there is anything better than to be loved, it is loving." ~ Anonymous

7088. Experiment: Is it *really* better to give than to receive? Try it for one month

7089. If you want your partner to be more loving, *you* start the romantic ball rolling

---

7090. Take her on a *Gone with the Wind* tour of Antebellum plantations

7091. For handymen in love: Install an On-Off switch on your doorbell

7092. Value your mate's opinions

Reminders for Wise Lovers

7093. The grass is *not* greener on the other side

7094. Valentine's Day is *not* the most romantic day of the year!

7095. Your love is unique in all the world

7096. Love must be *expressed*, otherwise it's just a nice-sounding-but-empty concept

7097. Time and effort expended are usually more appreciated than money spent

7098. Love is a matter of *skills*, not luck

7099. Arguing isn't about *winning*, it's about expressing frustration, then re-connecting

7100. Romantic gestures have no ulterior motive

7101. Relationships involve a lot of compromise

7102. Compromise is a two-way street
7103. While love is *universal*, your relationship is *unique*
7104. Your *relationship* needs as much attention as your *partner* does
7105. Romance is the expression of love

7106. Dance together at a restaurant, even when there's no music playing!
7107. Gals: A note to him: "Listen to tracks No. 1, No. 8, and No. 12 on Carole King's *Tapestry* CD"
7108. "Never change when love has found its home." ~ Sextus Propertius
7109. Decorate with Waterford crystal

7110. Keep your expectations reasonable
7111. But at the same time, dream big
7112. Hope and pray
7113. And put your whole heart and soul into your relationship

7114. Plan a series of weekends that will improve your relationship
7115. Weekend #1: Catch-up on all chores
7116. Weekend #2: Relax
7117. Weekend #3: Re-connect with your partner
7118. Weekend #4: Practice your communication skills
7119. Weekend #5: Explore your sexuality
7120. Weekend #6: Deal with tough issues
7121. Weekend #7: Deepen the intimacy

Relationship Myths Masquerading as Truth

7122. **Myth #1:** Men don't experience love as women do
Truth: Men experience the same longing, passion, and desire that women do
Explanation: It's the *outward expression* of love that often (but not always) differs

7123. **Myth #2:** Great relationships are 50/50
Truth: Great relationships are really 100/100
Explanation: It's more than meeting your partner halfway; sometimes you have to give a lot more

7124. **Myth #3:** Men are from Mars, and women are from Venus
Truth: You are not a *stereotype*, but an *individual* unique in all the world
Explanation: Your core personality is not simply gender-based, but a complex and unique mix of spiritual, psychological, genetic, and social factors

7125. **Myth #4:** There are "secret rules" that ensure lasting love
Truth: Nobody has all the answers; *everybody* is searching
Explanation: Poets, philosophers, psychologists, and scientists search constantly for rules and formulas to guide us. *Humans* and *love* simply aren't reducible to simple rules
Suggestion: Don't despair, but celebrate the glorious mystery of it all!

7126. **Myth #5:** Women are better communicators than men
Truth: *Some* women—about 60%—*are* better communicators
Explanation: Be careful of over-generalizations about the sexes! Many men are *great* communicators

Note: Don't forget that there are many different *styles* of communication

7127. **Myth #6:** It's wise to beware of "The Battle of the Sexes"
Truth: There ain't no such thing
Explanation: While there *is* a "gender gap"—*and* a lot of confusion—there's no "war" between the sexes.
Note: The phrase *itself* sets a dangerous mode of thinking; your thinking creates your reality!

7128. **Myth #7:** Real men aren't romantic
Truth: Real Men are *human*—not just *male*—and don't follow "rules" set-down in cute books
Explanation: Being a "Real Man" doesn't mean being a Neanderthal
Note: Guys in *groups* act more macho than they really are when you get them one-on-one

7129. Guys: Buy one item in each of the following stores; giftwrap in individual boxes
7130. A bath shop
7131. A lingerie boutique
7132. A card shop
7133. A flower shop
7134. A jewelry store

7135. Express the *spiritual* plane of your love by attending church together
7136. Express the *emotional* aspect of your love by communicating more
7137. Express the *physical* side of your love

7138. Regardless of the gift, thank your partner
7139. But if it's really *awful*, tell him/her the truth *the very next day* (You're obligated to tell the truth—but be *gentle* about it)

7140. Share feelings freely with your partner
7141. Let him/her know your likes and dislikes
7142. Help him/her differentiate between your *wants* and *needs*
7143. List your ten favorite restaurants
7144. Post pictures of your dream vacation spots on the refrigerator
7145. Show him/her what you like and dislike in various gift and clothing catalogs

---

Favorite Love Songs from 1972

7146. "Happiest Girl in the Whole USA," Donna Fargo
7147. "Lean on Me," Bill Withers
7148. "Let's Stay Together," Al Green
7149. "Nice to Be with You," Gallery
7150. "Precious & Few," Climax
7151. "Without You," Harry Nilsson
7152. "The First Time I Ever Saw Your Face," Roberta Flack

7153. Be child*like*…
7154. But not child*ish*

7155. Dedicate one week to improving your lovemaking skills…
7156. Monday: Get the book *Mating in Captivity: Unlocking Erotic Intelligence*, by Esther Perel

7157. Tuesday: Talk about your best lovemaking
7158. Wednesday: Talk about what turns you on
7159. Thursday: Talk about specific sexual techniques that work for you
7160. Friday: Practice foreplay for two hours
7161. Saturday: Make love all morning long
7162. Sunday: Make love in a way you've never practiced before

7163. Musical lovenote: "Play *Please Please Me*, by The Beatles; my message to you is song No. 11"
7164. Enjoy Dim Sum in San Francisco's Chinatown
7165. Travel to all seven continents during your life together
7166. On a whim, get a discount fare to London for the weekend
7167. Love Enhancer: A good therapist/counselor
7168. For Teddy Bear lovers: The White Swan Inn in San Francisco: www.jdvhotels.com/white_swan_inn

7169. For women only: Take his last name
7170. For men only: Don't make a fuss if she wants to keep her maiden name

Items for a *Daily* Romantic Checklist

7171. Compliment your partner
7172. Spend twenty minutes of uninterrupted time together
7173. Call on your way home
7174. Perform one small—and *unexpected*—gesture
7175. Say "I love you" at least three times
7176. Thank your partner for *something*
7177. Take one extra minute when kissing good-bye

7178. List the three things you want to change about your relationship habits
7179. Create a very specific two-year plan for enacting those changes
7180. Read three good relationship books to help you
7181. Talk with a good counselor to give you some direction

Ways to (Literally) Say "I Love You"

7182. English: "I love you"
7183. Apache: "Shi ingôlth-a"
7184. Arabic: "'Ahebbek"
7185. Armenian: "Sírem zk ´ez"
7186. Aztec: "Nimitzlaco'tla"
7187. Bengali: "Ami tomake bhalo basi"
7188. Bulgarian: "Obícom te"
7189. Burmese: "Chítte"
7190. Cambodian: "Khñoms(r)alañ 'neak"
7191. Cantonese: "Kgoh òi nei"
7192. Cherokee: "Kykéyu"
7193. Cheyenne: "Ne-méhotatse"
7194. Chinese: "Wo ài nei"
7195. Czech: "Miluji vás"
7196. Danish: "Eg elskar dig"
7197. Dutch: "It hous van jou"
7198. Egyptian: "Anna bahebek"
7199. Eskimo: "Nagligivaget"
7200. Finnish: "Mínä rákistan sínua"
7201. French: "Je t'aime"
7202. Gaelic (Irish): "Mo ghradh thú"

7203. German: "Ich liebe dich"
7204. Greek: "Sàs agapo"
7205. Gypsy or Romany: "Mándi komova toot"
7206. Hawaiian: "Aloha wau ia oe"
7207. Hebrew: "Aní ohev otakh"
7208. Hindi: "Mayn toojh ko pyár karta hun"
7209. Hungarian: "Szeretlék"
7210. Icelandic: "Eg elska pig"
7211. Indonesian: "Saja tjinta padamu"
7212. Irish: "Thaim in grabh leat"
7213. Italian: "Ti amo"
7214. Japanese: "Ai shite imasu"
7215. Korean: "Na nun tangshinul sarang hamnida"
7216. Kurdish: "Asektem"
7217. Latin: "Ego Te amo"
7218. Mandarin: "Wo ài ni"
7219. Mohawk: "Konoronhkwa"
7220. Norwegian: "Jeg elsker deg"
7221. Persian: "Aseketem"
7222. Polish: "Ja cie kocham"
7223. Portugese: "Eu te amo"
7224. Russian: "Ya lyablyu tyebya"
7225. Samoan: "O te alofa ya te oe"
7226. Sanskrit: "Aham twan sneham karomi"
7227. Sioux: "Techi 'hila"
7228. Somali: "Wankudja'alahai"
7229. Spanish: "Te amo"
7230. Swahili: "Mimi nakupenda"
7231. Swedish: "Jag älskar dig"
7232. Taiwanese: "Ngùa ai dì"
7233. Thai: "Pom rak khun"

7234. Tibetan: "Khyod-la cags-so"
7235. Turkish: "Seni severim"
7236. Ukranian: "Ya vas kikháyu"
7237. Vietnamese: "Anh yêu em"
7238. Welsh: "Rwy'n dy garu di"
7239. Yiddish: "Ich libe dich"
7240. Yugoslavian: "Ja te volim"
7241. Zulu: "Ngi ya thandela wena"

7242. Fill the cookie jar with love notes
7243. Fill his briefcase with cookies
7244. Browse in a good used clothing shop
7245. "On wings of song, my dearest, I will carry you off."
       ~ Heine
7246. Wear a top hat and a bowler
7247. Ask your partner to dress in a way that fulfills a
       fantasy
7248. Get some funny outfits for Halloween

Favorite Love Songs from 1973

7249. "Behind Closed Doors," Charlie Rich
7250. "Dancing in the Moonlight," King Harvest
7251. "I'm Gonna Love You Just a Little More," Barry
       White
7252. "Pillow Talk," Sylvia
7253. "Let's Get It On," Marvin Gaye

7254. Peruse some classic erotic books...
7255. *Lady Chatterley's Lover*, by D.H. Lawrence
7256. *Tropic of Cancer*, by Henry Miller
7257. *Tropic of Capricorn*, by Henry Miller

7258. Most Underutilized Loving Gesture: The *wink*
7259. Wear "Fahrenheit" cologne—And create a night of *hot* sex
7260. A+ Romance Rating: The Raffles Hotel, in Singapore
7261. Give a red rose on the first day of *every* month

Customized Gifts for Lovers

7262. Get a custom perfume created just for her
7263. A monogrammed bathrobe
7264. Get a *custom* love song written and recorded: http://www.customlovesongs.com/
7265. Create a custom mix of romantic music
7266. Create a custom mix of twelve songs that remind your partner of you
7267. Create a custom mix of romantic dinner music
7268. Create a custom mix of "seduction" music
7269. Create a custom mix of sexy music
7270. Create a custom mix to inspire his/her libido
7271. Get her a *customized* romance novel! www.yournovel.com
7272. Monogrammed underwear!
7273. Custom-made, monogrammed dress shirts
7274. Monogrammed cufflinks
7275. Cufflinks with *his* initials on one side, and *your* initials on the other
7276. A monogrammed handkerchief
7277. Have a favorite photo of the two of you made into a Christmas card
7278. Get your poems, lyrics, vows, invitations, etc., rendered in calligraphy: http://pendragonink.com/

7279. Custom balloons with your names on them
7280. Monogrammed golf balls
7281. Give him/her a funny caricature of yourself
7282. Insert your *own* messages into fortune cookies
7283. Wine with custom labels: www.personalwine.com
7284. Get jewelry custom designed for her
7285. Monogrammed towels
7286. Monogrammed boxer shorts
7287. Have her car custom detailed with stripes and designs in her favorite colors
7288. Get a rubber stamp made with her name on it
7289. Have custom jewelry made from *casts of your fingerprints!*
7290. An elegant letter opener—engraved with a short love quote
7291. Get a book signed by his/her favorite author
7292. An oil painting made from your favorite wedding photo

7293. Get her "Safari" perfume
7294. Along with tickets for an African safari
7295. Or just go to the local zoo

7296. Create your own Summer Celebration
7297. Soundtrack: George Winston's *Summer*
7298. Activity: Sleep under the stars together on a warm summer night
7299. Quote: "Shall I compare thee to a summer's day?" ~ William Shakespeare

7300. *Tiny* changes often produce *major* results

7301. Sports Analogy: It's like changing the grip on your golf club. Try changing your "grip" on your relationship

7302. Cooking Analogy: It's like the importance of one *small*—but *important*—ingredient. *All* the ingredients are important!

7303. Guys: Listen to her. Just *listen*.

7304. Don't problem-solve; don't give advice

7305. Validate her; her feelings; her experience

7306. True listening creates *connection*—and connection keeps love alive

7307. Gals: Send him a letter sealed with a kiss

7308. Use your reddest lipstick

7309. Don't position yourself against his passions

7310. Don't make him choose between you and golf/football/fishing, etc.

7311. There's time enough for sports *and* love

7312. Take the opportunity to develop your *own* passions.

7313. Love Enhancer: Gifts that touch the heart

7314. Slow dance in your bedroom at midnight

7315. "Life is short. Be swift to love! Make haste to be kind!" ~ Henri F. Amiel

7316. Dedicate a song to him/her on the radio

7317. Create a web hunt for your partner. Have them go to various websites to try and figure out your surprise (vacation, jewelry, etc.)

7318. Learn what he/she considers *special*

7319. Give three *blue* gifts, wrapped in *blue*, along with a note saying you'll always be "True Blue"

7320. Favorite gifts for women: An item for whatever she collects

7321. Favorite gifts for women: A subscription to her favorite magazine

7322. Favorite gifts for women: A gift certificate for her favorite boutique

7323. Honor her with a cherished family heirloom…

7324. A classic family portrait

7325. A relative's favorite piece of jewelry

7326. Your grandmother's engagement ring

7327. An antique music box

7328. For women only: No male bashing!

7329. For men only: Don't tell jokes about your partner

7330. For women only: Gaze at him with *love* in your eyes

7331. For men only: *Always* be gentlemanly toward her

7332. For women only: Whisper to him in public, "Let's make love tonight!"

7333. For men only: Whisper to her in public, "You're the *best.*"

Books *About* Women, *For* Women, *By* women

7334. *The Feminine Mystique*, by Betty Friedan

7335. *Real Sex for Real Women*, by Laura Berman

7336. *A Woman's Worth*, by Marianne Williamson

7337. *For Women Only, Revised Edition: A Revolutionary Guide to Reclaiming Your Sex Life*, by Jennifer Berman, Laura Berman, and Elisabeth Bumiller

7338. *Emotional Freedom*, by Judith Orloff, MD.

7339. *Happy for No Reason*, by Marci Shimoff
7340. *The Art of Extreme Self-Care*, by Cheryl Richardson
7341. *The Woman's Comfort Book: A Self-Nurturing Guide for Restoring Balance in Your Life*, by Jennifer Louden

7342. *The Museum of Bad Art: Masterworks*, by Michael Frank and Louise Reilly Sacco
7343. Giftwrap that new car with a big red bow
7344. Guys: Perform the classic "Chippendale Dancer Fantasy"
7345. In the spring, hide a love note in the pocket of her winter coat for her to discover next season
7346. Dream (sleeping) together
7347. For your "control freak" partner: Prepare a *detailed itinerary* for a romantic three-day weekend

Best Romantic Comedies

7348. *10* (♥ ♥ ♥ ♥ Romance Movie Rating)
7349. *10 Things I Hate About You* (♥ ♥ ♥)
7350. *The 40-Year-Old Virgin* (♥ ♥ ♥)
7351. *50 First Dates* (♥ ♥)
7352. *About a Boy* (♥ ♥ ♥)
7353. *A Midsummer Night's Sex Comedy* (♥ ♥)
7354. *Annie Hall* (♥ ♥ ♥ ♥)
7355. *Arthur* (♥ ♥ ♥ ♥)
7356. *Blind Date* (♥ ♥)
7357. *Bridget Jones's Diary* (♥ ♥)
7358. *Broadcast News* (♥ ♥ ♥)
7359. *Crocodile Dundee* (♥ ♥ ♥)
7360. *The Cutting Edge* (♥ ♥)
7361. *Definitely, Maybe* (♥ ♥ ♥)

7362. *Father of the Bride* (♥ ♥ ♥)
7363. *Frankie and Johnny* (♥ ♥ ♥ ♥ ♥)
7364. *Garden State* (♥ ♥ ♥)
7365. *The Goodbye Girl* (♥ ♥ ♥ ♥ ♥)
7366. *Groundhog Day* (♥ ♥ ♥ ♥)
7367. *He's Just Not That Into You* (♥ ♥)
7368. *Hitch* (♥ ♥)
7369. *Hope Floats* (♥ ♥)
7370. *How to Lose a Guy in 10 Days* (♥ ♥ ♥ ♥)
7371. *Knocked Up* (♥ ♥ ♥ ♥)
7372. *Legally Blonde* (♥ ♥)
7373. *Little Manhattan* (♥ ♥ ♥)
7374. *Love Actually* (♥ ♥ ♥ ♥)
7375. *Manhattan* (♥ ♥ ♥)
7376. *Mrs. Doubtfire* (♥ ♥ ♥)
7377. *My Best Friend's Wedding* (♥ ♥ ♥)
7378. *My Big Fat Greek Wedding* (♥ ♥ ♥ ♥)
7379. *Overboard* (♥ ♥)
7380. *The Philadelphia Story* (♥ ♥ ♥ ♥)
7381. *Pillow Talk* (♥ ♥ ♥ ♥)
7382. *Play It Again, Sam* (♥ ♥ ♥)
7383. *Pretty in Pink* (♥ ♥ ♥ ♥)
7384. *Pride and Prejudice* (♥ ♥ ♥ ♥)
7385. *The Princess Bride* (♥ ♥ ♥)
7386. *Risky Business* (♥ ♥ ♥)
7387. *Roxanne* (♥ ♥ ♥ ♥ ♥)
7388. *Serendipity* (♥ ♥)
7389. *Shakespeare in Love* (♥ ♥ ♥)
7390. *Shampoo* (♥ ♥ ♥)
7391. *Sixteen Candles* (♥ ♥ ♥ ♥)
7392. *So I Married an Axe Murderer* (♥ ♥)

7393.   *Some Kind of Wonderful* (♥ ♥)
7394.   *Splash* (♥ ♥ ♥)
7395.   *Sweet Home Alabama* (♥ ♥ ♥)
7396.   *Tootsie* (♥ ♥ ♥ ♥)
7397.   *The Wedding Planner* (♥ ♥)
7398.   *What Woman Want* (♥ ♥)
7399.   *The Woman in Red* (♥ ♥ ♥)
7400.   *You've Got Mail* (♥ ♥ ♥ ♥)

7401.   Set your alarm clock thirty minutes early—enjoy the morning together
7402.   Buy a DVD of his favorite show

7403.   Never open your mate's mail
7404.   Always have *some* body part touching your partner as you fall asleep
7405.   Always give him/her a phone number where you can be reached when you're traveling
7406.   Never argue in public
7407.   Always talk to one another with *respect*
7408.   Never sulk

7409.   Guys: Always treat her like a lady
7410.   Never, never, *never* disrespect her
7411.   Gals: Always, always, *always* honor his masculinity
7412.   Never, never, *never* embarrass him in public

7413.   "'Faith' in the language of heaven is 'Love' in the language of men." ~ Victor Hugo
7414.   Love is a quality that connects the material world with the spiritual world

7415. Light candles to symbolize your love
7416. Attend a church service together

The 10 Commandments for Loving Couples

7417. Thou shalt give 100%
7418. Thou shalt treat your partner as the unique individual he/she truly is
7419. Thou shalt stay connected through word and deed
7420. Thou shalt accept change and support growth in yourself and your mate
7421. Thou shalt live your love
7422. Thou shalt share: The love and fear, the work and play
7423. Thou shalt listen, listen, listen
7424. Thou shalt honor the subtle wisdom of the heart and listen to the powerful insights of the mind
7425. Thou shalt not be a jerk or a nag
7426. Thou shalt integrate the purity of spiritual love with the passion of physical love and the power of emotional love

7427. Write a "Love Warranty" to guarantee your devotion
7428. Attach a small love note to a bunch of balloons
7429. Send a bouquet of your partner's favorite flowers
7430. Hide a little gift so well that he probably won't find it for *months*
7431. Reassure her

Favorite Love Songs from 1974

7432. "A Very Special Love Song," Charlie Rich
7433. "The Best Thing That Ever Happened," Gladys Knight & Pips

7434. "Feel Like Makin' Love," Roberta Flack
7435. "Hooked on a Feeling," Blue Swede
7436. "I Will Always Love You," Dolly Parton
7437. "If You Love Me," Olivia Newton-John
7438. "Let Me Be There," Olivia Newton-John
7439. "Love's Theme," Love Unlimited Orchestra
7440. "Then Came You," Dionne Warwick
7441. "You Make Me Feel Brand New," Stylistics

7442. Work to *understand* your relationship
7443. But don't *analyze* it to death
7444. Love is an experience to be *cherished*, not scrutinized
7445. Get a huge umbrella-built-for-two
7446. Travel to Alaska to watch the Aurora Borealis (Northern Lights)

7447. Drive up the California coast
7448. Ski down Mount Aspen
7449. Climb up Mount Washington
7450. Raft down the Colorado River
7451. Climb up the Statue of Liberty
7452. Slide down a giant water slide
7453. Rise up in a hot air balloon
7454. Dive down into the Great Barrier Reef
7455. Lift up your spirits
7456. Hike down the Grand Canyon

Ways to Love an Aquarius
(21 January–18 February)

7457. Aquarius is an *air* sign: Cater to his/her light, funloving nature

7458. Gift tip: Whimsical and unusual
7459. Quirky pottery, costume jewelry
7460. Almost anything custom-made
7461. Orchids; cherry trees
7462. Subtle flavors, creamy textures
7463. The Taj Mahal, in India
7464. Wrap gifts in electric blue and turquoise

7465. Identify *very specific* problem areas in your relationship, *and vow to clear them up*
7466. Come up with a system for balancing the checkbook—*and never argue about it again*
7467. Bring those little sexual frustrations out into the open—before they become *big* problems
7468. Write a household budget—*with enough flexibility built-in*—and stick to it
7469. Divide-up the household chores—*fairly*—and just get on with it
7470. Discuss how you allocate your time—leisure time versus work time
7471. Enemy of Love: Shyness
7472. Turn your anniversary into a *week-long* celebration
7473. Write in tiny letters on a wooden yardstick: Thirty-Six Ways to Measure Your Love for Her
7474. Insert a love note into your mate's morning newspaper
7475. Greet him at the airport with a balloon bouquet

7476. "Make love not war": Well?!
7477. "Love makes the world go round": Do your part to keep it moving!

7478. "Two heads are better than one": Consult one another more often

7479. "It's not *what* you do, but *how* you do it": But you gotta *do* it!

7480. "The way to a man's heart is through his stomach": Cook his favorite meal

7481. "Two steps forward, one step back": This is how we usually make progress in our relationships

7482. "When the going gets tough, the tough get going": Don't give up

7483. To connect your love and spirituality, read *The Road Less Traveled*, by M. Scott Peck

7484. Try "less traveled roads" with your lover

7485. Resource: *Off the Beaten Path: A Guide to More Than 1,000 Scenic & Interesting Places Still Uncrowded and Inviting* by the editors of *Reader's Digest*

7486. Get DVDs of *Mad about You*, one of the most romantic sitcoms ever

7487. Charter a luxury yacht for a Caribbean cruise

7488. "Inspiration starts in the home." ~ Alpha English

7489. Have a charm *custom-made* for her charm bracelet

7490. For marrieds only: Inscribe your wedding rings with a romantic verse

7491. Read *Romantic Fantasies: And Other Sexy Ways of Expressing Your Love*, by Gregory J.P. Godek

7492. Identify the strengths of your "type" of relationship, and "go with the flow"

7493. Are you a "Two peas in a pod" couple? Or an "Opposites attract" couple?

7494. Are you a "Platonic" couple? Or a "Passionate" couple?

7495. Become aware of the problems *inherent* in your "type" of relationship, and plan to deal with them

7496. Go in search of romantic views...

7497. The Golden Gate Bridge—at sunset

7498. Paris—from the top of the Eiffel Tower

7499. The Grand Canyon—at sunrise

7500. The Pacific Ocean—from a Hawaiian hut

7501. The Caribbean—from the deck of a cruise ship

7502. The New York skyline—from a suite at the Waldorf Astoria

7503. The moon—rising over the Fiji Islands

7504. Niagara Falls—from aboard the Maid of the Mist

7505. Keep your promises

7506. Keep your cool

7507. Keep it up

7508. Keep your big mouth shut (when you're tempted to criticize)

7509. Try a little aromatherapy together

7510. Treat commercials as "Romance Breaks"

7511. Freeze a tiny love note in an ice cube

7512. Buy a smartphone and download episodes of his favorite TV show

7513. Frame both of your baby photos together

7514. For singles only: Send your resume with a note: "I want you to get to know me better"

On Birthdays

7515.   #20: Send twenty stuffed animals to her

7516.   #30: Send thirty golf balls to him

7517.   #40: Send forty reasons why you love her

7518.   #50: Send fifty specially selected love songs to him

7519.   #60: Send sixty greeting cards to her

7520.   #70: Send seventy sunflowers to him

7521.   #80: Send eighty Hershey's Kisses to her

7522.   #90: Send ninety balloons to him

7523.   #100: Send one hundred red roses to her

Favorite Love Songs from 1975

7524.   "Best of My Love," Eagles

7525.   "Falling in Love," Hamilton, Joe Frank & Reynolds

7526.   "Love Will Keep Us Together," Captain & Tennille

7527.   "Some Kind of Wonderful," Grand Funk

7528.   "You're the First, the Last, My Everything," Barry White

7529.   "My Eyes Adored You," Frankie Valli & the Four Seasons

7530.   "He Don't Love You (Like I Love You)," Tony Orlando & Dawn

7531.   "Feel Like Makin' Love," Bad Company

7532.   "I Only Have Eyes For You," Art Garfunkel

7533.   Treat her to a shopping spree at Neiman-Marcus

7534.   Tip for How to Buy Gifts for Guys: Look for "Toys-for-Boys" (We never really grow up—our toys just get more expensive)

Kinds of Gifts to Give Your Guy or Gal

7535.   The Surprise Gift

7536.   The Trinket Gift

7537. The "Just what I always wanted" Gift
7538. The Classically Romantic Gift
7539. The Perfume Gift
7540. The Sexy Gift
7541. The "Oh, you *shouldn't* have!—But I *love* it!" Gift
7542. The Obligatory Gift
7543. The Optional Gift
7544. The Kooky Gift
7545. The Keepsake Gift
7546. The "How did you *find* it?!" Gift
7547. The Homemade Gift
7548. The Unbelievably Expensive Gift
7549. The Gag Gift
7550. The Gift that Keeps on Giving
7551. The One Gigantic Item Gift
7552. Theme-Gifts
7553. Personalized Gifts
7554. The Gift of Travel
7555. The Gift of Food
7556. The Gift in His/Her Favorite Color
7557. The Meaningful Gift
7558. The Funny Gift
7559. The Practical Gift
7560. The Frivolous Gift
7561. The First Class Gift
7562. The Custom Romance Certificate Gift
7563. The Gift-Within-a-Gift-Within-a-Gift Gift
7564. The Beautifully-Wrapped Gift
7565. Birthday Gifts
7566. Anniversary Gifts
7567. The Gift of Time

7568. The Gift of Cash
7569. The Gift Certificate
7570. The Gift of Yourself

7571. Tie a love note to her dog's collar
7572. Love Enhancer: Good role models
7573. The most important sex organ is the *brain*

Questions About Life & Love
(That Reveal a *Lot* About You)

People with A+ Relationships don't *assume* too much about each other: They *ask!*

7574. When do you feel most fully engaged in living?
7575. What do you do when you feel blue?
7576. What makes you angry?
7577. What makes you sad?
7578. Who is your mentor? Hero? Role model?
7579. What's the best relationship advice you've ever gotten?
7580. What one wish do you have for your children?
7581. What would you like your epitaph to read?
7582. How did you first learn about sex?
7583. What crazy misconceptions did you once have about sex?

7584. English: "You make me so happy"
7585. French (to a guy): "Tu me rends très heureux"
7586. French (to a gal): "Tu me rends très heureuse"
7587. Italian: "Tu mi rendi così felice"
7588. German: "Du machst mich sehr glücklich"
7589. Spanish: "Me haces muy feliz"
7590. Portugese: "Você me fax muito feliz"

7591.   Gift & Date Idea: Get the song "True Love," by Bing Crosby & Grace Kelly—

7592.   And rent *High Society*, featuring the song

7593.   Favorite gifts for men: Tools!

7594.   Favorite gifts for men: Wristwatches!

7595.   Favorite gifts for men: Cash!

7596.   Be silly

7597.   Learn to tie a "Lover's Knot"

7598.   Share *everything:* Your secret dreams and desires

7599.   "However rare true love is, true friendship is even rarer." ~ La Rochefoucauld

7600.   Teach your parrot to say her name

7601.   Don't just *work* at it—*play* at it, too!

7602.   Eat finger foods and feed each other

7603.   Take your teddy bear collector to http://www.buildabear.com/

7604.   Attend a seminar together to build your relationship skills

The Most Romantic Movie Soundtracks

7605.   *About Last Night*

7606.   *Against All Odds*

7607.   *Bed of Roses*

7608.   *Casablanca*

7609.   *Crazy for You*

7610.   *Dirty Dancing*

7611.   *Love Affair*

7612.   *Somewhere in Time*

7613.   *Titanic*

7614. Buy a new car together
7615. View every anniversary as a new chapter of *The Story of Your Lives Together*
7616. Never, never, *never* say, "I told you so"
7617. Re-design your bedroom with the help of *Pottery Barn Bedrooms (Pottery Barn Design Library)*, by Sarah Lynch, Prue Ruscoe, and Clay Ide

7618. Know *all* of your anniversaries—
7619. And celebrate *several* of them…
7620. The day you first met
7621. Your first date
7622. Your first kiss
7623. The first time you said, "I love you"
7624. The first time you made love
7625. The day you moved-in together
7626. The day you bought your first home
7627. The day you conceived your child

7628. The gift: A four-leaf clover
7629. The note: "I got lucky when I found you."

7630. "Civilized people cannot fully satisfy their sexual instinct without love." ~ Bertrand Russell
7631. Sexual knowledge will *enhance* sex—but human sexuality isn't complete without love
7632. If you want to keep your *sex* life active, keep your love—*emotional*—life active!

7633. Splurge on a $100 shopping spree at Radio Shack

7634. Have a drawer-full of Hallmark cards ready to mail
7635. Replace *birth*days with "*mirth*-days"
7636. Perform the classic "Sexy Masseuse Fantasy"
7637. For singles only: Fantasize together about what your wedding might be like
7638. Ritual: Always hand her a towel after her shower
7639. Tape a love note to the center of the rear windshield, and wait for him to see it

---

7640. Give *him* a variety of jewelry…
7641. Cufflinks
7642. Tie tacks
7643. Earrings

Gemstones and Their Symbolic Meanings

Give jewelry with *symbolic* and *romantic* meaning! Write a poem that reflects the symbolic meaning of the gemstone in the jewelry. Find a love song that matches the meaning of the gemstone—and create a theme gift

7644. Agate: *calmness, eloquence, health, virtue, wealth*
7645. Amethyst: *deep love, happiness, sincerity*
7646. Aquamarine: *happiness in love, hope, courage*
7647. Beryl: *everlasting youth, happiness, hope*
7648. Bloodstone: *brilliance, courage, generosity, health*
7649. Carbunkle: *energy, self-confidence, strength*
7650. Carnelian: *courage, joy, friendship, peace*
7651. Cat's Eye: *long life, platonic love*
7652. Chrysolite: *wisdom, curiosity*
7653. Coral: *attachment, faithfulness*
7654. Diamond: *joy, life, love, purity, innocence*
7655. Emerald: *spring, hope, peace, tranquillity*

7656.   Garnet: *faith, loyalty, strength*
7657.   Hyacinth: *constancy, love, faithfulness*
7658.   Jade: *intelligence, longevity, strength*
7659.   Jasper: *courage, joy, wisdom*
7660.   Lapis Lazuli: *ability, cheerfulness, truth*
7661.   Moonstone: *pensiveness, intelligence*
7662.   Onyx: *clearness, dignity*
7663.   Opal: *confidence, happiness, hope, tender love*
7664.   Pearl: *beauty, purity, faithfulness, wisdom, wealth*
7665.   Peridot: *happiness*
7666.   Ruby: *beauty, dignity, nobility, happiness, love, passion*
7667.   Sapphire: *calmness, contemplation, hope, purity, truth*
7668.   Sardonyx: *divine love, joy, marital happiness, vivacity*
7669.   Topaz: *eager love, fidelity, friendship, gentleness*
7670.   Tourmaline: *courage, generosity, thoughtfulness*
7671.   Turquoise: *success, depth, understanding*
7672.   Zircon: *respect, joy*

7673.   For your chocoholic: *Chocolate Obsession*, by Michael Recchiuti, Fran Gage, and Maren Carus
7674.   Find some old Victorian-style greeting cards
7675.   Spouses *forever*: Have a "wedding band" tattooed on your ring finger
7676.   Remember: You get 1,440 minutes every day. How many do you spend expressing love?
7677.   A "Ride in the Country" Coupon: Good for a lazy Sunday afternoon of cruising the countryside. A relaxing day is promised
7678.   Don't sweat the small stuff (It's *all* small stuff)

Favorite Love Songs from 1976

7679. "Afternoon Delight," Starland Vocal Band
7680. "Let Your Love Flow," Bellamy Brothers
7681. "Love Hangover," Diana Ross
7682. "I Honestly Love You," Olivia Newton-John
7683. "I'll Have to Say I Love You in a Song," Jim Croce
7684. "Help Me," Joni Mitchell
7685. "Let's Stick Together," Bryan Ferry

7686. For women only: Let your hair grow long, if he desires it
7687. For men only: Shave off your mustache, if she doesn't care for it
7688. For women only: Wear one of his dress shirts—with lingerie underneath
7689. For men only: Wear bikini underwear just for her
7690. For women only: Wear his favorite lingerie under your work outfit today
7691. For men only: Write suggestive notes in her Victoria's Secret catalog

Questions We *Dare* You to Discuss With Your Partner!

A+ Couples share all kinds of "secrets" with each other

7692. Have you ever had sex in the back seat of a car?
7693. What was your most *embarrassing* moment in the presence of a member of the opposite sex?
7694. Under what conditions would you consider divorce?
7695. How did you lose your virginity?
7696. What sexual fantasy would you *love* to enact?
7697. What are you afraid of?

7698. How are you *just like* your father? Mother?

7699. What are your *fondest* childhood memories?

7700. What is your *worst* childhood memory?

7701. Whose ego is more fragile—yours or your partner's?

7702. Get a copy of *The Kama Sutra*

7703. Read parts of it aloud to each other

7704. Try some of its suggestions

7705. Take your Judy Garland fan to the Judy Garland Museum in Grand Rapids, Minnesota

7706. Wake her at 3 A.M. by gently kissing her

7707. Get a massage table, and get *serious* about those backrubs!

7708. Take your mystery lover to visit the Sherlock Holmes Museum at 221b Baker Street, London

---

A to Z Romantic Gifts

Dedicate yourself to finding one romantic gift for each letter of the alphabet

7709. **A** is for Artwork, Azaleas, Antiques, Aphrodisiacs

7710. **B** is for Balloons, Books, Beatles albums

7711. **C** is for Chocolate, Candles, Cards, Cookies, CDs, Cameras, Concerts

7712. **D** is for Donuts, Dining out, Diamonds, Dom Perignon

7713. **E** is for Earrings, Escape weekends, Engagement rings

7714. **F** is for Films, Flowers, Ferris wheel rides, Furs, Fishing

7715. **G** is for Gemstones, Gold, Garter belts, Guitars

7716. **H** is for Hats, Hawaiian vacations, Honeymoons

7717. **I** is for Ice cream, Italian vacations, Island escapes

7718. **J** is for Jewelry, Jacuzzis, Jazz music, Jamaican vacations
7719. **K** is for Kites, Kinky toys, Kiss coupons, Earl Klugh
7720. **L** is for Licorice, Lingerie, Luggage, Limousine rides
7721. **M** is for Movie tickets, Motorcycles, Music
7722. **N** is for Nightgowns, Necklaces, Nature, Novels
7723. **O** is for Opals, Oil lamps, Ornaments, Opera
7724. **P** is for Perfume, Picnic baskets, Popcorn, Poppies
7725. **Q** is for Quilts, Quiet afternoons, Queen Mary cruises
7726. **R** is for Rings, Roses, Robes, Reggae music
7727. **S** is for Satin Sheets, Spas, Skates, Silk boxer shorts
7728. **T** is for Tickets, Tools, Tents, T-shirts, Tea
7729. **U** is for Umbrellas, U2 albums, Unconditional love
7730. **V** is for Vacations, Vases, VCRs, Violin concertos
7731. **W** is for Waterfalls, Weekend get-aways, Watches
7732. **X** is for eXtra consideration, eXtravagant gifts
7733. **Y** is for Yachts, Yukon vacations, Year-of-romance
7734. **Z** is for Zany gifts, Zanzibar vacations, Zorro

7735. There's always romantic music by Yanni...
7736. Selected CDs: *Keys to Imagination; Tribute*
7737. *Optimystique; Out of Silence*
7738. *Reflections of Passion; Heart of Midnight*

7739. Mail a lock of your hair to your lover
7740. Encase a special memento (ticket stub, wedding invitation, etc.) in acrylic
7741. Get a pendant that honors his/her religious beliefs
7742. Enemy of Love: Resentment
7743. Leave the world a better place because you've raised your kids to be loving
7744. Play "sexy-words-only" Scrabble

7745. For plumbers in love: Install a luxurious Jacuzzi in your home

7746. Kidnap your partner for a surprise three-day weekend

7747. When you've got money to spend, *spend it!*

7748. On caviar

7749. Antique fountain pens

7750. Mink teddy bears

7751. Original artwork

7752. 24-karat gold *anything*

7753. Ask your partner to describe his/her "Dream Vacation"

7754. Let your imaginations run wild

7755. Picture this vacation down to the *smallest* detail

7756. Create a long-term plan to make this dream come true

7757. Periodically give gifts that relate to the destination, such as:

7758. Clothes and books

7759. Travel posters and brochures

7760. And finally, make this "Dream Vacation" a reality

7761. English: "You're sweet"

7762. French: "Tu es gentille"

7763. Italian: "Sei dolce"

7764. German: "Du bist süß"

7765. Spanish: "Eres dulce"

7766. Portugese: "Você é gentil"

7767. Turn on the heating blanket before your sweetie gets in bed

7768. Thumbtack a little love note to a beam in the attic—which may not be found for *years*!

7769. Experiment with some love potions (couldn't hurt—might help!)

7770. Get a custom street sign made with her name on it

7771. Surprise her with a briefcase stuffed with Milk Duds

7772. Include a love note in his lunchbox

Travel Websites to Help
You Plan a Romantic Vacation

7773. *Adventure Road*: http://adventure.nationalgeographic.com/

7774. *Hawaii Magazine*: www.hawaiimagazine.com

7775. *Asia Pacific Travel: www.CathayPacific.com/us*

7776. *California Highways*: www.californiatourandtravel.com

7777. *Conde Nast Traveler*: www.condenasttraveler.com

7778. *Endless Vacation:* www.endlessvacation.com

7779. *National Geographic Traveler*:
www.traveler.nationalgeographic.com

7780. *Railways*: http://www.modern-railways.com/

7781. *Romantic Traveling*: www.romantictraveling.com

7782. *The Discerning Traveler*: www.discerningtraveler.com

7783. *Travel & Leisure*: www.travelandleisure.com

7784. *TravelTips*: www.travltips.com

7785. Buy her a historical romance novel set in a time period and location she loves

7786. Buy her two tickets to that location

7787. Stay there for a long weekend

7788. Follow in the footsteps of the hero and heroine

7789. Stop using lame excuses, like "Real Men aren't romantic"
7790. And "I don't have time"
7791. And "I forgot"
7792. And "Maybe next week"
7793. And "Romance is for teenagers"
7794. And "I don't know what to do"
7795. And "I'm not very creative"
7796. And "I'm too tired"
7797. And "We're *parents* now"
7798. And "I have a career to think about"
7799. And "Romance is going to cost me a fortune"

7800. At a seafood restaurant: Hide a real pearl in an oyster
7801. Make love 33% more often
7802. Give freely of yourself
7803. Watch the lights of Broadway from the window seats of a restaurant
7804. Eat dinner at the restaurant with the best food at cheap prices
7805. Give one rose for every *day* you've been together!

Favorite Love Songs from 1977

7806. "Best of My Love," The Emotions
7807. "Handy Man," James Taylor
7808. "Feels Like the First Time," Foreigner
7809. "So in to You," Atlanta Rhythm Section
7810. "You're My World," Helen Reddy
7811. "You Light Up My Life," Debby Boone

7812. Guys, you may want to check out: *If Only He Knew: What No Woman Can Resist*, by Gary Smalley

7813. You'll be relieved to learn about: *What Men Say, What Women Hear: Bridging the Communication Gap One Conversation at a Time*, by Linda Papadopoulos

7814. What guys desire *and* fear: *Women Can't Hear What Men Don't Say: Destroying Myths, Creating Love*, by Warren Farrell Ph.D.

7815. Required reading: *Men's Health Guide to the Best Sex in the World*, by Editors of *Men's Health*

7816. Talk more; spend more time together

7817. "Shared joy is double joy; shared sorrow is half a sorrow." ~ Swedish proverb

7818. Don't keep the hard stuff to yourself: Two hearts are better than one

---

Bits of Advice from Happy Couples

7819. "Do *silly stuff*—like going trick-or-treating together on Halloween."

7820. "Celebrate *every single day.*"

7821. "Quit being so damn selfish!"

7822. "Sometimes a simple hug says more than words possibly can."

7823. "Count to ten before expressing anger."

7824. "Don't believe the cynics: You *can* keep love alive for a lifetime."

7825. "Be the most romantic couple in your neighborhood."

7826. "Don't assume you know each other inside out—even after many years together."

7827.   "Don't follow anybody's 'formula' for love: You gotta live your own love."

7828.   "Be best friends."

7829.   "Don't get stuck in your roles."

7830.   "Hold quarterly 'Relationship Meetings' to discuss what's going on."

7831.   "Never miss your yearly vacation."

7832.   "Relationships have cycles—so never despair."

7833.   "Arguing is God's pressure release valve for couples."

7834.   "Don't get stuck in a 'Saturday Night Sex Rut'"

7835.   "Travel together: It broadens your horizons."

7836.   "Lots and lots of little surprises."

7837.   "Most men won't admit it, but *we* like to receive flowers, *too.*"

7838.   "Don't sleep in separate bedrooms, it thwarts intimacy."

7839.   "Treat your wife like a *girlfriend*, not like a *wife.*"

7840.   "Share a hobby or sport."

7841.   "Don't keep secrets."

7842.   "Remember the reasons why you first fell in love with the little devil!"

7843.   "Love is a journey, not a destination."

7844.   "A great relationship is a place to 'come home' to."

7845.   "A relationship is God's gift; it's our job to make the most of it."

7846.   "I've learned that when you give love, you give from an infinite reservoir."

7847.   Music from romantic crooner Luther Vandross—

7848.   Selected CDs: *The Night I Fell in Love*

7849.   *Power of Love; I Know*

7850.   *Any Love; Never Too Much*

7851. Try making love as *quietly* as you possibly can…the skill may come in handy some day

7852. Try making love as *loudly* as you possibly can…don't hold *anything* back!

Favorite Love Songs from 1978

7853. "I Go Crazy," Paul Davis

7854. "Our Love," Natalie Cole

7855. "You Needed Me," Anne Murray

7856. "How Deep Is Your Love," Bee Gees

7857. "You're The One That I Want," John Travolta & Olivia Newton-John

7858. "Missing You," Rolling Stones

7859. "Take A Chance on Me," ABBA

7860. "Summer Nights," John Travolta & Olivia Newton-John

7861. "Wonderful Tonight," Eric Clapton

7862. "Is This Love?" Bob Marley and the Wailers

7863. Play romantic music after work

7864. Try some Kenny G or Al Jarreau

7865. Create your own custom holidays. For example…

7866. Wife Appreciation Day

7867. Redhead Day

7868. A Holiday for Workaholics

7869. Lefthander Day

7870. Beer Lovers of America Day

7871. Create unique rituals for your holiday—and take the day off work to celebrate

Best Love Songs by Stevie Wonder

7872. "For Once in My Life"
7873. "I Just Called to Say I Love You"
7874. "I Was Made to Love Her"
7875. "Nothing's Too Good for My Baby"
7876. "My Cherie Amour"
7877. "Signed, Sealed, Delivered I'm Yours"
7878. "You Are the Sunshine of My Life"

7879. Play sexy, sultry music when she/he comes home from work
7880. Try some Sade, Enigma, or Madonna

7881. Send her a note: "I knead you"—then bake bread together
7882. Frame posters from favorite vacation spots
7883. Invite him out by giftwrapping the song "I Wanna Dance with Somebody (Who Loves Me)," by Whitney Houston

7884. Favorite gifts for men: Cameras
7885. Favorite gifts for men: Power tools
7886. Favorite gifts for men: Really cool briefcases

7887. When your kids go back-to-school, send *yourselves* "back-to-school" too
7888. Take a relationship seminar together
7889. Or read a good relationship book, like *The Heart of the Five Love Languages*, by Gary Chapman

7890. Gift & Date Idea: Get the song "Can't Help Falling in Love," by UB40—
7891. And rent the movie *Sliver*, featuring the song

Things to Thank Your Partner For

Write a series of "Thank You" cards to him/her.

7892. "Thank you for falling in love with me"
7893. "Thank you for believing in me"
7894. "Thank you for your gentle touch"
7895. "Thank you for being by my side"
7896. "Thank you for putting up with me"
7897. "Thank you for being an awesome mom/dad to our children"
7898. "Thank you for the chocolate chip cookies"
7899. "Thank you for teaching me what love is really all about"
7900. "Thank you for hanging in there through thick and thin"
7901. "Thank you for that time in bed when you…"
7902. "Thank you for getting up at 3 A.M. with the kids"
7903. "Thank you for your emotional support"
7904. "Thank you coming to my rescue and…"
7905. "Thank you for the hugs"
7906. "Thank you for balancing the checkbook"
7907. "Thank you for being the best kisser in the world!"
7908. "Thank you for the way you hold me"

7909. Read *Romantic Dates: Ways to Woo & Wow the One You Love*, by Gregory J.P. Godek
7910. Special note to the overwhelmed: Remember the 80/20 Rule: "80% of your results come from 20% of your effort."
7911. Enemy of Love: Patronizing your partner

7912. "I am my beloved's, and his desire is toward me."
~ Song of Solomon 7:10
7913. For engaged couples only: Write your wedding vows together
7914. Expand your Romantic Music Library with Billy Ocean
7915. Remember, when it comes to love, "actions speak louder than words"

Favorite Love Songs from 1979

7916. "A Little More Love," Olivia Newton-John
7917. "Babe," Styx
7918. "Reunited," Peaches & Herb
7919. "Love You Inside Out," Bee Gees
7920. "Baby, I Love You," The Ramones
7921. "I Was Made For Lovin' You," Kiss
7922. "Just the Way You Are," Barry White
7923. "My Forbidden Lover," Chic
7924. "Escape (The Pina Colada Song)," Rupert Holmes

7925. Get a copy of *The Joy of Sex*
7926. Mark your favorite pages
7927. Share them with your partner
7928. Reserve an entire weekend to "play"

Questions to Spark Your Sex Life

People with A+ sex lives aren't shy about asking—and answering—sexy questions:

7929. What is your *secret* sexual fantasy?
7930. *Where* would you like to have sex?
7931. What kind of *public* clothing do you find sexy?
7932. What kind of *bedroom* clothing do you find sexy?

7933. Do you know what your partner's favorite foreplay activity is?

7934. What is your favorite foreplay activity to *perform*?

7935. What is your favorite foreplay activity to *receive*?

7936. Do you have a fantasy that turns you on but you'd never actually do?

7937. What sexual activity have you never done before and would like to try?

7938. What movie scenes do you find sexy?

7939. Write messages using "shoe string licorice"

7940. While in Los Angeles, you may want to drive down Juliet Street or Romeo Canyon Road

7941. Take your tea lover to visit Celestial Seasonings, in Boulder, Colorado: www.celestialsesonings.com

7942. For your golfer: Celebrate Jack Nicklaus's birthday, January 21

7943. In a love note, tell him that you are full of "concupiscence" for him

7944. Spend a day at Disney World together

7945. A+ B&B Rating: The Inn at Long Lake, in Naples, Maine: www.innatlonglake.com

7946. "A kiss is the shortest distance between two." ~ Henny Youngman

7947. *Forget* "communicating"; don't *bother* with "empathy"—just *kiss!*

7948. English: "Sweet dreams"

7949. French: "Fais de beaux rêves"

7950. Italian: "Sogni d'oro"

7951. German: "Träum süß"
7952. Spanish: "¡Que sueños con los angelitos!"
7953. Portugese: "Durma bem"

Creativity Enhancers to Help You

These "creativity enhancers" will enliven your relationship:

7954. A playful attitude
7955. Belief that you're creative
7956. Ability to handle ambiguity
7957. Risk-taking
7958. Changing the rules
7959. Humor
7960. Willingness to consider "dumb" ideas
7961. Juxtaposing: Putting things together in odd ways
7962. Metaphorical thinking
7963. Awareness of your talents and skills
7964. In-depth knowledge about your partner
7965. Draw, doodle, and make lists

7966. A "Romantic ABC's" Coupon: You choose one letter of the alphabet. The coupon-giver will create a day of romance with gifts and gestures that all begin with that letter
7967. For statisticians: Analyze the number of your sexual encounters as a function of the frequency of your romantic gestures: Is there a correlation?

7968. The gift: A giant jar of nuts
7969. The note: "I'm nuts for you"

7970. If money is no object—go all out!
7971. Rent a Lear Jet for a quick trip
7972. Buy a Jaguar for a joy ride
7973. Fly the Concorde together to Europe
7974. Take a round-the-world trip

7975. Tour the vineyards in Napa Valley, California
7976. Guys: Curb your sarcastic wit with your lover (save it for your buddies)
7977. Get the song "I Dare You to Move" by Switchfoot
7978. And rent the movie *A Walk to Remember*, featuring the song
7979. Guys: Perform the "Sexy Cowboy Fantasy"

7980. Write him/her a check on something unusual
7981. On a brick or lingerie or mattress

7982. Make love in every room in your house
7983. Don't forget to include the stairways and closets
7984. For the adventurous: Include the porches and backyard

Best Love Songs by Mariah Carey

7985. "Can't Let Go"
7986. "Dreamlover"
7987. "Emotions"
7988. "I'll Be There"
7989. "Love Takes Time"
7990. "Vision of Love"
7991. "Without You/Never Forget You"

7992. "All, everything that I understand, I understand only because I love." ~ Leo Tolstoy

7993. Like education, love is a major doorway to understanding and wisdom

7994. Calculate how many years you spent in school, becoming "educated." Now plan to spend the same amount of time learning love

Favorite Love Songs from 1980

7995. "(Just Like) Starting Over," John Lennon

7996. "Magic," Olivia Newton-John

7997. "Sailing," Christopher Cross

7998. "Please Don't Go," KC & The Sunshine Band

7999. "Lady," Kenny Rogers

8000. "Crazy Little Thing Called Love," Queen

8001. "Could You Be Loved," Bob Marley & the Wailers

8002. "Could I Have This Dance," Anne Murray

8003. "Tunnel of Love," Dire Straits

8004. Visit local coffeehouses

8005. Visit restaurants featuring live music

8006. Visit bars with live bands

8007. Go ice skating together

8008. For marrieds only: Treat him/her like you did while dating

8009. "A simple enough pleasure, surely, to have breakfast alone with one's husband, but how seldom married people in the midst of life achieve it." ~ Anne Morrow Lindbergh

"Couple Questions" to
Discuss with Your Partner

Don't avoid the tough questions...

8010. What do the two of you argue about most often?
8011. What is your "style" of arguing? (Logical, emotional, heated, calm)
8012. How do you balance *your* needs with your *partner's* needs?
8013. How do you balance kids and spouse?
8014. Can a person be "too much" in love?
8015. What made you fall in love?
8016. What are the three *best* things about him/her?

8017. Wear "Escape" perfume—The perfect accompaniment to a vacation
8018. Give a gift based on a favorite TV show
8019. "It doesn't matter who you love or how you love, but that you love." ~ Rod McKuen
8020. When traveling, write a love letter—one paragraph per day—and give it to him/her when you return home

---

8021. Find your passion and create your career around it
8022. Your satisfaction will make you a better partner/lover/friend

---

8023. Guys: *Triple* your time spent on foreplay—she'll adore you for it!
8024. Gals: Occasionally initiate a "quickie"—he'll adore you for it!

8025. Become a *magnet* for romantic ideas

8026. Look at the world through romance-colored glasses
8027. And ideas will *leap* out at you from newspapers, magazines, TV, etc.

8028. Memorize your wedding vows
8029. Erotic Book Alert! *Forbidden Flowers*, by Nancy Friday
8030. Make fresh-squeezed orange juice tomorrow morning
8031. A note: "Thank you for being the father of our children"
8032. For waiters/waitresses in love: Don your apron and serve your partner dinner at home, and provide *extraordinary* service

---

Things About You That
Your Partner Would *Love* to Know

Build intimacy by sharing more

8033. What was the single most significant turning point in your life?
8034. When/why/how do you lose your temper?
8035. How do you see your life in five years? Ten years?
8036. If you're so smart, why aren't you a millionaire?
8037. What feeling do you have the most difficulty controlling?
8038. What feeling do you have the most difficulty expressing?
8039. What are your pet peeves?
8040. How consistent are your actions with your beliefs?
8041. How do you handle your own inconsistencies?
8042. What accomplishments are you most proud of?
8043. Are you indecisive—or are you always *certain* that you're right?

8044. How do you handle being lost?

8045. What movie last brought tears to your eyes?

8046. Is it possible for a man and a woman to have a truly platonic relationship?

8047. What would you like most to change about yourself?

8048. What *really* makes you laugh?

8049. What makes you jealous?

8050. Have you ever had a broken heart? (Who? When? Why?)

8051. "How bold one gets when one is sure of being loved." ~ Sigmund Freud

8052. Slow down and think about how empowered you feel when you feel the love from your partner

8053. Love *literally* gives us strength and confidence; it's *not* just a metaphor

8054. Assure your partner of your love; leave no doubt about it—and watch him/her *flourish*

8055. Gift & Date Idea: Get the song "How Deep Is Your Love," by the Bee Gees—

8056. And rent *Saturday Night Fever*, featuring the song

8057. And then go out dancing on Saturday

8058. Turn your *house* (an architectural structure) into a *home* (a place where love lives)

8059. Eat in New Orleans' most romantic restaurant: The Grill Room

8060. Avoid pushing your partner's "Hot Buttons"

8061. English: "My love"

8062. French: "Mon amour"

8063. Italian: "Amore moi"
8064. German (to a guy): "Mein lieber"
8065. German (to a gal): "Meine liebe"
8066. Spanish: "Mi amor"
8067. Portugese: "Meu amor"

Her Name in a Song:
Hits Named for Gals

8068. "Amanda," Boston
8069. "Angelia," Richard Marx
8070. "Angie," The Rolling Stones
8071. "Annie's Song," John Denver
8072. "Beth," Kiss
8073. "Bernadette," The Four Tops
8074. "Cecilia," Simon & Garfunkel
8075. "Cindy, Oh Cindy," Eddie Fisher
8076. "Clair," Gilbert O'Sullivan
8077. "Come on Eileen," Dexy's Midnight Runners
8078. "C'mon Marianne," The Four Tops
8079. "Cracklin' Rosie," Neil Diamond
8080. "Delta Dawn," Helen Reddy
8081. "Diana," Paul Anka
8082. "Donna," Ritchie Valens
8083. "Georgia"
8084. "Georgia on My Mind," Ray Charles
8085. "Georgy Girl," The Seekers
8086. "Hello Mary Lou," Ricky Nelson
8087. "Hello, Dolly!" Louis Armstrong
8088. "Help Me, Rhonda," The Beach Boys
8089. "Hey Paula," Paul and Paula
8090. "Holly Holy," Neil Diamond

8091. "I Saw Linda Yesterday," Dickey Lee
8092. "Jenny, Jenny," Little Richard
8093. "867-5309 Jenny," Tommy Tutone
8094. "Joanna," Kool & the Gang
8095. "Julie, Do Ya Love Me," Bobby Sherman
8096. "Laura"
8097. "Lay Down Sally," Eric Clapton
8098. "Little Jeannie," Elton John
8099. "Long Tall Sally," Little Richard
8100. "Louise," Human League
8101. "Love Grows (Where My Rosemary Goes)," Edison Lighthouse
8102. "Lucille," Kenny Rogers
8103. "Maggie May," Rod Stewart
8104. "Mandy," Barry Manilow
8105. "Maria," from *West Side Story*
8106. "Marianne," Terry Gilkyson & The Easy Riders
8107. "Maybellene," Chuck Berry
8108. "Michelle," The Beatles
8109. "My Maria," B.W. Stevenson
8110. "Oh Julie," The Crescendos
8111. "Oh Sheila," Ready for the World
8112. "Oh Sherrie," Steve Perry
8113. "Oh! Carol," Neil Sedaka
8114. "Patricia," Perez Prado
8115. "Peggy Sue," Buddy Holly
8116. "Proud Mary," Creedence Clearwater Revival
8117. "Rosanna," Toto
8118. "Ruby Tuesday," The Rolling Stones
8119. "Sara," Fleetwood Mac
8120. "Sara," Starship

8121. "Sara Smile," Daryl Hall and John Oates
8122. "Sheila," Tommy Roe
8123. "Sherry," The Four Seasons
8124. "Sunny," Bobby Hebb
8125. "Susie Darlin'," Robin Luke
8126. "Sweet Caroline," Neil Diamond
8127. "Tammy," Debbie Reynolds
8128. "Think of Laura," Christopher Cross
8129. "Tracy," The Archies
8130. "Trudie," Joe 'Mr. Piano' Henderson
8131. "Wake Up Little Susie," Everly Brothers
8132. "Walk Away Renee," The Four Tops

8133. Buy three new lingerie outfits
8134. Model them for him
8135. Select sexy music to perform to
8136. Arrange the lighting just right

Ways to Love a Pisces
(19 February–19 March)

8137. Pisces is a *water* sign: Cater to his/her dreamy, romantic nature
8138. Gift tip: Sensuous
8139. Silk, velvet, soft
8140. Scarves and lingerie
8141. Feather beds and lots of pillows
8142. Sometimes shy, so enjoy couple-only activities
8143. Viburnum; willow trees
8144. Anything sweet, chocolate
8145. An island in the Mediterranean
8146. Wrap gifts in sea green

Favorite Love Songs from 1981

8147. "Celebration," Kool & the Gang
8148. "Keep on Loving You," REO Speedwagon
8149. "The One That You Love," Air Supply
8150. "Jessie's Girl," Rick Springfield
8151. "Endless Love," Diana Ross & Lionel Richie
8152. "Don't You Want Me," The Human League
8153. "Every Little Thing She Does Is Magic," The Police

8154. Write a list: "25 Clues We're Soul Mates"
8155. Along with the book *The Soulmate Secret: Manifest the Love of Your Life with the Law of Attraction*, by Arielle Ford
8156. Create a "soulmates" certificate for the two of you
8157. Create a soulmates card to carry in your wallet

Technological Tools for Saying in Touch

8158. Text messaging
8159. Email
8160. Cell phones
8161. Instant Messenger
8162. Faxes
8163. Facebook
8164. Twitter
8165. MySpace
8166. Blogs
8167. Skype

8168. Splurge on a $100 shopping spree at Victoria's Secret

8169. Surf http://www.filmmovement.com/index.asp for foreign and independent films
8170. Enemy of Love: Nagging
8171. Surprise her with stuffed animals from a favorite fairy tale

---

8172. Create a "Lingerie Fantasy" for him…
8173. You're a lingerie model
8174. He's a retail buyer
8175. Put on a private fashion show
8176. Use your imagination!

Ways to Put the *Sizzle* Back into Your Relationship

8177. Take a sauna together
8178. Make love three nights in a row—in three different places!
8179. Vacation in the Australian outback
8180. Barbecue a couple of juicy steaks on the grill
8181. Plan a surprise vacation to the French Riviera
8182. Go on a caravan in the Egyptian desert
8183. Share some of your "naughty" thoughts
8184. Frolic on a Hawaiian beach together
8185. Cook a hot, spicy meal
8186. Check out *Some Like It Hot: Spicy Favorites from the World's Hot Zones*, by Clifford A. Wright
8187. Make love in a semi-public place
8188. Guys: Spend a *solid hour* performing foreplay
8189. Visit Casablanca, Morocco
8190. Visit a nude beach
8191. Take a cruise in the Southern Pacific

8192. Go on an African safari
8193. Dance the Tango together
8194. Make love to "Principles of Lust," by Enigma

8195. Ask him to pick a number between one and fifty; reward him with that number of kisses
8196. "The opposite of love is indifference." ~ Rollo May
8197. Go to an *inexpensive* vacation spot—and get the *most expensive* accommodations
8198. Write one hundred love poems in haiku style
8199. For your spontaneous spouse: Go on an "open-ended" weekend: Hop in the car with no plans and no destination in mind
8200. Visit the Egyptian pyramids
8201. Gals: Never withhold sex to punish him

8202. The gift: A cactus
8203. The note: "I'm stuck on you."
8204. (Alternate gift): The song "Stuck on You," by Lionel Richie

8205. Name your child after her
8206. Celebrate the Winter Solstice (the longest night of the year) by spending it in *bed* together!
8207. Visit Aspen and stay at The Little Nell
8208. Love Coupon: This coupon entitles you to an *entire* week of romance! What's your pleasure?

Favorite Love Songs from 1982
8209. "One Hundred Ways," Quincy Jones & James Ingram
8210. "Turn Your Love Around," George Benson

8211. "Up Where We Belong," Joe Cocker & Jennifer Warnes
8212. "Why Do Fools Fall in Love," Diana Ross
8213. "Tainted Love," Soft Cell
8214. "Open Arms," Journey

8215. "Happiness is a present attitude—not a future condition." ~ Hugh Prather
8216. Don't wait! Not tomorrow, not in an hour—now!
8217. Pick up the phone and call!
8218. Pick up a pen and write a love letter
8219. Take him/her in your arms and whirl around
8220. Take a carefree walk in the park

Songs to Help You Express Your Feelings: *Friendship & Appreciation*

8221. "Bridge Over Troubled Water," Simon and Garfunkel
8222. "Stand by Me," Ben E. King
8223. "Thank You for Being a Friend," Andrew Gold
8224. "That's What Friends Are For," Dionne & Friends
8225. "You've Got a Friend," James Taylor

8226. Take a walk on the first day of spring—and talk about your hopes and dreams for the future
8227. Take a walk on the first day of summer—and talk about your relationship
8228. Take a walk on the first day of autumn—and talk about your best memories
8229. Take a walk on the first day of winter—and talk about everything you're thankful for

8230.   Explore aphrodisiacs together: Read *Aphrodite: A Memoir of the Senses*, by Isabel Allende, which combines recipes with eroticism

8231.   Dedicate your book to your partner

8232.   If she always misplaces her keys, get her *twelve* extra sets

8233.   Buy ten extra pillows to make your bed more luxurious

8234.   A+ B&B Rating: The Don Gaspar Compound, in New Mexico: www.dongaspar.com

Greatest Love Songs
from Broadway Musicals

8235.   "Almost Like Being in Love," from *Brigadoon*

8236.   "Can't Help Loving Dat Man," from *Showboat*

8237.   "Do I Love You Because You're Beautiful," from *Cinderella*

8238.   "Embraceable You," from *Crazy for You*

8239.   "All I Ask of You," from *Phantom of the Opera*

8240.   "I Could Have Danced All Night," from *My Fair Lady*

8241.   "I Have Dreamed," from *The King and I*

8242.   "I Wanna Be Loved By You," from *Good Boy*

8243.   "I'm in Love with a Wonderful Guy," from *South Pacific*

8244.   "I've Never Been in Love Before," from *Guys & Dolls*

8245.   "If I Loved You," from *Carousel*

8246.   "Just in Time," from *Bells Are Ringing*

8247.   "Love Song," from *Pippin*

8248.   "Me & My Girl," from *Me & My Girl*

8249.   "My Heart Is So Full of You," from *The Most Happy Fella*

8250.   "On the Street Where You Live," from *My Fair Lady*
8251.   "People," from *Funny Girl*
8252.   "People Will Say We're in Love," from *Oklahoma*
8253.   "She Loves Me," from *She Loves Me*
8254.   "So in Love," from *Kiss Me Kate*
8255.   "They Say It's Wonderful," from *Annie Get Your Gun*
8256.   "This Can't Be Love," from *The Boys from Syracuse*
8257.   "Til There Was You," the *The Music Man*
8258.   "Too Much in Love to Care," from *Sunset Boulevard*
8259.   "Try to Remember," from *The Fantastics*
8260.   "What I Did for Love," from *A Chorus Line*
8261.   "Wonderful Guy," from *South Pacific*
8262.   "You're the Top," from *Anything Goes*

8263.   For a Beatles fan: Get collector's original singles of all their No. 1 hits
8264.   Share a park bench on a sunny afternoon
8265.   "Love eagerly believes everything it wants to." ~ Jean Racine
8266.   Never buy cars with bucket seats
8267.   The Ultimate Gift for Audiophiles: A stereo system from Bang & Olufsen: www.bang-olufsen.com

Favorite Love Songs from 1983

8268.   "All Night Long (All Night)," Lionel Richie
8269.   "Baby, Come to Me," Patti Austin & James Ingram
8270.   "Heart to Heart," Kenny Loggins
8271.   "Straight from the Heart," Bryan Adams
8272.   "Total Eclipse of the Heart," Bonnie Tyler
8273.   "You Are," Lionel Richie

8274. Gift: A set of white satin sheets
8275. Presentation: Along with the song "Nights in White Satin," by The Moody Blues
8276. Activity: Make sweet love

Items for a *Monthly* Romantic Checklist

8277. Plan one romantic *surprise*
8278. Re-stock your stash of greeting cards
8279. Go out to dinner once or twice
8280. Rent at least *two* romantic movies
8281. Make plans for a romantic weekend sometime soon
8282. Plan one romantic event with a *seasonal* theme

8283. Read *The Lovers' Bedside Companion*, by Gregory J.P. Godek
8284. Snuggle in flannel sheets during the winter months
8285. Use the song "I Can't Give You Anything but Love" as the theme for a low-budget date
8286. Wake him gently at 3 A.M. by fondling him
8287. Wear "Dreamer" cologne—Give him something to dream about
8288. Take a stroll in the swirling snow

If You Read Only Seven Books to Improve Your Relationship, Read These Seven

8289. *The Soul's Code: In Search of Character and Calling*, by James Hillman
8290. *The Art of Loving*, by Erich Fromm
8291. *Emotional Intelligence: Why It Can Matter More Than IQ*, by Daniel Goleman

8292. *The Prophet*, by Kahlil Gibran
8293. *You Just Don't Understand—Women and Men in Conversation*, by Deborah Tannen
8294. *Iron John*, by Robert Bly
8295. *Love: The Course They Forgot to Teach You in School*, by Gregory J.P. Godek

8296. Gals: Do something *for* him that you hate to do
8297. It only counts as a loving gesture if you do it cheerfully and without complaint
8298. Iron his shirts, wash his car, cut the lawn

8299. English: "My honey"
8300. French: "Mon chou"
8301. Italian: "Mia dolcezza"
8302. German: "Mein schatz"
8303. Spanish: "Mi cariño"
8304. Portugese: "Meu bem"

8305. "A great flame follows a little spark." ~ Dante Alighieri
8306. Little Spark #1: Write a little note: "My fondest memory of you is…"
8307. Little Spark #2: Make gentle, gentle love together
8308. Little Spark #3: Turn off the TV tonight and *just be together*
8309. Most loving gestures are little, inexpensive, and easy
8310. Love, once ignited, rarely goes out altogether; it usually smolders quietly, waiting for something to fan the flames

Creative Ways to "Pop the Question"

8311. Write W.Y.M.M? on four separate cupcakes. Place them by the bed so she'll see when she wakes up

8312. Apply for the job of "Husband"

8313. Write an "Engagement Resume"—listing your qualifications!

8314. Hide a diamond ring in a rose bud—and wait for it to bloom!

8315. Return to the place where you first met

8316. Pop the question in the middle of lovemaking

8317. Gals: Don't wait for *him*—*you* do the asking!

8318. Get her the most perfect diamond your budget will allow

8319. Be *different:* Get a ruby, emerald, or sapphire engagement ring

8320. Be old fashioned: Ask her father's permission

8321. Hide the ring in a box of Cracker Jacks

8322. Choose the exact time based on specific astrological forecasts

8323. Ask her to marry you on a local radio show

8324. Place the ring in the bottom of a glass of champagne

8325. The outrageous skywriting proposal

8326. The insistent sky banner proposal

8327. The custom jigsaw puzzle proposal

8328. The really big billboard proposal

8329. The lucky Chinese fortune cookie proposal

8330. The classic get-on-one-knee-and-ask-her proposal

8331. Gift & Date Idea: Get the song "Love Me Tender," by Elvis Presley—

8332. And rent *Love Me Tender*, featuring the song
8333. (Then spend a night of tender lovemaking)

Favorite Love Songs from 1984

8334. "Almost Paradise," Mike Reno & Ann Wilson
8335. "Hello," Lionel Richie
8336. "Missing You," John Waite
8337. "Time After Time," Cyndi Lauper

8338. For romantic campers: *The Official Guide to America's National Parks*, by Fodor's
8339. Color Easter eggs together
8340. Discuss your family finances together
8341. "Great is the man who has not lost his child-like heart." ~ Mencius
8342. Get him a book on his favorite hobby

8343. For Christmas, give ten music CDs
8344. Then hang them on the tree like ornaments

8345. Learn the elegant art of Bonsai
8346. Grow and design two Bonsai trees together

8347. Watch the final scenes of the movies *Michael* and *All of Me*
8348. Allow yourselves to be inspired, and create a joyful dance of your own!

8349. For guys: A gift certificate from Radio Shack
8350. Or Sears
8351. Or Brookstone

8352. Or the local stereo shop
8353. Or the local auto parts store
8354. Or his favorite hardware store

More Relationship Dos and Don'ts

8355. Don't go out on New Year's Eve—
8356. Do stay home and cozy-up to your lover near the fireplace
8357. Don't buy roses for Valentine's Day—
8358. Do buy flowers that begin with the first letter of her name
8359. Don't go to the beach on crowded weekends—
8360. Do go mid-week
8361. Don't go to vacation spots during busy seasons—
8362. Do go right before or after the busy season
8363. Do make some sacrifices for each other—
8364. But don't turn yourself into a martyr
8365. Don't read the newspaper at the breakfast table—
8366. Do talk with one another over breakfast
8367. Don't give him a birthday present—
8368. Do give him seven gifts, one for each day of his birthday week
8369. Don't be afraid to share your feelings
8370. Don't leave lovemaking until just before sleeping
8371. Do schedule more time for foreplay
8372. Don't make love the same way every time
8373. Do eliminate distractions for two to three hours
8374. Don't try to change your partner
8375. Don't act your age

8376. Once every five years, do something incredible, outrageous, and truly memorable

8377. Daily affirmation: "I will make the most of my abilities"
8378. Visit a spiritually meaningful place, like Sedona
8379. As part of foreplay, read aloud a passage from *Little Birds*, by Anaïs Nin

Songs to Help You Express Your Feelings: *Love & Joy*

8380. "How Sweet It Is (To Be Loved By You)," James Taylor
8381. "It Had to Be You," Harry Connick, Jr.
8382. "Let's Hang On," The Four Seasons
8383. "Love Me Do," The Beatles
8384. "The Way You Do the Things You Do," The Temptations
8385. "What a Wonderful World," Louis Armstrong

8386. Collect prints of paintings by the great artists of the Romantic Period
8387. William Blake, Jean Baptiste Camille, John Robert Cozens
8388. Jacques Louis David, Eugene Delacroix, Francisco Goya
8389. Samuel Palmer, Johan Anton Alban Ramboux

Favorite Love Songs from 1985

8390. "Can't Fight This Feeling," REO Speedwagon
8391. "Everytime You Go Away," Paul Young
8392. "Method of Modern Love," Daryl Hall & John Oates
8393. "Part-Time Lover," Stevie Wonder
8394. "I Want To Know What Love Is," Foreigner
8395. "The Night I Fell in Love," Luther Vandross

8396. "Don't You (Forget About Me)," Simple Minds
8397. "Love on the Rise," Kenny G
8398. "Heaven," Bryan Adams
8399. "Say You, Say Me," Lionel Richie

8400. Create your own Winter Celebration
8401. Soundtrack: Windham Hill's *Winter Solstice I*
8402. Activity: Take a sleigh ride in the snow
8403. Quote: "One kind word can warm three winter months." ~ Japanese saying

8404. Find a local "romantic hideaway"—like a quiet aisle at the public library
8405. Nibble on her ear
8406. Take out a full-page ad in your local newspaper, declaring your love for your mate

Romantic Resources on the Internet

8407. The "CandyBouquet": www.candybouquet.com
8408. To locate classical music events: http://www.opus1classical.com/
8409. For tickets to rock concerts: Ticketmaster.com or http://www.rockonconcerts.com/
8410. To locate film festivals worldwide: filmfestivals.com/
8411. Beatle-related items, trivia and travel info: www.eecis.udel.edu/~markowsk/Beatles/
8412. Beatle-related items, trivia and travel info: http://www.thebeatles.com/core/home/
8413. For opera lovers: http://www.operainfo.org/
8414. For Shakespeare lovers: http://shakespeare.mit.edu/
8415. A B&B resource: http://www.bnbfinder.com/

8416. To get info on festivals, carnivals, etc.: www.
       fairsfestival.com

8417. A tea-lover's resource: www.tea-time.com

8418. A movie-lover's resource: www.hollywood.com

8419. For wine lovers: www.winespectator.com

8420. A book-lover's resource: amazon.com

8421. A Napa Valley Virtual Visit: www.freerun.com/cgi-
       bin/home.org

8422. London Theatre Guide: www.officiallondontheatre.
       co.uk/

8423. For animal lovers, info on every zoo in the world:
       www.goodzoos.com

8424. A great music resource: www.themusicresource.com

8425. For Broadway and Off-Broadway info: www.
       broadway.com

8426. For acoustic and New Age music: www.windham.
       com

8427. A resource for sports collectables: www.
       sportscardsplus.com

8428. The Erotic Prints: www.eroticprints.org

8429. For reviews and previews of current films: www.
       rottentomatoes.com

8430. Delight your mate with origami creations (Learn on
       the Internet: http://www.origami-club.com/en/)

8431. "I wonder, by my troth, what you and I did, till we
       lov'd." ~ John Donne

8432. For engaged folks only: Write a letter to your future
       in-laws, promising to love and care for their son/
       daughter

Songs to Help You Express
Your Feelings: *Gentle & Sweet*

8433. "All Right," Christopher Cross
8434. "Hearing Your Voice," Moody Blues
8435. "My Love," Paul McCartney & Wings
8436. "Strange Magic," Electric Light Orchestra
8437. "Summer Soft," Stevie Wonder
8438. "(They Long to Be) Close to You," The Carpenters

8439. Gift & Date Idea: Get the song "Can You Feel the Love Tonight," by Elton John—
8440. And rent *The Lion King*, featuring the song

8441. For his "second childhood," get him a Corvette!
8442. And the song "Little Red Corvette," by Prince

8443. Good song about kissing: "Kiss Me," Sixpence None the Richer
8444. Slow down your kissing
8445. Kiss with concentration
8446. Spend 10% as much time kissing as you spend watching TV every day

30 Years of Celebrity Birth-Years
Celebrate the celebrities that match your partner's age…

8447. **1946** Candice Bergen, Sally Field, Diane Keaton, David Lynch, Liza Minelli, Ozzy Osbourne, Dolly Parton, Linda Ronstadt, Susan Sarandon, Sylvester Stallone, Robert Urich
8448. **1947** Arnold Schwarzenegger, Elton John, David Bowie, Glenn Close, Billy Crystal, Ted Danson,

Farrah Fawcett, Kevin Kline, David Letterman, Olivia Newton-John, Steven Spielberg

8449. **1948** Mikhail Baryshnikov, James Taylor, Barbara Hershey, Jeremy Irons, Kate Jackson, Perry King, Stevie Nicks, Donna Summer, Steve Winwood

8450. **1949** Whoopi Goldberg, Billy Joel, Bruce Springsteen, Meryl Streep, Sigourney Weaver, Jeff Bridges, Richard Gere, Don Johnson, Jessica Lange

8451. **1950** Stevie Wonder, Cybill Shepherd, Tony Danza, John Candy, Peter Gabriel, William Hurt, Bill Murray, Randy Quaid

8452. **1951** Phil Collins, Sting, Timothy Bottoms, John Mellencamp, Elvira, Mark Hamill, Harry Hamlin, Mark Harmon, Michael Keaton, Joe Piscopo, Kurt Russell, Jane Seymour

8453. **1952** Robin Williams, Mr. T, Dan Aykroyd, Roseanne, David Byrne, Nora Dunn, Pee-Wee Herman, Grace Jones, Isabella Rossellini

8454. **1953** Kim Basinger, Jeff Goldblum, John Goodman, Cyndi Lauper, John Malkovich, Tom Petty

8455. **1954** Patrick Swayze, John Travolta, Ellen Barkin, Corbin Bernsen, Ron Howard, David Keith, Dennis Quaid

8456. **1955** Kevin Costner, Kirstie Alley, Jeff Daniels, Billy Idol, David Lee Roth, Bruce Willis, Debra Winger

8457. **1956** Mel Gibson, Tom Hanks, Larry Bird, Delta Burke, Carrie Fisher, Eric Roberts, Mickey Rourke, Joe Montana, Dale Murphy, Martina Navratilova

8458. **1957** Michelle Pfeiffer, Theresa Russell, Vanna White, Geena Davis, Spike Lee, Donny Osmond, Melanie Griffith

8459. **1958** Madonna, Prince, Michael Jackson, Arsenio Hall, Steve Guttenberg, Wade Boggs, Jamie Lee Curtis

8460. **1959** Judd Nelson, Rosanna Arquette, Sheena Easton, Holly Hunter, Victoria Jackson, Marie Osmond, Martha Quinn, Randy Travis

8461. **1960** Valerie Bertinelli, Eric Dickerson, Joan Jett, Nastassja Kinski, Apollonia Kotero, Sean Penn, Tracey Ullman

8462. **1961** Eddie Murphy, Jon Bon Jovi, Boy George, Rae Dawn Chong, Amy Grant, Wayne Gretzky, Daryl Hannah, Timothy Hutton, Don Mattingly

8463. **1962** Tom Cruise, Matthew Broderick, Emilio Estevez, Jodie Foster, Demi Moore, Meg Ryan, Ally Sheedy

8464. **1963** Whitney Houston, Michael Jordan, Julian Lennon, Andrew McCarthy, George Michael

8465. **1964** Tracy Chapman, Jose Canseco, Phoebe Cates, Melissa Gilbert, Robin Givens, Rob Lowe, Matt Dillon

8466. **1965** Brooke Shields, Nicolas Cage, Ronnie Gant, Mario Lemieux, Paulina Porizkova, Katarina Witt

8467. **1966** Justine Bateman, Tom Glavine, Janet Jackson, Dave Justice, Charlie Sheen

8468. **1967** Julia Roberts, Boris Becker, Lisa Bonet, John Cusak, Deion Sanders

8469. **1968** Mary Lou Retton, Molly Ringwald, Jonathan Knight

8470. **1969** Andrea Elson, Steffi Graf, Donnie Wahlberg, Danny Wood

8471. **1970** Kirk Cameron, Debbie Gibson, Jordan Knight, Emily Lloyd, Malcolm-Jamal Warner

8472. **1971** Minnie Driver, Kid Rock, Mary J. Blige, Ewan McGregor, Selena Quintanilla, Lance Armstrong, Jada Pinkett Smith, Winona Rider, Christina Applegate, Ricky Martin

8473. **1972** Drew Bledsoe, Denise Richards, Shaquille O'Neal, Mia Hamm, Dane Cook, Jennie Garth, Carmen Electra, Jennifer Garner, Wayne Brady, Selma Blair, Ben Affleck, Cameron Diaz, Gwyneth Paltrow, Jude Law

8474. **1973** Oscar De La Hoya, David Blaine, Heidi Klum, Carson Daly, Brian Austin Green, Kate Beckinsale, Paul Walker, Neve Campbell, Holly Marie Combs, Nick Lachey, Tyra Banks, Stephenie Meyer

8475. **1974** Kate Moss, Christian Bale, Jerry O'Connell, Mark Paul Gosselaar, Eva Mendez, Alyson Hannigan, Victoria Beckham, Penelope Cruz, Ken Jennings, Jewel, Alanis Morissette, Derek Jeter, Hilary Swank, Jimmy Fallon, Leonardo DiCaprio, Ryan Seacrest

8476. **1975** Drew Barrymore, Eva Longoria, Zach Braff, David Beckham, Enrique Iglesias, Lauryn Hill, Angelina Jolie, Tobey Maguire, Charlize Theron, Tiger Woods

8477. **1976** Keri Russell, Reece Witherspoon, Peyton Manning, Ja Rule, Colin Farrell, Joey Lawrence, Kevin Garnett, Fred Savage, Taylor Hicks, Alicia Silverstone, Rachel McAdams, Donovan McNabb

8478. **1977** Orlando Bloom, Shakira, Kanye West, Jason Mraz, Liv Tyler, Tom Brady, Fiona Apple, John Mayer, Ludacris, Laila Ali

8479. Recognize the Yin and Yang aspects of your relationship…

8480. Yin: Celebrate your differences—

8481. Yang: Take comfort in your similarities ☯

8482. Yin: Actions speak louder than words

8483. Yang: Communication is the cornerstone of a good relationship ☯

8484. Yin: Live in the present—

8485. Yang: Keep your memories alive ☯

8486. Yin: Read books (They contain great wisdom)

8487. Yang: Throw the books away! (Listen to your Inner Voice) ☯

8488. Yin: Say what you feel when you feel it—

8489. Yang: Choose your words carefully ☯

8490. Yin: Treat her like your best friend (You'll build intimacy)—

8491. Yang: Treat her like your girlfriend (You'll build passion) ☯

8492. Yin: Lighten up! (Have more fun)—

8493. Yang: Get serious! (Relationships are work) ☯

8494. Yin: Travel inspires romance (Exotic locales, adventure!)—

8495. Yang: Home is where the heart is (Cozy, comfortable) ☯

8496. Yin: Shake-up your life! (Do something different and exciting!)—

8497. Yang: Slow down your life (Meditate, find your center) ☯

8498. Rent a horse and suit of armor—and surprise the *heck* out of her!

8499. Watch classic cartoons on Saturday morning

8500. Take a stroll after dinner every evening
8501. Paint her toenails (bright red)
8502. "What greater thing is there for two human souls than to find that they are joined for life." ~ George Eliot
8503. Make love on a bearskin rug in front of a fire
8504. Collect jokes all month, and share them on the last day of each month
8505. For your frequent flyer: Get an inflatable neck pillow
8506. *Never* take off your wedding ring
8507. Hide her favorite stuffed animal in unexpected places around the house
8508. Take a mud bath together at a spa
8509. Get matching cashmere sweaters
8510. A+ Relationships are built equally of passion, commitment, and intimacy
8511. Passion alone is just a fling
8512. Commitment alone is a hopeless, aching relationship
8513. Intimacy alone is too fragile to last
8514. Passion and commitment without intimacy is a shallow relationship
8515. Commitment and intimacy without passion is flat and unexciting
8516. Passion and intimacy without commitment is short-lived

8517. Engrave a Cross pen with both of your names
8518. Install a mirror on your bedroom ceiling
8519. Make Tuesday "Game Night": Play board games instead of watching TV
8520. Use Skype or Windows Live to place video calls to each other

8521. Lover's Ritual: Hold hands and say a prayer of thanks at every meal
8522. Visit www.mrsfields.com for Mrs. Fields!
8523. Volunteer together
8524. Go for a midnight swim in the ocean
8525. Take a stroll on a foggy evening
8526. Make *s'mores* over a campfire in your backyard
8527. "Stroll" and "saunter"—it's more romantic than simply "walking"
8528. Host a formal "prom" for your friends
8529. Double-date with your *grandparents*
8530. Enjoy a "progressive dinner" by stopping at a series of street vendors

8531. Take her on a "Neiman-Marcus Shopping Spree"
8532. Take him on a "Radio Shack Shopping Spree"
8533. Take each other on a "Victoria's Secret Shopping Spree"

8534. Whisper "sweet nothings" in her ear
8535. Throw a themed birthday party based on his/her favorite movie
8536. Spend an afternoon on horseback
8537. Stuff his mailbox *full* of love notes
8538. Count your blessings; assign dollar values to them; add them up!
8539. Sleep in the buff
8540. Build sandcastles on the beach together
8541. Name a new mixed drink after her; serve it at your next party
8542. Play "Name That Tune" while taking a long road trip together

8543.   Hide a love note in a sea shell and place it on the
        beach where she will find it
8544.   "Women fall in love through their ears, men fall in
        love through their eyes." ~ Woodrow Wyatt
8545.   Spray paint "Welcome Home" on an old sheet; hang
        it on a tree

8546.   Imagine it's twenty-five years in the future: List your
        five favorite memories with your lover
8547.   List the great places you've visited together
8548.   List the great gifts you've given and received
8549.   List your favorite holiday memories you've shared
8550.   List the high points of your family life
8551.   Start working to make this future come true

8552.   Create two cartoon characters based on the two of you
8553.   Have a local artist draw them for you
8554.   Create a series of comic adventures that parallels
        your life
8555.   Occasionally paste them onto the newspaper
        comic page
8556.   After twenty-five years, collect them into a book

8557.   Chase rainbows—
8558.   Literally: Following a storm
8559.   Figuratively: Follow your dreams together

8560.   A themed "Dinner-and-a-Movie": Rent *Like Water
        for Chocolate*
8561.   Serve tacos and burritos
8562.   Drink margaritas

8563. Then take a siesta together

8564. Hold a "ribbon-cutting" to celebrate your new home
8565. Attend a stress management seminar together
8566. Accompany your partner inside the airport—don't just drop him/her off at the curb
8567. Get some motivation from Nightingale Conant: www.nightingale.com
8568. Find a special shady spot under a tree
8569. Pull taffy together
8570. Wade in a public fountain together
8571. Go horseback riding at dusk on a deserted beach
8572. Host a surprise birthday party for his/her dog/cat
8573. Take simultaneous sabbaticals from your jobs
8574. Watch holiday cartoon specials together
8575. Get him/her snacks during the commercials
8576. Go on a charity walk-a-thon together
8577. Make out "under the boardwalk" at a beach
8578. A lifetime goal: Dine at every five-star restaurant in the world!
8579. Don't just "meet"—have a "*rendezvous*"
8580. Wear the sexiest swimsuit that you dare
8581. On a hot summer day, have a water balloon fight
8582. Help her with her Christmas shopping
8583. Speak in a fake French accent throughout an entire date
8584. Create a snow sculpture together

8585. Offer your shoulder to cry on
8586. Offer your lap to sit on
8587. Give a hand

8588. Lend an ear

8589. Open your heart

8590. Whisper this: "You mean the world to me"

8591. Focus on being your lover's best friend

8592. Play footsie with your sweetheart

8593. Hang out at the local donut shop

8594. Vow to be more romantic in the 2020s than you were in the 2010s

8595. While watching *Titanic*, whisper to her: "I'd go down with the *Titanic* to save you"

8596. Watch Conan O'Brien's monologue together

8597. Get him a knick-knack, a tchochke, a bric-a-brac

8598. There's no cure for an incurable romantic

8599. But there is hope for the romantically impaired

8600. Give one Christmas gift that's "naughty"

8601. And one that's "nice"

8602. Attend the taping of a favorite TV show together

8603. Do some star gazing at Mann's Chinese Theater in Los Angeles

8604. Crash a wedding reception at a local hotel

8605. Write a letter to your unborn child together

8606. Go on a "backwards date": Kiss goodnight, then eat dessert, then eat dinner, etc.

8607. Stroll through a farmers market together

8608. Accompany your partner to his/her doctor appointments

8609. Find a cool jazz bar

8610. Make a custom homemade pizza together
8611. Rent a houseboat for a mini-vacation
8612. Serve a couple of piña coladas
8613. Take your sailor to view the America's Cup race
8614. Collect fresh rain water and wash her hair with it
8615. Attend a blue grass music festival
8616. Visit a garden maze in England
8617. "One word frees us of all the weight and pain of life: that word is love." ~ Sophocles

8618. Give her a diamond for *every* birthday
8619. Even if they're sometimes very, very small
8620. Or really, really imperfect

8621. For your book lover: A personalized embosser
8622. Shampoo her dog for her
8623. Wear matching running shoes
8624. Nibble on his ear
8625. Do her taxes for her
8626. Get your sweetheart a membership in a fan club
8627. Go on "Spring Break" even if you're not in school!
8628. Spend all day watching the ocean waves
8629. Hang out at a piano bar together
8630. Squeeze fresh orange juice for your lover

8631. Look through your high school and college yearbooks together
8632. And share stories of your best times
8633. And personal stories of heartbreak, too

8634. Get a proof set of coins from the year you married

8635.   Brew your own beer together
8636.   Get a special "Hearts on Fire" cut diamond
8637.   Put together a giant jigsaw puzzle
8638.   Over a weekend: Write, star-in, and record your own 10-minute movie
8639.   Teach your partner about the one topic you're an expert in
8640.   Create a sculpture for her out of Legos
8641.   Take your race fan to the Indianapolis 500
8642.   Visit the French Quarter of New Orleans
8643.   Whisper this: "I'm lucky I found you"
8644.   Watch the very first movie you saw together
8645.   Memorize the balcony scene from *Romeo and Juliet*
8646.   And act it out together

8647.   Date concept: Watch movies back-to-back
8648.   A good combination: *You've Got Mail* and *The Shop Around the Corner*

8649.   Go to a fortune teller together
8650.   Newlywed gift: A return address stamper with both of your names on it
8651.   Knit, crochet or needlepoint a gift
8652.   Organize his closet for him

8653.   Flip a coin: Heads you have sex—tails you go out to dinner
8654.   Heads you watch TV—tails you watch the sunset
8655.   Heads, *he* cooks dinner—tails, *she* cooks dinner
8656.   Heads you go to a movie theater—tails you rent a movie

8657. Heads, *he* chooses the rental movie—tails, *she* chooses

8658. Heads it's take-out *pizza*—tails it's take-out *Chinese*

8659. Heads, *he* gives a backrub—tails, *she* gives a backrub

8660. Heads it's an exciting night out—tails it's a quiet night in

8661. Heads it's red wine—tails it's white wine

8662. Heads it's Mozart—tails it's The Beatles

8663. Heads, *she* gets a "day off"—tails, *he* gets a "day off"

8664. Touch in many different ways—

8665. Softly, innocently, teasingly, sexually, quietly, daily, insistently, persuasively, sensually, lightly

Favorite Love Songs from 1986

8666. "Addicted to Love," Robert Palmer

8667. "True Colors," Cyndi Lauper

8668. "Glory of Love," Peter Cetera

8669. "Take My Breath Away," Berlin

8670. "This Could Be the Night," Loverboy

8671. Prepare a plate of luscious fruits and chocolates, and feed them to each other

8672. Give a *lifetime* subscription to his/her favorite magazine

8673. Create *incredible* gift wrappings: *Wrapped With Style: Simple, Creative Ideas for Imaginative Gift Wrapping*, by Leslie Carola

8674. Honor his/her individuality

8675. Go beachcombing together

8676. Get a cardboard crown at Burger King: Crown him King-for-a-Day

8677. Collect romantic acoustic music…
8678. *She Describes Infinity*, by Scott Cossu
8679. *Openings*, by William Ellwood
8680. *Down to the Moon*, by Andreas Vollenweider
8681. *A Winter's Solstice*, by various Windham Hill artists
8682. *Childhood and Memory*, by William Ackerman
8683. *Barefoot Ballet*, by John Klemmer

Creativity Blockers to Beware Of

Creativity is a spark that keeps relationships exciting. Beware of these "creativity blockers":

8684. Following the rules
8685. Looking for one right answer
8686. Logical thinking
8687. Fear of failure
8688. Giving in to peer pressure
8689. A narrow point-of-view
8690. Giving-up too soon
8691. Fear of embarrassment
8692. Belief that you're not creative
8693. Lack of self-confidence
8694. Being overly practical
8695. Concern over cost

8696. Write a list: "50 Reasons I Married You"
8697. Express each of those reasons with a small gift
8698. Renew your wedding vows, and include these reasons
8699. Keep this list handy when you've had an argument

Qualities That 5,000 Women
Dislike Most in Husbands

8700 Messy
8701 Sexually insensitive
8702 Dogmatic
8703 Overworked
8704 Sulking/The "quiet treatment"
8705 Macho attitudes
8706 Stubborn
8707 Self-centered
8708 Uncooperative
8709 Dresses poorly

8710. "As long as one can admire and love, then one is young forever." ~ Pablo Casals
8711. Forget exercise, vitamins and meditating: The *real* secret to staying young is *love*
8712. What do you *admire* about your partner? *Tell* him/her

---

8713. Create one *daily* ritual—to honor your spirituality
8714. Create one *weekly* ritual—to keep the two of you connected
8715. Create one *monthly* ritual—centered around turning the calendar page
8716. Create one *yearly* ritual—to mark the passage of time

Websites for
Romantic Gifts/Ideas/Inspirations

8717. Critics Choice video catalog: http://www.ccvideo.com/
8718. Movies Unlimited huge video catalog: http://www.moviesunlimited.com/musite/default.asp

8719. PBS Home Video: Free catalog:
http://www.pbs.org/video/
8720. Send muffins: http://www.montanamuffins.com/
8721. The Lladro collection of figurines:
http://www.lladro.com/
8722. Name a star: International Star Registry:
http://www.starregistry.com/
8723. Send flowers: www.ftd.com/ or 1800flowers.com
8724. Send fruit: www.ediblearrangements.com
8725. Visit beautiful Lexington, Kentucky: www.visitlex.com
8726. Vacation in the Florida Keys: http://fla-keys.com/
8727. Enjoy Palm springs: http://www.palm-springs.org/
8728. Visit Texas: http://www.traveltex.com/TexasMap.aspx

8729. For one week, give up 10% of your TV time, and
give it to your partner
8730. Gals: Be outrageous: "Flash" him when you're out in
public together

Best Love Songs by Rod Stewart
8731. "All for Love" (with Bryan Adams & Sting)
8732. "Have I Told You Lately"
8733. "Infatuation"
8734. "Love Touch"
8735. "Stay with Me"
8736. "Tonight's the Night (Gonna Be Alright)"
8737. "You're in My Heart (The Final Acclaim)"

8738. Don't forget the basics when it comes to sex!
8739. Read several books by Dr. Ruth
8740. (And share them with your lover)

8741. *Dr. Ruth's Top Ten Secrets for Great Sex: How to Enjoy it, Share it, and Love it Each and Every Time*

8742. *Dr. Ruth's Sex After 50: Revving up the Romance, Passion & Excitement! (The Best Half of Life)*

8743. *Dr. Ruth's 30 Days to Sexual Intimacy*

8744. *Sex for Dummies*, by Dr. Ruth K. Westheimer and Pierre A. Lahu

Favorite Love Songs from 1987

8745. "Lean on Me," Club Nouveau

8746. "Nothing's Gonna Stop Us Now," Starship

8747. "Nothing's Gonna Change My Love for You," Glenn Medeiros

Favorite Love Songs from 1988

8748. "Groovy Kind of Love," Phil Collins

8749. "Hungry Eyes," Eric Carmen

8750. "I Get Weak," Belinda Carlisle

8751. "I'm Gonna Be," The Proclaimers

8752. "Lost in You," Rod Stewart

8753. Build your partner's self-esteem—it will benefit *both of you*

8754. Get him a T-shirt with a Superman logo on it

8755. Create a *totally nonsensical* reason to go out and celebrate

8756. "Pains of love be sweeter far, than all other pleasures are." ~ John Dryden

8757. English: "I'll miss you"

8758. French: "Tu vas me manquer"

8759. Italian: "Mi mancherai"
8760. German: "Ich werde dich"
8761. Spanish: "Te echaré de menos"
8762. Portugese: "Eu vou sentir saudade sua"

8763. "I have found that if you love life, life will love you back." ~ Arthur Rubinstein
8764. People with the best *attitudes* have the best *lives*
8765. Embrace life, embrace your mate

12 Months' Notes from a Romantic's Planning Calendar

8766. January: Make one *romantic* resolution
8767. February: Plan your *summer* vacation
8768. March: Begin your Christmas shopping
8769. April: Plan a "Springtime Getaway"
8770. May: Begin looking for *next* year's Valentine gift
8771. June: Research exotic locations for a *major* vacation
8772. July: Plan to make your *own* "fireworks"
8773. August: Celebrate "Romance Awareness Month"
8774. September: Start making plans for New Year's Eve
8775. October: Plan a ski weekend for the upcoming winter
8776. November: Make reservations for Valentine's Day
8777. December: Get schedules for local theaters

8778. The gift, part 1: A classy beer mug engraved with his initials
8779. The gift, part 2: A six-pack of his favorite brew
8780. The gift, part 3: A custom Romance Coupon for one six-pack per month for a year

8781. Consciously "change gears" at the end of the day: From work mode to home mode

8782. Having rituals can help you get back in touch with your self—*and* your partner

8783. Meditate for half an hour

8784. Exercise till ya sweat

8785. Play with the kids (A great way to re-connect with your *own* fun-loving nature)

Naughty Books for Adventurous Couples

8786. *Erotic Tales of the Victorian Era*, from Prometheus Books

8787. *Dirty Girls: Erotica for Women*, by Rachel Kramer Bussel

8788. *Lust: Erotic Fantasies for Women*, by Violet Blue

8789. *Best Women's Erotica*, by Violet Blue

8790. *The Mammoth Book of Women's Fantasies*, by Sonia Florens

8791. *Gates of Paradise*, by Alberto Manguel

8792. *His Secret Life: Male Sexual Fantasies*, by Bob Berkowitz

8793. *Private Thoughts: Exploring the Power of Women's Sexual Fantasies*, by Wendy Maltz and Suzie Boss

8794. *My Secret Garden*, by Nancy Friday

8795. *Pleasures—Erotica for Women by Women*, edited by Lonnie Barbach

8796. *Beyond My Control: Forbidden Fantasies in an Uncensored Age*, by Nancy Friday

8797. *Who's Been Sleeping in Your Head: The Secret World of Sexual Fantasies*, by Brett Kahr

8798. *The Erotic Mind*, by Jack Morin

8799.   *Women on Top*, by Nancy Friday
8800.   *Arousal: The Secret Logic of Sexual Fantasies*, by
        Michael J. Bader
8801.   *Taboo: Forbidden Fantasies for Couples*, by Violet Blue

8802.   Guys: Have a new print made of the best photo of *her*
        from your wedding
8803.   Wrap it up, and give it to *yourself* for your birthday or
        the holidays

8804.   "And now these three remain: faith, hope, and love."
        ~ 1 Corinthians 13:13
8805.   From the Bible to rock 'n roll, the core message
        remains the same!
8806.   Demonstrate your *faith*: Get a gift that symbolizes
        your partner's faith
8807.   Express your *hope*: Write down three of your deepest
        hopes for your relationship
8808.   Live your *love*: Consciously decide to make "love"
        your Number One Priority

Favorite Love Songs from 1989

8809.   "Everlasting Love," by Howard Jones
8810.   "When I See You Smile," Bad English
8811.   "Don't Know Much," Linda Ronstadt & Aaron
        Neville

8812.   Create a custom soundtrack to accompany a Saturday
        evening date

8813. Greet her at the airport wearing a tuxedo, and carrying two dozen roses

8814. The "Ultimate Bubblebath" Coupon: One luxurious bubblebath complete with scented bath oils, soft music, champagne, and candles.

8815. Guys: Get all these items in coordinated fragrances:

8816. Body lotion and hand lotion

8817. Shampoo and conditioner

8818. Perfumed soap and bath gel

8819. Fragranced candle and dusting powder

8820. Remember: Love is a *feeling*. You feel love—you don't *do* love

8821. Remember: *Romance* is what you *do*. Romance is the expression of love

8822. Get some really cool "His" and "Hers" sunglasses

8823. Formally ask her to be your Valentine

8824. Get a copy of *People* magazine's "Top People of the Year" issue: Paste up photos of your partner and write a fun article

8825. Gals: Let the poor guy watch his favorite sports team in peace

8826. Guys: But it's unfair to claim that *every* team is your favorite team

The Best Love Songs of All Time

8827. "Colour My World," Chicago

8828. "Coming Around Again," Carly Simon

8829. "Crazy for You," Madonna
8830. "Endless Love," Diana Ross & Lionel Richie
8831. "(Everything I Do) I Do It for You," Bryan Adams
8832. "In Your Eyes," Peter Gabriel
8833. "(I've Had) the Time of My Life," Bill Medley & Jennifer Warnes
8834. "I Won't Last a Day Without You," Paul Williams
8835. "Just the Way You Are," Billy Joel
8836. "Lady," Kenny Rogers
8837. "At Last," Etta James
8838. "The Rose," Bette Midler
8839. "Something," The Beatles
8840. "Unchained Melody," Righteous Brothers
8841. "You Are So Beautiful (To Me)," Joe Cocker
8842. "You Light Up My Life," Debbie Boone
8843. "You're My Home," Billy Joel

8844. English: "Take me"
8845. French: "Prends-moi"
8846. Italian: "Prendimi"
8847. German: "Nimm mich"
8848. Spanish: "Me prendes"
8849. Portugese: "Me come"

8850. You can never go wrong with music from the fabulous Ms. Barbra Streisand…
8851. Selected CDs: *Memories; One Voice*
8852. *Songbird; Emotion; Till I Loved You*
8853. *The Way We Were; Higher Ground*

7 Romance Coupons for a Week of Love

8854. The "Sexy Saturday" Coupon: The coupon-giver will create a day of eroticism, sexiness, hedonism, delight, and loving for you

8855. The "Spiritual Sunday" Coupon: A day devoted to spiritual growth and deeper understanding

8856. The "Mellow Monday" Coupon: The coupon-giver is responsible for making Monday evening mellow and relaxing (with music and massage?)

8857. The "Togetherness Tuesday" Coupon: Do *everything* together, e.g., shower, prepare meals, do chores, make love

8858. The "Wonderful Wednesday" Coupon: *You* define "wonderful"—and your *partner* fulfills that definition this Wednesday

8859. The "Thankful Thursday" Coupon: Your partner expresses his or her thanks for you all day

8860. The "Funny Friday" Coupon: Your partner is responsible for making you laugh

---

8861. A+ Rating, Romantic Music Artist: Grover Washington, Jr.

8862. *Always* give her the seat in a bus, train, or subway

8863. Whisper softly while making love

8864. Help her create the wedding of her dreams

8865. Appreciate his quirks

8866. Go on a "Travel Date"

Favorite Love Songs from 1990

8867. "The Way You Do the Things You Do," UB40

8868. "Love Will Never Do Without You" Janet Jackson

8869. "Nothing Compares 2 U," Sinead O'Connor

8870. "Love has the patience to endure the fault it sees but cannot cure." ~ Edgar Guest
8871. Paste *this* quote on your refrigerator!
8872. Practice patience, understanding, and forgiveness

8873. Create your own Spring Celebration
8874. Soundtrack: George Winston's *Winter Into Spring*
8875. Activity: Plant a flower garden together
8876. Quote: "In the Spring a young man's fancy lightly turns to thoughts of love." ~ Alfred Lord Tennyson

Underwater Wonders of the World in Range of Snorkelers

8877. Crystal River, Florida: Swim side-by-side with manatees
8878. Providenciales Island, Turks and Caicos: Reefs like bonsai gardens
8879. Heron Island, Australia: A microcosm of the Great Barrier Reef
8880. Sting Ray City, Grand Cayman: Swim with sting rays
8881. The Red Sea's Gulf of Aqaba: Incredibly colorful coral reefs
8882. Qamea Island, Fiji: Some of the world's best soft corals
8883. Madang, Papua New Guinea: Vibrant with oceanic activity
8884. Yap, Micronesia: If you like manta rays
8885. Delos, Greece: Sunken ruins: Temple columns and mosaics
8886. La Paz, Mexico, in the Sea of Cortez: Consort with playful sea lions

8887. Write a list: "15 Reasons Why You're the Sexiest Thing Alive"
8888. Gals: Print the list on a pair of silk panties—
8889. Gals: Let him read the list while you're *wearing* them
8890. Guys: Print the list on fine parchment—
8891. Guys: Wrap it with a gift of elegant lingerie

8892. Train your subconscious mind to recognize romantic ideas when they pass your way
8893. Train your heart to speak loudly to your head
8894. Train your mind to be open
8895. Train your inner eye to "read between the lines" when your partner communicates with you

8896. Experiment: Gals, wear really nice lingerie every day for a week
8897. Does he notice? How does he react?

"Either-Or" Questions
(That Reveal A *Lot* About You)

Some questions are deceptively simple, yet reveal a lot
8898. Are you a peace-keeper or a trouble-maker?
8899. Do you tend to see things as black-and-white, or as shades of gray?
8900. Are you more or less thoughtful than most?
8901. Are you more or less sensitive than most people?
8902. Do you live to work—or work to live?
8903. Are you open or secretive?
8904. Are you a cat-person or a dog-person?
8905. Is it "love" or "money" that makes the world go 'round?

8906.   Are you humble or arrogant?
8907.   Are you an outdoors person or a homebody?
8908.   Are you good or bad with money?
8909.   Are you more or less intelligent than most?
8910.   Are you more or less competitive than most?
8911.   Do you evaluate things in terms of *time* or *money*?

8912.   Guys: Stuck for gift ideas? Ask her *mother*
8913.   Give one kiss for every day you've been a couple
8914.   Float a laminated love note in a punch bowl
8915.   "No disguise can mask love, nor feign it for long."
        ~ La Rochefoucauld
8916.   A+ Romantic Music Rating: Walter Beasley's *Intimacy*
8917.   Add to her collection of porcelain angels
8918.   The only acceptable prenuptial agreement:
        "Everything I have is yours"

8919.   Celebrate your similarities
8920.   Honor your differences
8921.   Practice your talents
8922.   Cherish your uniqueness

10 Ways to Love an Aries
(20 March–20 April)

8923.   Aries is a *fire* sign: Cater to his/her passionate, sexual
        nature
8924.   Gift tip: Intellectual, puzzling
8925.   As the head is ruled by Aries, give books and
        educational classes
8926.   Elegant hair brushes and ornaments are great gifts
8927.   Hats! (Sometimes gaudy)

8928. Aries likes brightly-colored clothes
8929. Honeysuckle; thistles
8930. Spicy and exotic foods
8931. The romance and history of Florence
8932. Wrap gifts in bright red

8933. Compromise over the little things
8934. (Choose your battles wisely)
8935. You'll be appreciated for your flexibility on the little things
8936. And you'll be respected for holding your ground on the big things

Favorite Love Songs from 1991
8937. "When a Man Loves a Woman," Michael Bolton
8938. "I'll Be There," The Escape Club
8939. "That's What Love Is For," Amy Grant

8940. Give him/her a homemade timeline of your lives together, highlighting your lives together with world events
8941. Draw it on poster paper
8942. Or have a calligrapher design it

8943. "'Tis not love that hurt my days, but that it went in little ways." ~ Edna St. Vincent Millay
8944. Beware of love slipping away while your attention is focused elsewhere
8945. Make love a habit

8946. For three weeks, be 25% more creative in your relationship

8947. Establish "your" table at a favorite restaurant
8948. Bana-gram: A love note on a banana
8949. Enemy of Love: "Humoring her"—Not really engaging your partner
8950. Re-create your wedding cake exactly for your 20th anniversary
8951. Tell your lover that he is the "crème de la crème"
8952. Visit the amazing Flower Fields at Carlsbad Ranch, California

8953. Gift & Date Idea: Get the song "Tonight," by Ferrante & Teicher—
8954. And rent *West Side Story*, featuring the song
8955. Or—surprise your partner with tickets to the musical, live on stage

8956. Drop hints
8957. Drop in unexpectedly
8958. Don't drop the ball

8959. Romantic music by Al Jarreau—
8960. *L Is for Lover; Glow*
8961. *Heart's Horizon; Tenderness*

Songs to Help You Express Your Feelings: *Falling in Love*

8962. "Could It Be I'm Falling in Love?" The Spinners
8963. "Could It Be Magic," Barry Manilow
8964. "Fallin' in Love," Hamilton, Joe Frank & Reynolds
8965. "If I Fell," The Beatles
8966. "Knocks Me off My Feet," Stevie Wonder

8967. Get her "Unforgettable" perfume
8968. And a copy of "Unforgettable," by Natalie Cole
8969. And write a poem about how she's so unforgettable
8970. Gals: What every guy *wants* you to know: *203 Ways to Drive a Man Wild in Bed*, by Olivia St. Claire
8971. Gals: *What both of you should know: Love & Respect: the Love She Most Desires, the Respect He Desperately Needs*, by Emerson Eggerich
8972. Gals: Required reading: *The Sensuous Woman*, by J
8973. Gals: You may want to explore: *For Women Only: What You Need to Know about the Inner Lives of Men*, by Shaunti Feldhaun
8974. Gals: More of what you ought to know: *What Every Woman Should Know About Men*, by Dr. Joyce Brothers

Ways to Learn More About Your Lover

8975. Have a three-session "Relationship Check-Up" with a relationship counselor
8976. Get astrological readings for the two of you
8977. Listen to your partner more closely and more often
8978. Review the list of "Favorite Things You Should Know About Your Lover" elsewhere in this book
8979. Review your photo albums together
8980. Be bridge partners on a regular basis
8981. Talk about your religious beliefs
8982. Attend a relationship seminar together
8983. Check out *Love by the Numbers*, by Glynis McCants to see if numerology has any insights
8984. "Frost Yourself" as seen in *How To Lose A Guy in 10 Days*—Splurge on expensive jewelry.

8985. Join a Marriage Encounter group
8986. Analyze your "personal styles" by reading *Please Understand Me: Character & Temperament Types,* by David Keirsey & Marilyn Bates
8987. Spend an "all-nighter" together: Talk and make love all night long
8988. Talk about your childhoods
8989. Read *Your Relationship Report Card*, by Gregory Godek

Favorite Love Songs from 1992

8990. "Save the Best for Last," Vanessa Williams
8991. "Ordinary Love," Sade
8992. "I Will Always Love You," Whitney Houston

8993. Send her on a "Blank Check Shopping Spree"—on Rodeo Drive in Beverly Hills
8994. Get her a replica of Rose's "Romantic Heart Necklace" as seen in *Titanic*
8995. "In the coldest February, as in every other month in every other year, the best thing to hold on to in the world is each other." ~ Linda Ellerbee
8896. A+ Rated music from Eric Tingstad & Nancuy Rumbel: *Homeland; Give and Take; In the Garden*
8997. Peruse a book of "toasts" for some inspiration
8998. Clip newspaper and magazine articles you know will amuse and interest your mate
8999. Turn to your partner in public and whisper, "There's no one I'd rather be with!"
9000. Try to set the record for the world's longest kiss

Songs to Help You Express Your Feelings: Adoration

9001. "Cherish," The Association

9002. "Heaven Must Be Missing an Angel," Tavares

9003. "I Just Want to Be Your Everything," Andy Gibb

9004. "My Eyes Adored You," Frankie Valli

9005. "My Love," Paul McCartney & Wings

9006. "Wind Beneath My Wings," Bette Midler

9007. Buy her a reproduction of the sculpture "The Kiss," by Auguste Rodin

9008. Give him a poster of the painting "The Kiss," by Gustav Klimt

---

9009. Write your own wedding vows

9010. If your partner was formerly in the military, give him/her a "Lover's Medal of Honor," "Bravery in the Face of Parenthood," etc.

9011. For Married Folks: Think like a single person: *Date* your spouse

9012. Save some sand in a jar from beach vacations

9013. "We don't remember the days; we remember the moments." ~ Cesare Pavese

9014. Forget about *extravagant* romantic gestures—focus on individual *moments*

9015. Stop. Hold her face in your hands. Gaze into her eyes. Tell her you love her. And really, really, really mean it

9016. Create a special moment of intimacy—not sexuality—in bed tonight

9017. Find a copy of "This Magic Moment," the 1960 hit by The Drifters

9018. Guys: Don't demean her by saying to your kids, "Oh, you know how your mother is"

9019. Gals: Don't make him the bad guy by threatening your kids with "Wait until your father gets home!"

Reasons to Be Romantic

9020. You'll be happier

9021. Your *partner* will be happier

9022. You'll have sex more often

9023. You'll enjoy sex more

9024. You'll keep your love alive

9025. You'll experience the spark of infatuation again

9026. You'll reduce the chance your partner might cheat on you

9027. You'll increase the probability that you'll stay married

9028. You'll add meaning to your relationship

9029. You will create a safe haven

9030. You will be truly heard and deeply understood

9031. You'll save money by expressing your love in lots of little, creative ways

9032. Exercising your creativity will benefit you in other areas of your life

9033. You'll probably live longer

9034. You'll be better parents

9035. You'll be great role models for your children

9036. You'll be great role models for friends

9037. Your children will understand love better than most kids

9038. Your children will experience what love is really all about

9039. Your children will have a better chance of choosing partners wisely

9040. Your children will be better able to create healthy love relationships

9041. You'll make the world a better place

9042. You'll come to appreciate your own uniqueness

9043. You'll come to appreciate your partner's uniqueness

9044. You'll reduce or eliminate therapy bills!

9045. You'll get more of what you want out of life

9046. You'll strengthen your self-esteem

9047. You'll never have to write to Dear Abby for love advice

9048. You'll be better able to live your faith (love is central to every religion)

9049. You will have the quiet confidence that you've achieved something that few people accomplish

9050. You'll create a truly mature relationship

9051. You'll move beyond treating your partner like a stereotype

9052. You'll have more energy for your career

9053. You'll surprise your skeptical in-laws!

9054. You'll deepen your understanding of the opposite sex

9055. You'll reconnect with your creative, impulsive, spontaneous, childlike nature

9056. You'll live up to your true potential in life

9057. You'll never again be panic stricken on Valentine's Day

9058. You'll never again have to feel guilty for having forgotten a birthday or anniversary

9059. You'll stay young-at-heart

9060. Love makes the world go 'round

9061. Your partner *wants* you to be romantic—What more reason do you *need*?

9062. Why *not*?

9063. For cat lovers: http://www.i-love-cats.com/
9064. For dog lovers: http://www.dogchannel.com/
9065. For horse lovers: http://www.horseloversgifts.com/
9066. For butterfly fans: http://www.thebutterflysite.com/
9067. And for *exotic* pet lovers: http://www.exoticpetcenter.com/

Favorite Love Songs from 1993

9068. "Breathe Again," Toni Braxton
9069. "Dreamlover," Mariah Carey
9070. "(I Can't Help) Falling in Love with You," UB40
9071. "Have I Told You Lately," Rod Stewart

9072. Use the three most powerful words in the world: "I love you"
9073. (The *second* most powerful: "Let's eat out")

9074. Spend a week at a spa together: The Spa at Cordillera, in Colorado: www.cordilleralodge.com
9075. Discuss your core values and beliefs
9076. "Love is…an endless mystery, for it has nothing else to explain it." ~ Rabindranath Tagore
9077. For your Judy Garland fan: *Judy*—a four-CD retrospective
9078. Enemy of Love: Stereotyping
9079. Set your alarm clock thirty minutes early—make love as the sun rises
9080. Give her a hand massage

Breathtaking-But-Smaller Waterfalls in America

"Bigger" is not necessarily better:

9081. Amicalola Falls State Park, Georgia

9082. Cumberland Falls State Resort Park, Kentucky

9083. DeSoto Falls, DeSoto State Park, Alabama

9084. Gorman Falls, Colorado Bend State Park, Texas

9085. Issaqueena Falls, Stumphouse Tunnel Park, South Carolina

9086. The Kaanapali area on Maui, Hawaii

9087. Linville Falls, Brue Ridge Parkway, North Carolina

9088. Turner Falls Park, Oklahoma

9089. "We kiss. And it feels like we have just shrugged off the world." ~ Jim Shahin

9090. Tender kisses communicate caring

9091. Passionate kisses connect emotional love with physical sexuality

9092. Long, lingering kisses slow you down

9093. Deep kisses connect you—on *several* levels

9094. Quick kisses keep you connected

9095. Guys: Approach the subject of lingerie with her *gently*

9096. Don't: Start by giving her a peek-a-boo bra

9097. Do: Attach a one hundred dollar bill to a Victoria's Secret catalog along with a note saying, "You choose"

9098. "Don't hate. It's too big a burden to bear." ~ Martin Luther King Jr.

9099. "Don't look for love; give love—and you will find love looking for you." ~ Beth Black

9100. "I don't want to live. I want to love first, and live incidentally." ~ Zelda Fitzgerald

9101. "Don't Go Breaking My Heart," Elton John & Kiki Dee

9102. "Don't Fall in Love with a Dreamer," Kenny Rogers & Kim Carnes

9103. "Don't Let the Sun Go Down on Me," George Michael & Elton John

9104. "Don't Ever Leave Me," Helen Morgan

9105. "Don't Sit Under the Apple Tree," The Andrews Sisters

9106. "Don't Get Around Much Anymore"

9107. "You Don't Know What Love Is"

9108. "Why Don't You Do Right?" Peggy Lee

9109. "You Don't Have to Be a Star," Marilyn McCoo & Billy Davis Jr.

9110. "Baby Don't Go," Sonny & Cher

9111. Remember: It requires no effort to *fall* in love

9112. But *staying* in love requires two things: 1) Conscious decision, and 2) consistent action

9113. Soundtrack for a summer celebration: Paul Winter's *Sun Singer*

9114. Write a love note on a rock, then toss it into the deep end of your pool

9115. An "Adult Ed" Coupon: The coupon-giver will pay for and accompany you to an adult education class of your choosing

Items for a *Yearly* Romantic Checklist

9116. Make a New Year's Resolution to be more loving next year

9117. Make plans for your next anniversary

9118. Think of an *unusual* way to celebrate your partner's birthday

9119. Review your plans for your next vacation

9120. Create a "Romance" category in your household budget

9121. Make plans for Valentine's Day at least six months in advance

9122. Write "Relationship Goals" for the next five years

9123. Watch the snow from a cozy cabin window

9124. Love and learn: Read *Hold Me Tight: Seven Conversations for a Lifetime of Love*, by Sue Johnson

9125. Spend your entire holiday gift budget on lottery tickets—You may just win enough for some *great* gifts

9126. "How vast a memory has love." ~ Alexander Pope

9127. For your ice cream lover: Tour Ben & Jerry's factory: www.benjerry.com

9128. Write a sexy haiku

9129. Have a poem delivered to your table at a restaurant

9130. Rent a beach bungalow on Cape Cod

Favorite Love Songs from 1994

9131. "All for Love," Bryan Adams & Rod Stewart & Sting

9132. "I'll Make Love to You," Boyz II Men

9133. "When Can I See You," Babyface

9134. "You Mean the World to Me," Toni Braxton

9135. "At Your Best (You Are Love)," Aaliyah

9136. "Can You Feel the Love Tonight," Elton John (*Lion King* soundtrack)

9137.   Gift & Date Idea: Get the song "Call Me,"
        by Blondie—
9138.   And rent *American Gigolo*, featuring the song

9139.   And there's always Wynton Marsalis for some jazzy
        romantic music…
9140.   Selected CDs: *Intimacy Calling*
9141.   *Carnival; Jump Start and Jazz*
9142.   *The Majesty of the Blues*

4 Aspects of Love—Based on the Ancient 4 Elements

A well-rounded relationship incorporates aspects of all four
elements. Where are your strengths and weaknesses?

9143.   *Earth:* Grounded, solid, dependable, strong
9144.   *Air:* Light, free flowing, flexible
9145.   *Fire:* Passionate, powerful, sexual
9146.   *Water:* Soothing, filling, comforting

9147.   English: "Will you marry me?"
9148.   French (to a gal): "Tu veux être ma femme?"
9149.   French (to a guy): "Tu veux être mon mari?"
9150.   Italian: "Vuoi sposarmi?"
9151.   German: "Heiratest du mich?"
9152.   Spanish: "¿Te casarías conmigo?"
9153.   Portugese: "Você quer casar comigo?"

9154.   "A loving heart is the truest wisdom." ~ Charles Dickens
9155.   What a mistake we make when we believe that
        wisdom comes from the *head*
9156.   Trust your heart. Listen for that Inner Voice.

9157. Get a stone Cupid to place in her garden
9158. Remember: 5 = 1 (5 minutes devoted to love equals 1 day of harmony)
9159. Go whitewater rafting on the Gauley River, in West Virginia
9160. See a couple's counselor: Not because you've got problems, but simply to help you deepen your relationship
9161. A luscious surprise: Ice cream made from flowers! www.outofaflower.com
9162. "Any time that is not spent on love is wasted." ~ Torquato Tasso
9163. Discuss with your partner: Is this an overstatement, or the truth?
9164. Experiment: For the next thirty days, spend thirty additional minutes per day being loving

Top Public Golf Courses

For your golf nut: Plan great golfing vacations

9165. Bethpage, Farmingdale, New York
9166. Blackwolf Run (River Course), Kohler, Wisconsin
9167. Cog Hill (Number 4), Lemont, Illinois
9168. Pebble Beach, Pebble Beach, California
9169. Pinehurst (Number 2), Pinehurst, North Carolina
9170. Pumpkin Ridge (Ghost Creek), Cornelius, Oregon
9171. Spyglass Hill, Pebble Beach, California
9172. TPC at Sawgrass (Stadium), Ponte Vedra Beach, Florida
9173. Troon North (Monument), Scottsdale, Arizona
9174. World Woods (Pine Barrens), Brooksville, Florida

9175. Turn to him in public and whisper, "I'm not wearing any panties"
9176. Enemy of Love: Emotional withdrawal
9177. A+ Romance Rating: *Kiss Under the Moon*, Warren Hill's jazzy, romantic music
9178. Nurture your partner in as many ways as possible
9179. Carve your Halloween pumpkin with *hearts*
9180. After you've talked on the phone for a long time, call back in three minutes to say you miss her
9181. Remember: Romance isn't just a weekend sport!
9182. Spend an afternoon at MOMA in NYC

Favorite Love Songs from 1995

9183. "Have You Ever Really Loved a Woman," Bryan Adams
9184. "I Can Love You Like That," All-4-One
9185. "On the Verge," Colin Raye
9186. "Only Wanna Be with You," Hootie & the Blowfish
9187. "Dreaming of You," Selena
9188. "Can't Stop Lovin' You," Van Halen

9189. Gift & Date Idea: Get the song "April Love," by Pat Boone—
9190. And rent the movie *April Love*, featuring the song

9191. Send a bouquet of *mistletoe*!
9192. Kiss in at least five different countries over the next ten years
9193. Turn to her in public and whisper, "I wouldn't trade you for *anything*"

9194. Take an inn-to-inn hike through the Grand Canyon: www.hiddentrails.com
9195. Hire a celebrity look-alike of his/her favorite actor to entertain at a party
9196. Anticipate her desires

Songs to Help You Express Your Feelings: *Forgive Me/Don't Leave Me!*

9197. "Baby Come Back," Player
9198. "Don't Give Up on Us," David Soul
9199. "Hard to Say I'm Sorry," Chicago
9200. "If You Leave Me Now," Chicago
9201. "One More Night," Phil Collins
9202. "Sorry Seems to Be the Hardest Word," Elton John

9203. Guys: On your wedding anniversary, re-create her wedding bouquet
9204. Show a wedding photo to your florist
9205. Present her with the photo and bouquet together

9206. "As we think in our hearts, so we are."
   ~ Proverbs 23:7
9207. This Biblical quote elegantly unites the *heart* (emotions) and the *head* (thinking)
9208. The popular notion that the head and heart are *separate* is just plain *wrong*
9209. It is not true that "being in love" is *entirely* a matter of the heart
9210. True love involves a *dynamic balance* of both
9211. Clarification: *Infatuation* is about heart and sex—and ignoring the head

9212. Note: Boredom and cynicism result when the head leaves the heart behind

9213. Always have one set of tickets to an upcoming event tacked to your bulletin board

9214. "May you live all the days of your life." ~ Jonathan Swift

9215. Participate in something that you hate just to make your partner happy

9216. Get him box seats for the local pro baseball team

9217. Put a tiny love note inside a walnut; seal it up

9218. Hang a world map on the wall, and place little flags on spots you want to visit

9219. "Life is a paradise for those who love many things with passion." ~ Leo Buscaglia

9220. Wear matching Hawaiian shirts

9221. Do something just plain *ZaNy*

9222. Take your rock fan to the Rock & Roll Hall of Fame in Cleveland

9223. Make flags from toothpicks and tiny squares of paper; write tiny love notes on them and stick them in pancakes, rolls, etc.

Favorite Love Songs from 1996

9224. "If You Could Only See," Tonic

9225. "(I Love You) Always Forever," Donna Lewis

9226. "One Sweet Day," Mariah Carey and Boyz II Men

9227. "You Were Meant for Me," Jewel

9228. "And I will make thee beds of roses. And a thousand fragrant posies." ~ Christopher Marlowe

9229. Want romantic inspiration? Read poetry!
9230. In poetic form, this is the classic romantic strategy of "overdoing something"
9231. Start *literally*: Cover your bed with roses…
9232. Or *fill a room* with posies for your partner
9233. Or bring home a bouquet of flowers every day for a month
9234. Or every Friday for the rest of your life!

Ways for Women to Get Men to Be Romantic

9235. *Barter* with him for romantic favors
9236. Get a buddy of his (who "gets it" when it comes to relationships) to have a talk with him
9237. Stop using the word "romance" altogether—And replace it with the word "fun"
9238. Be a good role model—*You* be romantic first
9239. Give him this book—with your favorite items circled
9240. Give him a list of all your "favorite things"
9241. Ask him for a list of *his* "favorite things"
9242. Give him three "Romance Coupons" for things you want him to do for you
9243. Schedule one lunch "meeting" a month for the two of you
9244. You be romantic *first*, then take turns
9245. Appeal to his competitive nature: Hold a "Who Can Be More Romantic" contest

9246. Visit America's West Coast Romantic Hideaway Island: Catalina
9247. Live your wedding vows
9248. For anyone in or into the performing arts: The Music Stand: www.themusicstand.com

9249.   The Red-Hot "Kiss" Coupon: Redeemable for one
        hour of "making-out"

9250.   "I love thee with the breath, smiles, tears, of all my
        life." ~ Elizabeth Barrett Browning

9251.   Romantic piano by Peter Kater: *Two Hearts* CD

9252.   Place a single red rose in his/her briefcase

9253.   Make a ten-foot-tall greeting card

9254.   Attend a live production of *Romeo and Juliet*

9255.   Do something that's sexy to the point of being illegal

Sexy Ways to Celebrate the Holidays

9256.   Christmas: Wrap yourself in a red bow and wait
        underneath the Christmas tree

9257.   Independence Day: Wrap yourself in a flag—and see
        if he salutes!

9258.   Halloween: Dress-up as favorite fantasy characters

9259.   Thanksgiving: Give thanks for your relationship by
        giving sexual favors

9260.   Groundhog Day: Go "underground": Skip work and
        stay in bed all day together

9261.   Memorial Day: Create a sexual encounter that will be
        truly *memorable*

9262.   Valentine's Day: Treat your partner (and yourself) to
        edible massage lotion!

9263.   St. Patrick's Day: Wear green underwear

9264.   Musical lovenote: "Play the CD *Mud Slide Slim and
        the Blue Horizon*, by James Taylor. My message to
        you is song No. 2"

9265.   Tour the French countryside

9266.   Remember: Romance isn't about "giving in"

9267. Use romantic gestures to create a bridge between the two of you

9268. Mood music: Create a peaceful, thoughtful mood with the *Canon in D*, by Johann Pachelbel

9269. Create your own Autumn Celebration

9270. Soundtrack: George Winston's *Autumn*

9271. Activity: Watch the blazing colors of the trees in Maine

9272. Quote: "Autumn's flaming colors inspire passion in lovers' hearts." ~ Anonymous

---

9273. When apart, think about one another for one minute at a pre-determined time

9274. Re-visit your childhood and paint a picture together

9275. Eat in the most romantic inn in Edinburgh: Prestonfield House

9276. Add a bottle to his wine cellar

9277. Write a detailed "Job Description" for your role as husband or wife

9278. Cook him the same meal you first cooked as husband and wife

---

Books *About* Men, *For* Men, *By* Men

9279. *For Men Only: A Straightforward Guide to the Inner Lives of Women*, by Shaunti Feldhahn and Jeff Feldhahn

9280. *Why Do Men Have Nipples? Hundreds of Questions You'd Only Ask a Doctor After Your Third Martini*, by Mark Leyner and Billy Goldberg

9281. *Why do Men Fall Asleep After Sex? More Questions You'd Only Ask a Doctor After Your Third Whiskey Sour*, by Mark Leyner and Billy Goldberg

9282. *Love Letters of Great Men*, by John C. Kirkland
9283. *For Young Men Only: A Guy's Guide to the Alien Gender*, by Jeff Feldhahn, Eric Rice, and Shaunti Feldhahn

9284. Write a love note in macaroni
9285. Dance in the living room to your wedding song
9286. Leave little notes on the windshield of his car for a week
9287. Recreate your wedding day meal

9288. Name your boat after her
9289. Never, never, *never:* Teach your partner to drive a car
9290. Gift resource for wine enthusiasts: www.wineenthusiast.com
9291. Adopt his/her kids from a previous marriage

Poignant Love Songs
9292. "Do You Love Me?" from *Fiddler on the Roof*
9293. "One More Night," Phil Collins
9294. "Truly," Lionel Richie
9295. "Without You," from the Broadway musical *Rent*

9296. Kidnap him from work on a Friday afternoon
9297. Visit a spiritually meaningful place, like Mecca
9298. Create your own "Romance Game" using an old Monopoly Game
9299. Believe that the best is yet to come
9300. Erotic Book & Movie Alert! *The Unbearable Lightness of Being*
9301. "Motivation is what gets you started. Habit is what keeps you going." ~ Jim Ryun

9302. Romantic piano concerto: Beethoven's Piano Concerto No. 5 in E flat

9303. Tuck a love note in his baseball glove

9304. Hold a "His" and "Hers" Weekend: On Saturday you both do whatever *she* wants to do and on Sunday, you both do whatever *he* wants to do

9305. Unlearn the attitude "Give her an inch and she'll take a mile."

Favorite Love Songs from 1997

9306. "How Do I Live," LeAnn Rimes

9307. "My Heart Will Go On (Love Theme from *Titantic*)," Celine Dion

9308. "Truly Madly Deeply," Savage Garden

9309. "Something About the Way You Look Tonight," Elton John

9310. "The Light in Your Eyes," LeAnn Rimes

9311. "I'll Never Break Your Heart," Backstreet Boys

9312. "It's the thought that counts"

9313. Pay attention to the details

9314. Be 10% more thoughtful/considerate

9315. Remember how you thought about your mate when you first met

9316. Put your thoughts on paper: Write a love note

9317. Enemy of Love: Fear of rejection

9318. Give a subscription to *Sports Illustrated*

9319. Tell your mate you think he/she is "pulchritudinous"

9320. Press some flowers that you've received

9321. Share *everything:* Your ice cream and snack foods

9322. Get a professional massage table

"Love Codes" for Lovers

9323. SWAK—Sealed With A Kiss
9324. X's stand for kisses; O's stand for hugs (Often used to sign letters)
9325. *Red* roses symbolize love and passion
9326. *Pink* roses symbolize friendship
9327. *Yellow* roses symbolize respect
9328. *White* roses symbolize purity
9329. Point to your eye; then point to your heart; then point to your partner
9330. Learn the sign language gesture for "I love you"
9331. Three soft taps on the shoulder mean "I love you"
9332. Three soft taps on the thigh mean "Let's make love"

9333. Gift & Date Idea: Get the song "Baby I Love Your Way," by Big Mountain—
9334. And rent *Reality Bites*, featuring the song

9335. Soundtrack for a winter celebration: Paul Winter's CD *Wintersong*
9336. Have mimosas with breakfast
9337. A little follow-up gift to a night of great love-making: A copy of "You Make Lovin' Fun," by Fleetwood Mac
9338. Call when you're running late
9339. Enemy of Love: Thoughtlessness
9340. Give her Chanel No. 5
9341. Enemy of Love: Short-term thinking
9342. Stay at the fanciest hotel in Rome: Sole al Pantheon

9343. Gift & Date Idea: Get the song "(Everything I Do) I Do It for You," by Bryan Adams—

9344. And rent the movie *Robin Hood: Prince of Thieves*, featuring the song

Best Love Songs by The Four Tops

9345. "Ain't No Woman (Like the One I've Got)"

9346. "Baby I Need Your Loving"

9347. "I Can't Help Myself (Sugar Pie, Honey Bunch)"

9348. "Reach Out I'll Be There"

9349. "River Deep—Mountain High" (with The Supremes)

9350. "Something About You"

9351. "Sweet Understanding Love"

9352. A "Happy Anniversary!" Coupon: Choose *one* of the following: 1) Dinner for two, 2) A romantic movie date, or 3) A sexy lovemaking session

9353. Love Coupon: Flowers! Your choice: One dozen of any kind. Flowers to be delivered within three days of issuance of coupon

9354. For sports fans: Birthday cakes in the shape of footballs, basketballs, etc.

9355. Say "I love you" in Morse Code:
.. / . _ .. _ _ _ ... _ . / _ . _ _ _ _ _ .. _

9356. Carry a lock of her hair in your wallet

9357. Be frugal all year so you can *live it up* on vacation

9358. If you're talkative by nature, talk 20% less, and listen 20% more

9359. Keep handy left-handed scissors, etc., for your southpaw spouse

9360. A note: "Time and time again you amaze me because…"

Favorite Love Songs from 1998

9361. "I'll Be," Edwin McCain
9362. "Iris," Goo Goo Dolls
9363. "I'm Afraid This Might Be Love," Linda Eder
9364. "You're Still the One," Shania Twain
9365. "All My Life," K-Ci and Jo Jo

9366. "As soon as you cannot keep anything from a woman, you love her." ~ Paul Geraldy
9367. Lovers don't keep secrets from each other
9368. Picture the two of you as the *center* of a series of concentric circles that comprise your life

9369. Help her study for a class she's taking
9370. Sing duets in the shower together
9371. If he's a former Boy Scout: Award him with some custom "Merit Badges"—for "Loving Skills," "20 Years of Loyal Service," etc.
9372. Send a mysterious "Treasure Map" to lead her to a secret rendezvous

9373. Write an entire love letter on the surface of a balloon, with a magic marker
9374. FYI: Arguments between A+ Couples end with *two* winners
9375. Go "Garage Sale Hopping" and buy $25 of junk for each other
9376. Prepare an Easter basket with plastic eggs filled with love notes and tiny gifts
9377. Expand your Romantic Music Library with Anita Baker

9378. Experiment: For two weeks, set aside one hour every evening to do "romantic homework"; your partner gets to choose the "assignment"

9379. Create a "Count-Down Calendar" anticipating your 10th anniversary

9380. Give your partner permission to play

9381. Take off work on Valentine's Day and make it extra special!

9382. Love Enhancer: Listening with your heart

9383. Attach a note to his calculator: "Count on me"

9384. Get your space nut a piece of jewelry that incorporates a meteorite

9385. A+ Rating, Romantic Music Artist: Tom Scott

9386. Into astrology? Check out http://www.astrojewelry.com/

Songs to Help You Express
Your Feelings: *Hot Passion*

9387. "All I Wanna Do Is Make Love to You," Heart

9388. "Deeper and Deeper," Madonna

9389. "Do You Wanna Make Love," Peter McCann

9390. "Hot Stuff," Donna Summer

9391. "I Do What I Do," John Taylor

9392. "I'm Your Baby Tonight," Whitney Houston

9393. "Kiss You All Over," Exile

9394. "Light My Fire," The Doors

9395. "Make Me Lose Control," Eric Carmen

9396. "Touch Me (I Want Your Body)," Samantha Sang

9397. Attend a Renaissance Fair together

9398. Visit America's East Coast Romantic Hideaway Island: Martha's Vineyard

9399.   If you both play piano, play Mozart's *Sonata in F*—a piece for *4 hands*

9400.   Plant one rose bush for every anniversary

9401.   "If it is not erotic, it is not interesting." ~ Fernando Arrabal

9402.   Attach a note to a bottle of Tabasco Sauce: "You're *hot stuff!*"

9403.   Create a romantic screen-saver for his computer

9404.   Share *everything:* Your meals and desserts

9405.   Bring home Häagen-Dazs Rum Raisin

9406.   A "Classic Romance" Coupon: You will be treated to a weekend of champagne, romantic movies, dinner, and dancing

9407.   Stay at the fanciest hotel in Monte Carlo: Hôtel de Paris

9408.   Trek through the Himalayas together

9409.   Use Alpha-Bits cereal to spell-out love messages

9410.   Hold a "Romantic Idea Brainstorming Party" with ten friends

Best Love Songs by Marvin Gaye

9411.   "Ain't Nothing Like the Real Thing" (with Tammi Terrell)

9412.   "How Sweet It Is to Be Loved by You"

9413.   "If I Could Build My Whole World Around You"

9414.   "Let's Get It On"

9415.   "Too Busy Thinking About My Baby"

9416.   "You're a Special Part of Me" (with Diana Ross)

9417.   "You're All I Need to Get By" (with Tammi Terrel)

9418.   Go in search of little-known vacation spots

9419.   Roll-up a little love note and insert it in a tube of her lipstick

9420.   Kiss at the top of the Eiffel Tower

9421.   Watch the tide go out on a Jamaican beach

9422.   Have a trophy made: "World's Best Wife"

9423.   Hang a fancy, Victorian Christmas stocking, filled to the brim with goodies

9424.   Order a 14K gold pin of two geese (symbolizing "Geese Mate for Life"): From Cross Jewelers: www.crossjewelers.com

9425.   Paint "I love my wife" in two-foot letters on the side of your pick-up truck

9426.   For tea lovers: Share afternoon tea

9427.   Give a case of wine from the country of his/her ancestors

9428.   Have the face of his wristwatch engraved with "Time for love"

9429.   Don't just buy her *perfume*, get her a "fragrance wardrobe"

9430.   Keep extra batteries for his electronics

Favorite Love Songs from 1999

9431.   "Angel of Mine," Monica

9432.   "I Knew I Loved You," Savage Garden

9433.   "You'll Be in My Heart," Phil Collins

9434.   "I Do (Cherish You)," 98 Degrees

9435.   "The One," Aaron Skyy

9436.   "All I Want is You," U2

9437.   Romantic music by Kenny G…

9438.   Selected CDs: *Silhouette; Kenny G*

9439. *G-Force; Duotones*

9440. Enemy of Love: Speed (modern life's fast pace)

9441. Try a new *position* the next time you make love

9442. Put quarters in her parking meter

9443. Present your partner with a movie poster signed by his/her favorite star

9444. Make love on top of the washer/dryer (while it's running)

9445. Remember: Romance is the language of love

9446. "Nothing is worth more than this day." ~ Johann Wolfgang Von Goethe

9447. Expand your Romantic Music Library with Mike Howard CDs

9448. Spray your "signature" perfume in his car

9449. When traveling for a week, leave behind seven wrapped boxes filled with trinket gifts labeled with the days of the week

9450. Watch the sunset from an Italian villa

9451. Get great clothing for him/her from J. Peterman: www.jpeterman.com

9452. Musical lovenote: "Play the CD *To Our Children's Children's Children*, by The Moody Blues. My message to you is song No. 13"

9453. Take her off the pedestal and place her by your side

9454. Wrap seven *shoe boxes* for her: Each box contains a gift certificate for a new pair of shoes

9455. Make fun "deals" with your lover:

9456. She'll accompany him to a topless beach—

9457. If he'll buy her diamond earrings

9458. He'll treat her to a shopping spree at Saks Fifth Avenue—
9459. If she'll buy him a wide screen TV
9460. She'll give him a backrub—
9461. If he'll do the week's grocery shopping
9462. He'll forego his Sunday golf game—
9463. If she'll serve him breakfast in bed

9464. Send an "S.O.S." message ("Sex On Saturday")
9465. Is he a Blue Ribbon lover? Give him one!
9466. Love Enhancer: Appreciation for *life*
9467. Secretly pass a love note to her
9468. Perfume his pillow as a signal that you want to make love tonight
9469. The "Romantic Cuddle" Coupon: You are entitled to one solid hour of cozy cuddling
9470. Spend two weeks together at a French villa
9471. Stop the elevator between floors to make out
9472. Sign her up for the Panty-of-the-Month Club: www.pantiesclub.com
9473. Get her a little gold Cupid pin
9474. Take a paddle boat down the Mississippi River
9475. Prepare a perfumed milk bath for her
9476. "Perseverance is not a long race; it is many short races one after another." ~ Walter Elliott
9477. Attend the grand opening of a new restaurant
9478. Turn to your partner in public and whisper, "You look *wonderful* tonight!"
9479. "The more I wonder…the more I love." ~ Alice Walker
9480. Spoil her
9481. Romantic piano concerto: Schumann's Concerto in A Minor for Piano & Orchestra

9482. Learn some little magic tricks to amuse her
9483. Enemy of Love: Inattentiveness
9484. Eat in the most romantic restaurant in Amsterdam: De Goudsbloem
9485. Work together to complete the *New York Times* Sunday Crossword Puzzle
9486. Share a good laugh together

Favorite Love Songs from 2000

9487. "Your Everything," Keith Urban
9488. "Thank God I Found You," Mariah Carey
9489. "Everything," Lifehouse
9490. "Breathless," The Coors
9491. "The Way You Love Me," Faith Hill
9492. "I Need You," LeAnn Rimes

9493. Photograph all the stages of her pregnancy
9494. Don't let a single day go by without telling her how beautiful she is

9495. "Re-frame" your relationship
9496. She's not your wife—she's your *lover*
9497. He's not your husband—he's that handsome devil you flipped for

9498. A "Day of "Kissin'-an'-a-Lovin'" Coupon: No directions necessary for this one!
9499. For your gourmet: A kitchen gadget he's been lusting after
9500. For electricians in love: Install dimmer switches in your bedroom

9501. Come down with a case of "Spring Fever"; the cure is to spend all day in bed with your mate

9502. Give yourself permission to be sexy

9503. Note: If love is really your top priority, then you never really "sacrifice" for it

9504. Gals: Don't use "feminine wiles" on him: It's deceitful

9505. If you're quiet, open up and talk 20% more

9506. Eat in the most romantic restaurant in Budapest: Paradiso

9507. Create a "Romance Credit Card": Establish two types of credit—time and money—and chart your expenditures

9508. Get a shower head built-for-two

9509. Celebrate the Spring Equinox by watching a sunrise together

9510. Celebrate the Summer Solstice by taking a stroll together

9511. Celebrate the Autumn Equinox by watching a sunset together

9512. Celebrate the Winter Solstice by cuddling in front of a fire together

9513. To help you celebrate: The Celebration Fantastic Catalog: http://www.celebrations.com/

9514. Write a love note in French/German/Swedish/etc.— and wait for her to translate it!

9515. Get your pianist partner a Steinway baby grand

9516. Listen to Frank Sinatra's *Songs for Young Lovers*: Widely known as the best of his albums

9517. Eat in Boston's most romantic restaurant: The Hungry I

9518. "There's more to love than love, when it's right."
~ John O'Hara
9519. While at parties and dinners, share one glass all evening
9520. Love Enhancer: Time—*Quantity* of time
9521. In a love note, describe your lover as "sui generis"
9522. Create a "Count-Down Calendar" anticipating your wedding
9523. For two weeks, compliment your partner 50% more than usual
9524. Make a wish on the first star
9525. Eat in the most romantic restaurant in Venice: Da Fiore
9526. Send a telegram. Western Union: www.westernunion.com
9527. Enemy of Love: Poor time management
9528. Write down your excuses for not being romantic, put a big red "X" through them, and give the list to your partner

Favorite Love Songs from 2001
9529. "Fallin'," Alicia Keys
9530. "Love Letters," Diana Krall
9531. "Hero," Enrique Iglesias
9532. "Love of My Life," Brian McKnight

9533. "If you love somebody, tell them." ~ Rod McKuen
9534. We often need to be reminded of the basics, the ABCs, of love
9535. No one ever tires of hearing "I love you"
9536. Tell your partner you love him/her with just a look

9537. Tell your partner you adore him/her with just a touch

9538. Tell your partner you're crazy about him/her with a little gesture

9539. Musical lovenote: "Play *A Hard Day's Night*, by The Beatles. My message to you is song No. 2"

9540. Erotic Book Alert! *Stories to Make You Blush*, by Marie Gray

9541. Before vacationing in Venice, watch the movie *Summertime* together

9542. For four weeks, be 20% more communicative

9543. Create a Build-A-Bear for your loved one. Dress it up in something she'll love and record a romantic message: www.buildabear.com

9544. "It is a beautiful necessity of our nature to love something." ~ Douglas William Jerrold

9545. Provide "turn-down service" for her at home: Place little chocolates on her pillow

9546. Play valet, and lay out your partner's night clothes on the bed

9547. Send a series of postcards picturing romantic movie couples

9548. For two weeks, be 10% more considerate to your partner

9549. Brush her hair for her

9550. Make this a regular nightly ritual

9551. Use this as a time to slow down and re-connect

9552. Buy her an antique silver plated hair brush

9553. Wednesday is "Hump Day": Celebrate!

9554. Guys: Never give her the "silent treatment"

9555. Visit the best bar for watching sunsets in Italy: The Casina Valadier, on Pincio Hill in the Villa Borghese Gardens
9556. Love Enhancer: Time—*Quality* time
9557. Stop trying to change your partner
9558. "Soul meets soul on lovers lips." ~ Percy Bysshe Shelley

9559. English: "You're so beautiful"
9560. French: "Tu es très belle"
9561. Italian: "Sei molto bella"
9562. German: "Du bist sehr schön"
9563. Spanish: "Eres preciosa"
9564. Portugese: "Você é muito bonita"

9565. The "Ultimate Pizza" Coupon: Good for one date at the best pizza joint in town
9566. Gals: Wear his favorite perfume
9567. Some people prefer gifts over gestures. What does *your* partner prefer?
9568. Make love, have sex, sleep together
9569. Write ten romantic ideas on a board game "spinner": Take a romantic spin once-a-week
9570. Create a Things To Do Before I Die list for yourself
9571. Create a Things To Do Before I Die list for your partner
9572. Buy raffle tickets together
9573. Create a collage of photos of the two of you

9574. Give your Texas gal one huge yellow rose
9575. And the song "The Yellow Rose of Texas," by Johnny Desmond

9576. Plant a flower garden consisting *entirely* of flowers in her favorite color

9577. Have a plaque made: "Lover of the Year Award"

9578. Go in search of her G-Spot

9579. Attach a note to the TV remote control: "Turn *me* on instead!"

9580. If she's a former Girl Scout: Award her with some custom "Merit Badges"—for "Friendship," "Communication Skills," etc.

Favorite Love Songs from 2002

9581. "A Sorta Fairytale," Tori Amos

9582. "A Thousand Miles," Vanessa Carlton

9583. "Come Away with Me," Norah Jones

9584. "Your Body is A Wonderland," John Mayer

9585. Create your own rituals around bubblebaths

9586. Enemy of Love: Blaming—Refusing to take responsibility for your part

9587. Give an "Expand Your Sexual Horizons" Coupon: You get to ask the coupon issuer to participate in a sexual activity that is slightly outrageous and/or positively scandalous

9588. Fly together in a chartered private plane

9589. "None is so near the gods as he who shows kindness." ~ Seneca

9590. Make his favorite cookies

9591. Use spray paint to write in the snow

9592. Read *Hug Time*, by Patrick McDonnell, a fun little book

9593. Enemy of Love: Feelings of powerlessness

9594. Renew your wedding vows in a public ceremony
9595. Write your own "Updated Marriage Vows" reflecting on what you've learned
9596. Create an altar of meaningful symbols
9597. Invite *everyone* you'd invited to your first ceremony—plus new friends
9598. Eat in the most romantic restaurant in Rome: Girone VI
9599. Remember this: Love is simple, but *people* are complicated
9600. Hold a "Spring Fling" on the first day of Spring
9601. Engrave Cupid on the back of his watch (so only he'll know!)
9602. Be a good sport: Attend your partner's high school/college reunions

Favorite Love Songs from 2003

9603. "Forever and For Always," Shania Twain
9604. "Amazing," Josh Kelley
9605. "With You," Jessica Simpson
9606. "Crazy in Love," Beyonce

9607. Stay in romantic splendor in Paris: La Tremoille
9608. Save sea shells from your beach vacations
9609. Gals: Get an engagement ring for *him*
9610. Call each other by private "pet names"
9611. Take your "Parrot-Head" to a Jimmy Buffett concert
9612. Insert three lottery tickets into her birthday card
9613. Enemy of Love: Stinginess with *money*
9614. Don't play "relationship games" with each other

9615. Stay at the Ritz

9616. For married men: Ask her to marry you—*again*
9617. And *this* time, give her a *huge* diamond ring
9618. (But buy smart! Read *How to Buy a Diamond*, by Fred Cuellar)

9619. Wallpaper a room with greeting cards you've exchanged
9620. "Let your hair down": No games, no masks
9621. Make purely physical, passionate love
9622. Frame a travel poster from your honeymoon
9623. "I have enjoyed the happiness of the world; I have lived and loved." ~ Johann von Schiller
9624. For one week, listen with 20% more attentiveness
9625. Love Enhancer: Respect for your partner
9626. Love Coupon: An evening of "Classic Romance." Included: The movie *Casablanca*, music by Glenn Miller, candlelight, and champagne
9627. Read her favorite book to get to know her better— Surprise her by asking to discuss it!

9628. Gals: Treat him as if he were your Prince Charming
9629. Guys: Treat her as if she were your Princess

9630. Visit a secret romantic garden: El Capricho Park, in Madrid, Spain
9631. Wish her "Good Luck" before a big presentation
9632. Familiarity often leads to laziness; be a little more polite, like when you were dating

---

9633. "'Tis better to have loved and lost, than to never have loved at all." ~ Alfred Lord Tennyson

9634. Thought Experiment: Imagine having *everything*—wealth, power, prestige, comfort, talent—*except* love. What good would it do you?

9635. In addition to color, space, and style when designing your home, use "romance" as an element

9636. Get a custom wine-label printed honoring her; wrap around her favorite bottle of wine

9637. Wrap her gently in your arms

9638. Create a homemade Hawaiian lei

9639. Make more time for your lover: Read *The 4 Hour Work Week*, by Tim Ferriss

9640. Enemy of Love: Modern life's complexity

9641. Love Enhancer: Presents that *symbolize* your love

9642. Spend a week at a spa together: Saybrook Point Inn, in Connecticut: www.saybrook.com

9643. The Chocoholic's Coupon: Redeemable for five pounds of your favorite chocolate treats

9644. Stay in a Baroque palace in Vienna: Romischer Kaiser

9645. Thank your love for being patient with you

9646. Thank your love for being there for you

9647. Thank your love for all the good times

9648. Thank your love for being a *friend*

9649. Thank your love for caring for you

9650. Thank your love for persevering through the bad

9651. Thank your love for *being* your love

9652. Learn to barbecue burgers *exactly* the way she likes them

9653. Musical lovenote: "Play *Angel Clare*, by Art Garfunkel. My message to you is song No. 6"

9654. Stay at the fanciest hotel in Milan: The Grand Hotel Et de Milan

9655. Make love in the most romantic setting and in the most romantic manner you can imagine

9656. "There is more pleasure in loving than in being loved." ~ Thomas Fuller

9657. Write an article describing your love; paste it into his paper

9658. Send a bouquet made of little love notes fashioned into flowers

9659. "In order to love simply, it is necessary to know how to show love." ~ Fyodor Dostoevsky

9660. Kiss at the top of the Empire State Building

9661. Make love without using your hands

9662. Increase the *quality* of your lovemaking by 21%

9663. Make love using a silk scarf

9664. Watch your wedding video on your anniversary

9665. Roll out a real red carpet to welcome him/her home

Favorite Love Songs from 2004

9666. "She Will Be Loved," Maroon 5

9667. "If I Ain't Got You," Alicia Keys

9668. "Accidentally In Love," Counting Crows

9669. "Collide," Howie Day

9670. "Absence makes the heart grow fonder." ~ Sextus Propertius

9671. "Absence sharpens love, presence strengthens it." ~ Thomas Fuller

9672. Enemy of Love: Macho attitudes
9673. Build a "Rube Goldberg" device for presenting an engagement ring to her
9674. Can't get him to write a love letter? Create a *fill-in-the-blanks* love letter for his use
9675. Get a 50th anniversary card from the President!
       The White House
       Attn: Greetings Office
       Washington, D.C.
       20502-0039
       (do not email)
9676. Wrap yourself around your partner like a pretzel
9677. Celebrate the moment you fell in love
9678. Have a birthday cake delivered to her at work
9679. A+ Romance Rating: The Hotel Hassler, in Rome, Italy

9680. Favorite gifts for men: High-powered stereo equipment
9681. Favorite gifts for men: Silk boxers
9682. Favorite gifts for men: Tickets to sporting events

9683. Enemy of Love: Superior attitudes
9684. A Theme-Gift: Give her one pink rose, a pink lingerie outfit, and a bottle of pink champagne
9685. Give him chili peppers with a note: "I'm hot for you!"
9686. Note: Little white lies in the service of creating romantic surprises don't really count as lies
9687. Give her a Lladro figurine that reflects her personality

9688. Get off the "career treadmill" and lead a more balanced, loving life
9689. Write "I love you" on a cake with icing
9690. For two weeks, be 15% less inhibited in your lovemaking
9691. Travel on the fabled Orient Express
9692. Stencil a cryptic love message on your driveway
9693. Stay at the fanciest hotel in Tokyo: The Imperial Hotel
9694. Give him a makeover but let him give you one afterwards!
9695. Make love with the only goal being to help your partner achieve orgasm
9696. Enemy of Love: Condescending attitudes
9697. Tape a love note to the inside of her bedroom closet door

---

9698. Gals: Do something *with* him that you hate to do
9699. It only counts as a loving gesture if you do it cheerfully and without complaint
9700. Go fishing, bowling, bird-watching, or hiking

9701. A "Happy Anniversary!" Coupon: You are entitled to a day of True Togetherness. This means a day just for the two of you: no kids, no job, no responsibilities, no chores
9702. Perform the classic "Doctor-Patient Fantasy"
9703. "Keep me as the apple of the eye, hide me under the shadow of thy wings." ~ Psalms 17:8
9704. Romantic piano concerto: Mozart's Piano Concerto No. 21 in C

9705. Send a birthday greeting via telegram
9706. FYI: Outrageous behavior is contagious
9707. Romantic piano: Grieg's Concerto in A Minor for Piano & Orchestra
9708. Slow down: Take the scenic route
9709. Enemy of Love: Fear of intimacy
9710. Get your partner a cardboard standup of his/her favorite celebrity
9711. Make him a custom gingerbread man
9712. During a winter walk, surprise him with a thermos full of hot cocoa
9713. Share a milkshake
9714. Eat in San Francisco's most romantic restaurant: Masa's
9715. Buy a new digital camera and spend an afternoon on a "Photo Safari"

9716. Have two photos of her in one frame: A photo of her as a baby, and a current photo
9717. Give it to her along with a recording of "You Must Have Been a Beautiful Baby ('Cause Baby Look at You Now!)"
9718. When he's traveling, give him a sexy wake-up call
9719. Wear "Obsession" perfume—To help you express your infatuation
9720. Give her a face massage
9721. Create a "Romantic Weekend-on-a-Budget"
9722. Create a custom ritual: Give a little gift *every* Wednesday
9723. Go whitewater rafting on the Salmon River, in Idaho
9724. Change one of your habits that really bugs your partner

Favorite Love Songs from 2005

9725. "Making Memories of Us," Keith Urban
9726. "We Belong Together," Mariah Carey
9727. "You and Me," Lifehouse
9728. "Inside Your Heaven," Carrie Underwood

9729. A+ Rating, Romantic Music Artist: Stan Getz
9730. Musical lovenote: "Play the CD *Beatles '65*; my message to you is song No. 8"
9731. Ask a "Magic 8 Ball" questions about your relationship
9732. Learn the hand gesture for "Live long and prosper" (from *Star Trek*)
9733. Spend a lazy Saturday in a hammock together
9734. Clip or email relationship cartoons from *The New Yorker* magazine
9735. A great music resource: cdnow.com
9736. Eat in the most romantic hotel in Zurich: Ermitage
9737. Enemy of Love: Escalating *discussions* into *arguments*

9738. Love your partner *unconditionally*—
9739. When you slip, love *yourself* unconditionally

9740. Charter a luxury yacht for an evening cruise
9741. Learn how to make his favorite mixed drink
9742. Hum "your song" together
9743. Hire an organizational consultant to straighten up his out-of-control office
9744. When traveling for a week, leave behind seven greeting cards, labeled with the days of the week

9745. Place friendly $5 bets when you disagree over factual trivia

9746. Love Enhancer: Playful attitude

9747. Never return his car with an empty gas tank

9748. Gals: Let him keep his macho facade in public—as long as he lets you see the "real him" when you're alone together

---

9749. Have a graphic designer create a logo out of her name

9750. And have custom stationery made: letterhead, thank you cards, etc.

9751. Enemy of Love: Assuming a *parental* role in your relationship

9752. Kiss on a chairlift

9753. For Married Folks: *Flirt* with your spouse

9754. Go to an *expensive* vacation spot—and get the *least expensive* accommodations

9755. Never watch TV during dinner!

9756. "Lips only sing when they cannot kiss." ~ James Thomson

9757. Spend a weekend together baking everything you can possible think of

9758. Use scented oil while giving a massage

9759. A "Formal Dinner" Coupon: You both dress in formal attire. Your partner will prepare and serve an elegant dinner-for-two at home

9760. "We two form a multitude." ~ Ovid

9761. Don't let your chores be divided by gender

9762. Share in the grocery shopping

9763. Share in the lawn care

9764. Share in the housework

9765. Share in the auto maintenance

9766. Help with the cooking

9767. Help with the snow shoveling

9768. Do the laundry together

9769. Pay the bills together

9770. A+ Rated romantic music: *The Sacred Fire*, by Nicholas Gunn

9771. Guys: Yes, there's a "fine line" between being *tenderhearted* and being a *wimp*, but women *love* tenderhearted guys

9772. Compliment him

Favorite Love Songs from 2006

9773. "You're Beautiful," James Blunt

9774. "For You I Will (Confidence)," Teddy Geiger

9775. "My Love," Justin Timberlake

9776. "Let Love In," Goo Goo Dolls

9777. Love Enhancer: Eye contact

9778. Help him conduct research for a big work project

9779. Guys: Watch *The Full Monty* as inspiration—and then perform a private show for her!

9780. Garnish a special dinner with *edible flowers*: Nasturtiums, calendulas, or pineapple sage

9781. Gift & Date Idea: Get the song "Love Theme from Romeo and Juliet," by Henry Mancini—

9782. Rent Romeo and Juliet the movie (1996 is the most current. Get the 1968 version for a flash of the past)

9783. Or—surprise your partner with tickets to the musical, live on stage

9784. Create romantic gestures based on "Eight Days a Week" by The Beatles

9785. Share comfort food

9786. Purchase the newest GPS system for his or her car. Check out http://www.garmin.com/garmin/cms/site/us

9787. Topics to be avoided during romantic interludes: Work, money, parents, kids

9788. Dribble a liqueur on your body; invite your partner to lick it off

9789. The "Instant Celebration" Coupon: *At any time* you may demand that your partner create an *instant*, romantic celebration

9790. For a fan of rock and classical music: A cool CD called *What If Mozart Wrote "Born to Be Wild"*

9791. Enjoy a campfire in your own backyard

9792. Keep a journal of your life together

9793. Keep a journal of your best memories

9794. Keep a "Joint Journal," in which you *both* write

9795. For your gourmet: A bottle of fine wine

9796. Use your typing skills to help speed along his/her weekend work

9797. Stay at the fanciest hotel in Hong Kong: The Peninsula

9798. Make her proud of you at family reunions

9799. Single gals: The first Saturday in November is Sadie Hawkins Day—Tradition says *you* can propose

9800. "Kissing is the most pleasant way of spreading germs yet devised." ~ Anonymous

9801. Hold a truly magical wedding at Disney World

9802. Shop for costume jewelry

9803. Put your partner's phone number in the No. 1 place on your "speed dial"

9804. Be her sex slave

9805. Serve dinner amid clouds of dry ice

9806. See your relationship as a safe place to stretch yourself

9807. Get classy gifts from the Museum of Fine Arts, Boston: www.mfa.org

---

9808. English: "Take your clothes off"

9809. French: "Déshabille-toi"

9810. Italian: "Spogliati"

9811. German: "Zieh dich aus"

9812. Spanish: "Desnúdate"

9813. Portugese: "Tire sua roupa"

9814. A+ Rating Gift Resource: The Parkleigh, in Rochester, New York: www.parkleigh.com

9815. Send him a pair of oven mitts in the mail, with this note attached: "I'm going to be *too hot to handle* tonight, so wear these!"

9816. Note for a love letter: Describe your relationship as "the *quintessential* love affair"

9817. Dinner-and-a-movie tip: Always see the movie *first*. This way you won't have to rush dinner

9818. Bring home her favorite style of bagel

9819. Go on a "New Activity Date"

9820. Buy *anything* from Tiffany's

9821.   Make love to the rhythm of background music
9822.   Make dried flower arrangements from bouquets you've received
9823.   Turn to your partner in public and whisper, "I can't wait to be alone with you!"
9824.   Keep candles at your bedside at all times
9825.   Make love as Rhett Butler and Scarlett O'Hara

9826.   Learn to say what's on your mind
9827.   Learn to say what's in your heart
9828.   Learn to say "I'm sorry"

9829.   A great love song: "Chagall Duet," by Jon Anderson & Sandrine Piau, on *Change We Must*
9830.   Help him find things, instead of complaining about his forgetfulness
9831.   Create a "Count-Down Calendar" anticipating your baby's birth
9832.   Wear matching sweatshirts when you work out
9833.   Hire a barbershop quartet to sing "Happy Birthday" to her

Favorite Love Songs from 2007

9834.   "First Time," Lifehouse
9835.   "Our Song," Taylor Swift
9836.   "Bleeding Love," Leona Lewis

9837.   Practice "emotional generosity"
9838.   Give an antique bottle with a special love note in it based on Jim Croce's song "Time in a Bottle"
9839.   A+ Rating, Romantic Music Artist: David Benoit

9840. Shout your love into a valley; listen for the echo

9841. Flash a love message on a ballpark's scoreboard

9842. Favorite gifts for men: Fishing rods

9843. Favorite gifts for men: Golf clubs

9844. Favorite gifts for men: Bowling balls

9845. Love Coupon: This coupon entitles you to one evening of "stimulation." You define what *kind* of stimulation you want—intellectual or physical!

9846. Sensual Music Alert: *Embrya*, by Maxwell

9847. A+ Rated loving lyrics: In "State of Independence," on *The Friends of Mr. Cairo* CD by Jon Anderson

9848. "Love unreciprocated is like a question without an answer." ~ Kathryn Maye

9849. Make love by the light of a full moon

9850. Go on a "Surprise Week-Night Date"

9851. Learn the art of slowly undressing your lover

9852. Copy some of your body parts on a Xerox machine and mail the pages to her

9853. Spell out "I Love You" in Play Doh

9854. Read *Why I Love You*, by Gregory E. Lang, then write about your relationship

9855. Make love to him *the way he wants*

9856. Visit someplace new in your state

9857. Carry the groceries

9858. If you have the same argument over and over and over again, dedicate yourselves *once-and-for-all* to get to the bottom of it!

9859. Read books, talk more, try different approaches...

9860. Talk to a counselor, minister, therapist
9861. Give yourselves plenty of time (several years!) but stay focused and dedicated

---

9862. Eat in the most romantic restaurant in Stockholm: Min Lilla Tradgard
9863. Talk with your partner openly about sex
9864. Give her a tiara
9865. Surprise him with an antique desk for his home office
9866. A great love song: "Lend Your Love to Me," by Emerson Lake & Palmer, on *Works II*
9867. Translate your pet name for her into French, Italian, or Japanese
9868. Give *fragrant* flowers: Stock, Roses, Gardenias
9869. Go to a drive-in movie together and make out

Qualities that 5,000 Men Want *Most* in Wives

9870. Loving/Demonstrative
9871. Attentive
9872. Sexiness
9873. Confident
9874. Caring
9875. Independent
9876. Intelligent
9877. Beauty
9878. Romantic
9879. Sense of humor

9880. For tea lovers: Get a special tea pot
9881. "Breakfast-in-Bed" Coupon: Redeemable sometime within a year

9882. When it's raining, place a love note inside a Ziplock bag, and place it under her windshield wiper of her car

9883. Charter a small plane to fly you to the nearest major city for dinner

9884. Order room service

9885. Say "Yes" to your relationship every morning

9886. Save the decorative metal cap from the top of a special bottle of champagne, and have it made into a jewelry pin

9887. Bring her a stack of her favorite magazines when she's home sick

9888. Make love in a pool

9889. Always stop what you're doing to greet your mate

9890. Order a huge *wedding cake* for a special *birthday*

9891. Honor him with a cherished family heirloom…

9892. An oriental rug

9893. An antique pocket watch

9894. A grandfather clock

9895. Sing a lovesong duet at a Karaoke bar

9896. Brainstorm romantic ideas with your partner

9897. Musical lovenote: "Play the CD *Coming Around Again*, by Carly Simon. My messages to you are songs No. 2 and No. 4"

9898. Give her a written bill for repairing her car: "Oil change: Four kisses. Check battery: Two hugs. Tighten belts: One backrub"

9899. Share many private jokes

9900. Hold an extravagant surprise party—for her *beloved pet*

9901. Design an Old West "Wanted" poster that describes why you *want* him/her
9902. Stay a week in Buenos Aires
9903. Spend all day at a giant flea market together
9904. Feed her grapes on a lazy Saturday
9905. Create a personal holiday based on her most charming quirk
9906. Buy greeting cards in foreign languages
9907. Buy your partner clothes that flatter his/her shape

Favorite Love Songs from 2008

9908. "Love Story," Taylor Swift
9909. "You Found Me," The Fray
9910. "I'm Yours," Jason Mraz

9911. Watch the Hawaiian surf from a hotel balcony
9912. Share a picnic lunch in the park
9913. "They love indeed who quake to say they love."
      ~ Philip Sidney
9914. Honor your partner with a "This Is Your Life" party
9915. Organize a great tailgating party for him and his sports buddies

9916. What does your lover need—*right now*?
9917. Appreciation? Security? Enchantment?
9918. Understanding? Sex? Friendship?
9919. Passion? Food? Gifts?
9920. Time? Answers? Excitement?
9921. Affection? Adventure? Solitude?
9922. Exercise? Music? Escape?
9923. Toys? Tools? Candy?

9924. Hugs? Kisses? Compliments?

9925. Return her movies to Blockbuster
9926. For the New Year: Give a calendar with pre-marked "Mystery Dates"
9927. Go apple picking in the autumn
9928. Go beachcombing in the summer
9929. Give memories as gifts
9930. Take a classic winter sleigh ride together
9931. "The heart that loves is always young." ~ Greek proverb
9932. Attend an outdoor art festival
9933. Go tidepooling at the beach

Pairs of Gender Generalizations:

Do You Agree or Disagree?
9934. Women hear "love" when you say "romance." Men hear "sex" when you say "romance"
9935. Women connect many emotional issues with their sexuality. Men can easily separate their sexuality from their feelings
9936. Women communicate to create relationships. Men communicate to gather information
9937. Women cooperate. Men compete
9938. Women tend to be "right-brained"—emotional, creative thinkers. Men tend to be "left-brained"— logical, compartmentalized thinkers
9939. Women view relationships as a vast interlocking network. Men view relationships as hierarchical
9940. Women often treat men as emotional children. Men often treat women as incompetents in the real world

9941. Women put men in shining armor on a white horse. Men put women on a pedestal
9942. Women are aroused through sensation. Men are aroused visually
9943. Women arouse slowly. Men arouse quickly
9944. Women have been taught to hide their angry feelings. Men have been taught to hide their tender feelings
9945. Women have been taught to suppress their aggressive side. Men have been taught to suppress their gentle side

9946. Give her your frequent flyer miles
9947. Frequently give him a pat on the back
9948. "Keep your eyes wide open before marriage, and half-shut afterwards." ~ Benjamin Franklin
9949. Before getting out of bed, say: "I'm so thankful I have you in my life"

9950. Get your country western guy a new pair of cowboy boots
9951. Get your country western gal a fancy new cowgirl hat
9952. Go on a glass-bottom-boat tour
9953. List twelve sexual activities. Roll two dice to determine which activity you'll share tonight!
9954. Ride an old-fashioned carousel together
9955. Play on a co-ed softball team together
9956. Splash through rain puddles together
9957. Kiss in mid-air while skydiving
9958. "Love doesn't make the world go 'round. Love is what makes the ride worthwhile." ~ Franklin Jones
9959. Go "4-wheeling" together

9960. Create a home version of "Sexy Bingo"
9961. Join a health club together
9962. Do Tai Chi together
9963. Attend a craft fair together
9964. Eliminate from your vocabulary: "Yes, but—"
9965. Note: If you've been together ten years or more, you should be an *expert* on your partner!
9966. Build a tree fort together
9967. "Love is not love until love's vulnerable." ~ Theodore Roethke

---

9968. *Talking* is not necessarily "communicating"
9969. Sharing *feelings* is only *part* of communicating
9970. *How* you say what you say is just as important as *what* you say
9971. *Half* of communicating is simply listening
9972. There are as many communication "styles" as there are people

---

9973. A romantic weekend at the elegant Plaza Hotel in NYC: www.fairmont.com
9974. "Shared laughter is erotic, too." ~ Marge Piercy
9975. Rent every movie that stars her favorite actor
9976. Get an elegant canopy bed
9977. "The first duty of love is to listen." ~ Paul Tillich

Favorite Love Songs from 2009

9978. "Come Back to Me," David Cook
9979. "No Surprise," Daughtry
9980. "Halo," Beyonce
9981. "You Belong With Me," Taylor Swift

9982. Slip a little love note into her purse
9983. Do one of your partner's chores
9984. Grow her favorite flowers in your garden
9985. Make love in all fifty states
9986. Have a band play "your song"
9987. Buy a book on time management: Create more time for love
9988. Believe in one another
9989. Use one of his pet names for your ATM password
9990. Kiss at stop signs and red lights
9991. Write a love note, fold it into a paper airplane, and sail it across the room
9992. Write "I love you" on the bathroom mirror with soap
9993. Think about this one! "I hate to be a failure. I hate and regret the failure of my marriages. I would gladly give up my millions for just one lasting marital success." ~ J. Paul Getty
9994. When he/she calls you at work, always interrupt whatever you're doing to take the call
9995. Save all the "slow dances" for each other
9996. Buy her one big, humongous diamond
9997. Decorate the bedroom with one balloon for every year you've been together
9998. Turn to him in public and whisper, "On a scale of 1 to 10, you're a 12"
9999. Kiss the palm of her hand; close her fingers into a fist; say "Save this"
10000. Live happily ever after

ABOUT THE AUTHOR

13 Facts About Gregory J.P. Godek

1. Greg has taught romance on *Oprah*
2. He has counseled the "romantically impaired" on *Donahue*
3. Greg has been featured in the *New York Times, Cosmopolitan, Glamour, Playboy*, and *Harper's Bazaar*
4. He has authored 12 books in 8 years
5. More than 2 million copies of his books have been sold worldwide
6. Greg is a teacher and role model, not a therapist or theorist
7. He is a researcher, questioner, and listener
8. He studies successful couples and happy people
9. He not only believes that love *can* be taught, but that it *must* be taught
10. Greg's is a synergistic and quirky path that combines a novelist's eye for character and motivation with a teacher's passion for connecting and communicating with students
11. Greg has been invited to teach his Romance Seminar to the U.S. Army
12. He has consulted with the flower, chocolate, diamond, and movie industries
13. For Greg, this was not a chosen profession, but the following of a muse, the expression of universal truths as experienced by one individual

4 Curious Things Said About Gregory J.P. Godek

1. "Greg Godek should be nominated for the Nobel Peace Prize for teaching *1001 Ways To Be Romantic*." *~ Boston Magazine*

2. "Godek is *ruining* things for us guys!" ~ Joe Magadatz, author of the parody *1001 Ways NOT To Be Romantic*

3. "Greg Godek is a *thirtysomething* Leo Buscaglia." *~ Evening Magazine*

4. "Greg teaches the truth." ~ Mark Victor Hansen, co-author of *Chicken Soup for the Soul*

6 Personal Facts About Gregory J.P. Godek

1. The "J.P." stands for John Paul
2. Greg is a classic, romantic Pisces
3. Yes, he really *did* have a girlfriend in kindergarten
4. No, his father was *not* a romantic role model
5. But Greg combined his father's passion for life with his mother's creativity
6. His favorite TV show is *Babylon 5*